All Things Reconciled

All Things Reconciled

Essays on Restorative Justice, Religious Violence, and the Interpretation of Scripture

Christopher D. Marshall

FOREWORD BY Willard M. Swartley
AFTERWORD BY Thomas Noakes-Duncan

CASCADE *Books* • Eugene, Oregon

ALL THINGS RECONCILED
Essays on Restorative Justice, Religious Violence,
and the Interpretation of Scripture

Copyright © 2018 Christopher D. Marshall. All rights reserved. Except for brief quotations in critical publications or reviews, no part of this book may be reproduced in any manner without prior written permission from the publisher. Write: Permissions, Wipf and Stock Publishers, 199 W. 8th Ave., Suite 3, Eugene, OR 97401.

Cascade Books
An Imprint of Wipf and Stock Publishers
199 W. 8th Ave., Suite 3
Eugene, OR 97401

www.wipfandstock.com

PAPERBACK ISBN: 978-1-62564-370-4
HARDCOVER ISBN: 978-1-4982-8753-1
EBOOK ISBN: 978-1-60608-789-3

Cataloguing-in-Publication data:

Names: Marshall, Christopher D. | Swartley, Willard M., 1936–, foreword. | Noakes-Duncan, Thomas M. I., afterword.

Title: All things reconciled : essays in restorative justice, religious violence, and the interpretation of scripture / Christopher D. Marshall ; foreword by Willard M. Swartley ; afterword by Thomas M. I. Noakes-Duncan.

Description: Eugene, OR : Cascade Books, 2018 | Includes bibliographical references and indexes.

Identifiers: ISBN 978-1-62564-370-4 (paperback) | ISBN 978-1-4982-8753-1 (hardcover) | ISBN 978-1-60608-789-3 (ebook)

Subjects: LCSH: Restorative justice—Religious aspects—Christianity. | Christian ethics. | Christianity and justice.

Classification: BR115.J8 M27 2018 (print) | BR115.J8 M27 (ebook)

Manufactured in the U.S.A.   JUNE 8, 2018

For Howard Zehr

humble trailblazer, mentor and friend, with respect and appreciation

καρπὸς δὲ δικαιοσύνης ἐν εἰρήνῃ σπείρεται τοῖς ποιοῦσιν εἰρήνην
(Jas 3:18)

Contents

Foreword by Willard M. Swartley ix

Acknowledgments xiii

Introduction xv

1. The Use of the Bible in Ethics:
   A Starting Point for a Restorative Reading of Scripture 1
2. Re-engaging the Bible in a Postmodern World 39
3. What Language Shall I Borrow?
   The Bilingual Dilemma of Public Theology 62
4. Crime, Crucifixion, and the Forgotten Art of Lament 80
5. Prison, Prisoners, and the Bible 93
6. Satisfying Justice: Victims, Justice, and the Grain of the Universe 110
7. The Violence of God and the Hermeneutics of Paul:
   Wresting with God's Retributive Violence in the Bible 128
8. Atonement, Violence, and the Will of God 159
9. For God's Sake!
   Terrorism, Religious Violence, and Restorative Justice 184

Afterword by Thomas Noakes-Duncan 209

Bibliography 217

Scripture Index 231

Subject Index 243

Author Index 253

Foreword

IT IS MY PLEASURE to contribute a foreword to this book of essays by my esteemed and treasured friend, Professor Christopher D. Marshall. When Chris came to the Anabaptist Mennonite Biblical Seminary in 1991-92 on study leave, I realized we were blessed to have a unique student, one with a distinguished vita. He had earned a PhD in New Testament in 1985 at King's College London, one of the constituent colleges of the University of London, and his dissertation had subsequently been published in 1989 by Cambridge University Press as *Faith as a Theme in Mark's Narrative*. No other student with a completed PhD in biblical studies had ever come to AMBS to enroll in a Master's degree program in Peace Studies. I was familiar with Chris's book on Mark and recommended it to my students—my own doctoral dissertation from Princeton Theological Seminary in 1973 had also been on Mark's Gospel—so it was a special honor to have him not only as a student but also as a contributor to an independent study with me on "Peace in the New Testament." We had mutual scholarly interests, but most significantly, we became friends, sharing our spiritual journeys and praying for each other, including our spouses and children.

During his time in London as a graduate student, Chris had become acquainted with the London Mennonite Centre, then under the leadership of Alan and Eleanor Kreider. Chris had heard Alan speak at a conference celebrating five years of publication of the British magazine *Third Way* and was impressed with Alan's theological and ethical emphases. With his wife, Margaret, they soon began attending Sunday worship at the London Mennonite Fellowship, where they sensed they had "come home" theologically. Kinship between the Marshalls and Kreiders developed and deepened, and Chris soon began preaching and exercising leadership in the church.

After completing his doctoral studies, Chris returned home to New Zealand to take up a teaching position. After five years of service he had earned a sabbatical leave and decided, with his young family, to spend it at AMBS. He was attracted by the distinctive Master of Arts in Peace Studies program (MAPS), with its strong biblical and Anabaptist commitment to nonviolence. Chris's impressive academic background and commitment to arduous work enabled him to complete the course work in one year. His extraordinarily competent MAPS thesis, titled "Classed with the Criminals," demonstrated his mastery of both New Testament studies and peace studies, beyond the usual level of theses in the MAPS program.

Chris later revised and extended his thesis and published it as a book entitled *Beyond Retribution: A New Testament Vision for Justice, Crime and Punishment* (Wm. B. Eerdmans, 2001). I was only too happy to include this important contribution in the Studies in Peace and Scripture series, of which Ben Ollenburger and I were editors.

How did Chris become interested in restorative justice as a focus in peace studies? In his preface to *Beyond Retribution* he gives an account of this development:

> During a visit to the offices of the Mennonite Central Committee in Akron, Pennsylvania, in 1991, I was given a copy of Howard Zehr's book *Changing Lenses: A New Focus for Crime and Justice*. I didn't get around to reading this remarkable book until I returned to New Zealand the following year, and even then did so primarily because I was interested in the chapter on biblical justice. The book made a deep impression on me [xiii].

Chris wrote a review of *Changing Lenses* for the New Zealand journal *Stimulus* and helped convene a conference in 1994 to which Howard Zehr was invited as keynote speaker. Since then, Chris has been at the forefront of promoting restorative justice measures in New Zealand, drawing on the example of the Victim Offender Reconciliation Program pioneered in North America. Notably, in 2004 Chris won an International Community Justice Award from the British Home Office for his teaching and writing on restorative justice, an award presented by Princess Anne. As the essays in this book attest, the award was a well-deserved honor.

Also in 2004, Chris moved from Auckland to Wellington to take up an appointment as the St John's Senior Lecturer in Christian Theology in the Religious Studies Program at Victoria University of Wellington. Later he was appointed as Head of the School of Art History, Classics and Religious Studies and promoted to full professor. In 2013, he became inaugural holder of the Diana Unwin Chair in Restorative Justice in the School of Government at Victoria University, a position he still holds.

In all his scholarly contributions, Chris's strong biblical competence shines brightly. This is evident in his books on the biblical foundations of human rights (2001) and on the meaning of biblical justice (2005). It is also evident in the present collection, such as in chapter 8, an extended review of Denny Weaver's 2001 book, *The Nonviolent Atonement* originally published in the *Mennonite Quarterly Review* (2003). Marshall's adroit mastery of Scripture here is superb. His critique of Weaver's work is right on target.

In mid-2012, Chris informed me of his new book, *Compassionate Justice: An Interdisciplinary Dialogue*.[1] Only Chris could have written such a book, which excels in combining perceptive biblical exegesis with interdisciplinary expertise in restorative justice. The big surprise was to learn that Chris had dedicated the book to me, choosing the Greek text of Ephesians 6:21—"a beloved brother and faithful servant in the Lord"—as a lovely expression of appreciation for my life-example and our shared discipleship, and ending the dedication with the words "in friendship and fellowship." A tribute beyond my deserving! My copy of his book is well marked, with twenty sticky-notes to direct me to those portions I may sometime quote in future writings.

Our friendship has continued over many years, even though we are on opposite sides of the globe, with treasured interactions in both personal and published form. We share our life experiences, our scholarly pursuits, and our spiritual pilgrimage, and I feel Chris to be an upholding, praying brother. That's Chris, blessed and blessing others with sensitive pastoral care for people. When during a visit to our home in March 2013, he spoke of his son, Peter, a government lawyer, it occurred to me that a book in my library must go home with him. It was a book of Peter Marshall's sermons and prayers as chaplain to US government personnel in the 1940s, entitled *Mr. Jones Meet the Master: Sermons and Prayers of Peter Marshall*, published in 1949 by Catherine Marshall. I hope that Chris and Margaret's son, also a Peter Marshall, will treasure the book.

Finally I mention Chris's contribution to a Festschrift or "thanksgiving volume" published in honor of Perry Yoder's and my work on the

---

1. Cascade Books, 2012. Other noteworthy contributions are his biblically oriented ground-breaking book on human rights: *Crowned with Glory and Honor: Human Rights in the Biblical Tradition* (vol. 4 in the SPS series; Telford, Pa.: Pandora Press [now Cascadia Publishing], 2002) and *The Little Book on Biblical Justice* (Intercourse, Pa.: Good Books, 2005).

biblical meaning of peace and our lifelong contributions to peacemaking, entitled *Struggles for Shalom: Peace and Violence across the Testaments* edited by Laura Brenneman and Brad Schantz. Of course, Chris Marshall had to be one of the contributors to this volume—and he is, with an inspiring chapter on "'Making Every Effort': Peacemaking and Ecclesiology in Ephesians 4:1-6" (256-66). As usual, Chris mines the passage well and links it to similar emphases in Paul's writings, showing that "the power of the gospel . . . is a peaceful power . . . of spiritual transformation and spiritual freedom 'at work within us . . .'" (259) and that "the unity of the church is a divine fact, for Christ is not and can never be divided" (266). I am grateful for this fine contribution. It resonates with our friendship and mutual concern for the peacemaking and the unity of the church.

Readers will open this book *All Things Reconciled* with anticipation and not be disappointed. A careful scholar, Chris has kept abreast of several fields of study: biblical interpretation, the character of God and the question of divine violence, and, most crucially, peace studies, with a focus on restorative justice. The essays exemplify Chris's seamless movement from his biblical expertise to his passion for restorative justice. His emphasis on lament and the Gospels' portrayal of Jesus as a criminal segues into a stellar contribution on restorative justice. His essays, all grounded in biblical exposition, tackle pressing contemporary issues and global realities, including terrorism and the counter "war on terrorism." Where does restorative justice fit in this "war" mentality? Chris tells stories of how restorative justice efforts have worked. He beckons us all, including policy-makers, to consider the potential and peace-making fruit of a third way of responding to harm—not retributive justice or rehabilitation but restorative justice. His sources and bibliography confirm his wide reading and knowledge in several fields of expertise. But at the heart of it all, for Chris, is Jesus—his teachings and salvific work, which call us to work for reconciliation and for making peace.

May the "God of peace" continue to abundantly bless Chris, in his teaching, administration, and reconciliation work, which bridges several fields of scholarly study combined with compassionate praxis.

Willard M. Swartley
Professor Emeritus of New Testament,
Anabaptist Mennonite Biblical Seminary
Author of *Covenant of Peace: the Missing Peace in New Testament Theology and Ethics* (Eerdmans, 2006)

Acknowledgments

THE ESSAYS INCLUDED IN this book have all been previously published elsewhere and are reproduced here with permission. "The Use of the Bible in Ethics: Scripture, Ethics, and the Social Justice Statement," in J. Boston and A. Cameron (eds.), *Voices for Justice: Church, Law and State In New Zealand* (Palmerston North: Dunmore Press, 1994), 107-46; "Atonement, Violence and the Will of God," *Mennonite Quarterly Review* 76:1 (2003), 67-90; "Prison, Prisoners and the Bible," *Justice Reflections* 3/13 (2003), 1-18, reprinted in *Restorative Directions Journal* 2/1 (2006), 118-31; "Crime, Crucifixion and the Forgotten Art of Lament," *Justice Reflections* 6/43 (2004), 1-14; "Satisfying Justice: Victims, Justice and the Grain of the Universe," *Interface: A Forum for Theology in the World* 8/1 (2005), 35-55, reprinted in *Justice Reflections* 10/ 69 (2005), 1-19; "What Language Shall I Borrow? The Bilingual Dilemma of Public Theology," *Stimulus* 13/3 (2005), 11-18; reprinted in *Evangel* 24/2 (2006), 45-52; "Re-engaging the Bible in a Post-Modern World," *Stimulus* 15/1 (2007), 5-20; "Religious Violence, Terrorism and Restorative Justice," in Daniel van Ness and Gerry Johnston (eds.), *Handbook on Restorative Justice* (Uffculme Cullompton, Devon: Willan Publishers, 2007), 372-94; "The Violence of God and the Hermeneutics of Paul," in Alain Epp Weaver and Gerald J. Mast (eds.), *The Work of Jesus Christ in Anabaptist Perspective: Essays in Honor of J. Denny Weaver* (Telford, PA: Cascadia, 2008), 74-105.

Introduction

THE TERM RESTORATIVE JUSTICE denotes ways of responding to criminal offending that focus on emotional, relational, and material repair rather than on conviction and punishment. Emerging in North America in the early 1970s, its principal innovation was the practice of using facilitated victim-offender dialogue to explore the harm perpetrated by the offending and to determine what should be done to demonstrate accountability and promote healing. This soon spawned an entirely new theoretical paradigm for conceptualizing the nature of crime and the meaning of justice, and, by implication, the larger goals of the criminal justice system.

Initially the concept of restorative justice was used solely with respect to criminal justice concerns, and there are still theorists who insist the phrase should only be used for responses to criminalizable actions. But the semantic field of the term has expanded considerably over recent years and now includes a range of discursive and peacemaking practices beyond the criminal justice system as well—in schools, families, workplaces, social services agencies, voluntary associations, community groups, businesses, and regulatory bodies. It has become routine in the literature to speak not only of restorative justice but also of restorative practices and restorative organizations, and to view them as different facets of the same diamond, as varied applications of the same values, principles and relational philosophy, as distinct manifestations of an eclectic, global social movement for a more inclusive, peaceful, and participatory democracy.[1] On this understanding, restorative justice is more

---

1. "To refer to restorative justice as a social movement is not to say that restorative justice programs comprise a unified body of actors or that restorative justice philosophies form an undifferentiated body of ideas . . . This is clearly not the case for restorative justice, but this is also not true for most, if any, social movements. Social movements are networks in which actors with varying interpretations of what the movement is about, and different levels of commitment to the movement, negotiate the meaning of a linked set of 'big ideas' as well as their ideal application in everyday

than a novel approach to crime control or a new set of victim-sensitive justice practices. It is the tip of a very large iceberg, a project aimed at the creation of interpersonal relationships and societal institutions that foster human dignity, equality, freedom, mutual respect, democratic engagement, and collaborative governance.

The comprehensiveness of this vision, which calls to mind the biblical notion of *shalom*, is probably no accident.[2] Likely it is encoded in the DNA of the approach, for the modern restorative-justice movement was born in a Christian stable to Christian—specifically to Anabaptist Mennonite Christian—parents. Not that Christianity can claim exclusive proprietary rights to the restorative justice ideal. As it has grown and deepened, restorative justice has been molded by a wide array of influences and interests, ranging from indigenous conceptions of justice to the feminist ethics of care, from relational theory and positive psychology to affect theory, organizational psychology and the insights of modern neuroscience. Instead of a single taproot sinking ever deeper into its point of origin, the restorative seed sprouted a fibrous or tangled root system, fanning out in all directions to draw sustenance from sundry sources of knowledge and experience. This has given restorative justice from its inception a dynamic or synthetic quality, which remains a singular strength. Constantly evolving and expanding it has incorporated insights into human behavior and interpersonal relationships from diverse disciplinary sources and intellectual traditions, and has proved itself adaptable to a wide range of social and cultural settings.

Yet notwithstanding its heterogeneous character, it is not an extraneous detail that the first architects of restorative justice were Christian peace activists intentionally striving to put their Christian faith into practice in the public arena. Nor is it immaterial that the first major book in the field, Howard Zehr's *Changing Lenses: A New Focus for Crime and Justice* was written for a church audience, published by a denominational publishing house, and included an entire chapter on the biblical conception of justice.[3] Biblical theology, one might say, was midwife at the birth of the movement and without the influence of core Christian values and

---

life . . . Thus a social movement is not a single group or organization but rather a host of individual and collective agents engaged in a process of movement definition, issue or grievance articulation, activism and program implementation." Woolford, *Politics*, 19.

2. For a comprehensive analysis, see Swartley, *Covenant*.
3. Zehr, *Changing Lenses*, 4th ed.

beliefs the central tenets of restorative theory might not have emerged with such clarity and conviction.

One of the impressive features of *Changing Lenses* is the way it brings together historical and social-scientific analysis of the criminal justice system with biblical reasoning on law, crime, justice and peace (or *shalom*). In this respect it is a splendid example of public theology—which is the attempt to address issues of common concern in society in light of the special truth claims, insights, and moral convictions of Christian faith, and in a manner that is intelligible to all citizens.[4] Though addressed primarily to Christians, Zehr's analysis of the criminal justice dilemma resonated with secular readers as well, and the book went on to have a significant impact on criminological thought and public policy well beyond its target audience. Zehr's success in this regard may have been helped by the fact that he wrote as a historian and practitioner, not a professional theologian, and his primary goal was to promote social change, not to advance academic debate.

But a curious thing has happened in the quarter century since the book's appearance.[5] The two strands of analysis that are so tightly interwoven in the discussion—the sociological and the theological, the conceptual and the spiritual—have been teased apart again and gone their separate ways, with few commentators now appreciating the innovative nature and productive power of their original combination. The sociological or conceptual strand has given rise to an entirely new field of legal and criminological studies called "restorative justice," possibly the most fertile, and certainly the most hopeful, of all forms of contemporary criminal justice discourse. As Carolyn Hoyle, editor of the massive four-volume survey *Restorative Justice: Critical Concepts in Criminology*, observes, "over the last two decades there has been more written about restorative justice than almost any other criminological topic."[6]

Those writing on the topic frequently acknowledge Zehr's pioneering role in forging the analytical categories of this new field, such as the concept of crime as a harming of persons more than the breaking of rules, the construal of justice as relational rather than abstract, the emphasis on needs and obligations over rights and retribution, the crucial place of victims as well as perpetrators in the justice process, the role of the local

---

4. See Marshall, "Parables as Paradigms," 23-44.
5. For a fuller statement on this, see my article "Gracious Legacy," 439-44.
6. Hoyle, "General Introduction," 15.

community alongside the state in dispensing justice, and the overarching concern of restorative justice to make things right again, not simply to mark the wrongness of past actions. What is less frequently acknowledged or understood, however, is the extent to which this conceptual payload is deeply indebted to Zehr's Anabaptist Christian theological convictions. Not one of the almost 80 articles selected for reprinting in Hoyle's important collection deals with the religious resonances of the restorative agenda and the introductory essay attributes the rise of restorative justice simply to mounting disillusionment in America and elsewhere with the mainstream criminal justice process and to a growing desire to find ways to balance the needs of victims, offenders, and communities. It may well have been disillusionment that propelled the search for alternatives, but in Zehr's case at least, the form his alternative took was deeply conditioned by his Christian convictions.

These convictions are most obvious in the chapter on covenant justice, but they are evident elsewhere in *Changing Lenses* as well, such as in his reflections on the dynamics of repentance, forgiveness, and reconciliation; his emphasis on the collective nature of guilt and the place of atonement; his relational or covenantal conception of justice and its inseparability from peacemaking; his attempt to disentangle the concepts of crime and sin; his insistence, in company with the biblical prophets and legislators, on prioritizing the rights and needs of victims in face of their oppressors; his attraction to the language of healing that permeates the Gospel tradition; and in his emphasis on the role of the church as an alternative community of values. Even the term restorative justice itself, which Zehr appropriated to highlight the distinctiveness of the new approach, has theological origins. It may be traced back to a 1955 book on *The Biblical Doctrine of Law and Justice*.[7] Beyond all these details, there is a visionary or prophetic quality to the entire project that also derives from Zehr's theological presuppositions. In the final pages of the book, Zehr concedes the almost utopian nature of his proposal to reconceptualize justice in restorative or reparative terms and confesses his own failings to live up to this ideal in his personal life.

> Yet, I believe in ideals. Much of the time we fall short of them but they remain a beacon, something toward which we aim, something against which to test our actions. They point a direction.

---

7. H. Schrey et al., *Justice and Law*, 1. Cited in Van Ness and Strong, *Restoring Justice*, 22.

> Only with a sense of direction can we know when we are far off the path. The place to begin experiencing restoration is not from the top but from the bottom, in our homes and communities. I continue to have faith that the community of God's people can lead in this direction. Certainly we will often fail, as those in the biblical record did. But just as certainly God will forgive and restore us.[8]

Despite all these clues, subsequent restorative justice scholarship has largely ignored or discounted the importance of the confessional seedbed from which restorative justice has sprung. In most of the standard accounts of its origins, the spiritual impulse behind the restorative vision is almost entirely elided from the story. It is understandable that secular theorists, policymakers, and practitioners should not wish to engage with the biblical and theological content of *Changing Lenses* and focus instead on its criminological concepts. But this comes at a loss. Some observers have noted that as restorative justice has moved into the mainstream of criminological theory, the language of repentance, forgiveness, grace, reconciliation, mercy, peace, and love has become increasingly rare, and is sometimes actively resisted, partly because of the difficulties of transposing such virtues into public policy. Yet it is these qualities and commitments that contribute to the oft-called "magic" of restorative justice, without which it risks being reduced to just another program or procedure for crime control rather than what it actually is: an exercise in moral and spiritual truthfulness. This depth dimension is easier to sustain when we appreciate the spiritual side of justice making, and the capacity of faith traditions to illuminate and energize such spirituality.

Just as the mainstreaming of restorative justice theory and practice in criminological and legal studies has involved a severing of its theological roots and an unraveling of the theoretical and theological strands interwoven in *Changing Lenses*, in Christian circles a similar thing has happened. The enormous potential of restorative theory to better understand the big themes of the biblical story—the justice of God, the historical mission of Jesus, the work of atonement, the nature of grace, the dynamics of forgiveness, the meaning of resurrection and Last Judgment, the mission of the church, and so on—remains seriously under-realized. My own published work has sought to use the restorative paradigm to freshly illuminate these core Christian convictions,[9] and a handful of

---

8. Zehr, *Changing Lenses*, 228.

9. Marshall, *Beyond Retribution*; Marshall, *Little Book*; Marshall, *Compassionate Justice*.

other Christian theologians and ethicists have sought to do likewise.¹⁰ But we remain a minority. For the majority of theological scholars, as well as for most Christian social activists, biblical theology and restorative justice theory remain distinct fields of knowledge, with little interconnection. Few have followed Zehr's pioneering example of interweaving the two fields of discourse into a seamless and constructive unity.

This book is intended to further this integrative goal. It brings together nine essays written over the past thirty years and published in various journals, magazines, or edited volumes, some of which are no longer readily accessible to readers. The essays were chosen for inclusion here because they all deal with issues (especially of a methodological nature) of perennial relevance to anyone interested in exploring the mandate for Christian engagement in restorative justice or in peacemaking in general, since restorative justice is best understood as a peacemaking response to crime and conflict.

I first encountered Anabaptist peace theology in the early 1980s during my time as a doctoral student in New Testament at the University of London and a few years later became captivated by the vision of restorative justice set forth in *Changing Lenses*. Ever since then, my work as a New Testament scholar, a theological educator, a religious studies professor, and now as holder of a dedicated university Chair in Restorative Justice has been dominated by a desire to understand the relationship between my commitment to nonviolent ways of pursuing justice and the witness of the Christian Scriptures, including their apparently violence-endorsing strands. My goal has been to create a kind of dialogue between restorative justice theory and practice and biblical teaching on law, crime, justice, violence, and punishment. I think of it as a dialogue because dialogues are two-way conversations, in which each side is affected, even fundamentally changed, by what the other says. By bringing restorative theory into dialogical encounter with biblical teaching, the hope is that helpful new ways will emerge of understanding both the ancient text and modern justice discourse. Both sides will benefit from the other's insights and priorities.

The reason why such a dialogue is important is because of the privileged place Christians afford to the Bible in moral and theological discernment. It is true that Christians can be effective peace and justice

---

10. Book-length examples include Myers and Enns, *Ambassadors of Reconciliation*; Belousek, *Atonement, Justice, and Peace*; Broughton, *Restorative Christ*; Flood, *Healing the Gospel*; Noakes-Duncan, *Communities of Restoration*.

practitioners without ever consulting the Bible, and many never bother to do so. But if the Bible is truly to serve as God's word, "a lamp unto our feet and light unto our path" (Ps 119:105), its witness cannot be ignored without serious deficit. All the essays in this book acknowledge the supreme authority of Scripture in shaping Christian belief and practice, and all aspire to handle the text in a hermeneutically responsible manner.

The first three chapters look at how the Bible should function in Christian ethical reflection and how best to go about articulating its insights in the public arena of secular society, and in light of diminishing levels of biblical literacy in the church and a creeping loss of confidence in the Bible's truthfulness. The next three chapters focus specifically on criminal justice themes in the text. One considers Jesus' experience on the cross as a pattern for lamenting the damage done by criminal offending and by the violence of criminal punishment. Another looks at the role of prison and the plight of prisoners in the biblical accounts, and the third explores the bitterness of criminal victimization, proposing that restorative justice "works" because it reflects the nature of ultimate reality, as disclosed in the life, death, and resurrection of Christ.

The last three essays venture into the trickiest territory of all—what to do about the acts of retributive violence ascribed to God in the biblical record and presupposed in punitive theologies of atonement. It has always been a challenge to explain, or explain away, the violence recorded in sacred Scripture. But in our day of religiously inspired terrorism and counter terrorism, it is more important than ever to find some theologically sensitive way of managing this material that will prevent it from being used to justify death-dealing retribution today as the work of God. It is also important for Christians to find a means of reconciling God's violence in the biblical accounts with the peacemaking themes that pervade the Jesus story and that can inform, even require, a commitment to restorative justice and nonviolence as gospel imperatives.

Each of the nine essays contained here was originally written for independent publication, with a specific audience in mind. Accordingly, there is no progressively unfolding argument that unifies this book. One chapter does not build on the other or advance the case to the next level. Each chapter is a stand-alone piece, and inevitably there is a degree of repetition that comes from laboring similar themes, both here and in my later books. Apart from minor editorial adjustments to fit them to their present location, I have deliberately refrained from modifying the content of the original essays or updating the literature they cite. To do so would have been a mammoth task given the thirty-year period the publications cover. Countless works of importance have appeared since the material was first published, but I thought it unwise to attempt a selective updating of references, for fear of missing key contributors. Instead I have opted to let each essay be judged on its own merits, even if the secondary sources may be a little dated. The key issue before us is how peacemaking Christians can honor the witness and authority of Scripture, in all its pluriformity, as they strive to join in God's great work in Christ of "reconciling to himself all things, whether on earth or in heaven, by making peace through the blood of his cross" (Col 1:20).

1

The Use of the Bible in Ethics

A Starting Point for a Restorative Reading of Scripture

CHRISTIANS OFTEN DISAGREE ON moral and political issues, but they usually agree that Christian ethical judgments ought to be demonstrably consistent with the teaching of Scripture in general and with the message of the Christian gospel in particular. They accept that in wrestling with difficult moral questions, believers have a duty to reflect carefully on what the Bible has to say about the matter, much like the synagogue congregation in Berea that "welcomed the message very eagerly and examined the Scriptures every day to see whether these things were so" (Acts 17:11). Even as levels of biblical literacy in churches continue to plummet, and the extent of engagement with the biblical text in most Sunday sermons is modest at best, there remains an instinctive feeling among the faithful that the Bible is important, and that even the declarations of bishops, cardinals, and church leaders need ultimately to be tested against Holy Writ.

What is less clear is *how* to do this. How should the Scriptures properly function in Christian ethical reflection? How are the sometime discordant voices of the biblical writers to be rightly appropriated when considering contested moral issues, including those to do with the nature of justice? This is the starting point for any attempt to develop a biblical theology of restorative justice.

SOURCES OF ETHICAL GUIDANCE

The Components of Christian Ethics

Ethics may be understood as the systematic study of the moral principles, values, and obligations that guide human behavior. While "morality" concerns the evaluation of such behavior as right or wrong, good or bad, "ethics" is the theoretical analysis of the major ingredients that shape and validate these moral judgments.[1] "Christian" ethics is the attempt to understand and justify moral obligation in relation to the will of God, the Creator, Redeemer, and Sustainer of all. This makes Christian ethics a distinctive enterprise.[2] That is not to say that the content of Christian moral values is radically different from the content of non-Christian values. There *are* important differences,[3] but Christian attitudes to what is right and wrong are often widely shared by non-Christians. The distinctiveness of Christian ethics lies primarily in the way Christians understand the ultimate origin and sanction of these values. At the heart of Christian ethics lies an appeal to revelation. Christian ethical judgments are governed ultimately by belief in the self-disclosure of God's own moral character and will, pre-eminently in the person and work of Jesus Christ, not by the dictates of human reason, affections, volition or environmental conditioning.

In the attempt to clarify the ethical corollaries of divine revelation, Christian ethics draws on five main sources of guidance.

Scripture

The Bible serves as the primary record of God's self-disclosure in the events of salvation-history, as apprehended by the community of faith. Inasmuch as it presents God as a righteous Being who requires righteousness of his creatures, the Bible is profoundly concerned with ethics.

---

1. Cf. Birch and Rasmussen, *Bible and Ethics*, 35–65.
2. Cf. McGrath, "Doctrine," 145–46; Douma, "Use of Scripture," 113–14.
3. Certain demands are made of Christians in the New Testament that go beyond natural human prudence or philosophically justifiable morality—preference for the outcast, costly service even unto death, helping others with no expectation of recompense, loving one's enemies, taking others more seriously than oneself. Christian ethics does not just require us to love our neighbor, but to love in the way specifically modeled by Jesus in the Gospels. On the love commands, see the stimulating discussion by Ricoeur, "Golden Rule," 392–97.

According to biblical tradition, ethical behavior stands in a two-fold relationship to God's self-revelation. On the one hand, it is a response of gratitude for God's saving acts in history, while on the other hand those saving acts themselves provide the pattern and standard for human conduct. The people of God are enjoined to model their behavior on the actions of God; the covenant requires nothing less than the "imitation of God" (Lev 11:45). The meaning of "justice," for instance, is arrived at not by contemplating some abstract norm of justice, but by remembering how God delivered his people from oppression, and then acting accordingly.[4] For Christian ethics, the imitation of God centers on the imitation of Christ (1 Pet 2:21), whose concrete manner of living and acting is known to us only through the biblical record.[5]

Theological Tradition

Revelation, including biblical revelation, is received, reflected on, and interpreted by the people of God, down through history. This interpretation and application of revelation constitutes the theological and moral tradition of Christianity, which serves as a second source for discerning God's will. It is not only the Catholic church that so uses tradition; all branches of Christianity have appealed to historical precedents and experience in formulating moral and doctrinal teaching. Such tradition is more than a collection of dogmatic and moral propositions transmitted from the past; it is also the "story" of a particular people, handed on and re-appropriated by each generation. We cannot separate ourselves from our traditions and heritage. We enter into life in the midst of tradition; we are fundamentally shaped by tradition; and even our ability to question and change tradition comes from the tradition itself.

Moral Philosophy

The great moral traditions of Western philosophy, which have appealed principally to the exercise of human reason for the determination of right

---

4. Cf. Mic 6:3–5, 8; Exod 20:1–17.

5. The precise meaning of the *imitatio Christi* motif in the New Testament is debated, but it seems clear that the early Christians believed that by imitating Jesus, they were learning to imitate God (note, for example, the use of "perfect" in Matt 5:48 and 19:21). For a survey of later uses of the motif, see Miles, "Imitation of Christ."

and wrong, have also had a profound impact on both the content and methodology of Christian ethics (the very word "ethics" is the legacy of Greek philosophy). Of particular significance has been the concept of natural law, which has been very influential in Catholic moral theology. The extent to which natural law considerations should shape Christian ethics is much contested, but some concept of a "natural" revelation of God's moral will accessible to all humanity in virtue of creation has played a role in most expressions of Christian ethics, including New Testament ethics.[6]

Empirical Data

Christian ethics is more than a speculative exercise; it also requires attention to the full range of contextual factors that bear on each ethical situation. Indeed, the first task of moral analysis is to clarify the decision-making situation and identify the range of available options. The data furnished by the social sciences and by other empirical analyses thus has an indispensable role in ethical discernment. The special contribution of such descriptive research is to keep ethical evaluation in touch with reality, where the rubber hits the road.[7]

The Spirit-in-Community

The New Testament places great emphasis on a twofold role for the Holy Spirit in Christian ethical life—that of bringing about inner moral renewal in believers so that they spontaneously manifest ethical virtues,[8] and

---

6. For example, Matt 5:45–47; Rom 1:28; 2:14–16; Acts 17:16–34; 1 Cor 11:13–15. It is noteworthy that the first Christians were not especially concerned to maintain an "ethical distance" between themselves and their non-Christian environment, except in areas where contemporary values clashed with those of the gospel. Recent studies have shown that in their paraenesis, New Testament authors draw upon well-established *topoi*, and in so doing align themselves with ethically enlightened members of wider Jewish and Greco-Roman society. This is not to deny a genuine distinctiveness about certain Christian values, nor to weaken the oft-repeated call to Christian non-conformity in the New Testament (e.g., Rom 12:1–2). It is rather to discern two complementary themes in early Christian ethical teaching, one that recognizes the common humanity of Christian and non-Christian in virtue of creation, the other that stresses the eschatological distinctiveness of Christian lifestyle.

7. See Cahill, *Between the Sexes*, 5f., 145–48.

8. See, for example, Gal 5:16–26; 6:1; Rom 8:13, 28; 9:1; 14:17; 15:13, 30; 2 Cor 3:18; 6:6; Col 1:8.

of guiding them in ethical decision-making.[9] Moral character-formation and moral decision-making are inseparably linked within the Spirit's orbit. It is crucial to recognize that in the New Testament the Spirit's work is expressed in the context of the Church.[10] "Paul knows nothing of solitary religion or individual morality," explains W. D. Davies, "but rather sees the Christian firmly based in the community."[11] The gathered community provides the necessary checks and balances that prevent the Spirit's direction degenerating into individualistic subjectivism.

This list of the main sources of Christian ethics invites two immediate observations. The first is that while the five components may be conceptually distinguished, they are in practice inseparable. Scripture cannot be entirely distinguished from tradition, since Scripture is both the product of tradition and the shaper of tradition. Empirical data does not exist in isolation from the moral values and ideological commitments that govern the gathering, classification and interpretation of data. The Spirit's guidance of the community is not merely intuitive but often employs the text of Scripture and the wisdom learned from ecclesiastical tradition or scientific discovery.[12] The five sources, then, are intertwined. Yet there is still value in notionally distinguishing them, for in different Christian traditions different constituents have the dominant role, although in all traditions ethical arguments gain in persuasiveness by employing all five in an ongoing conversation.

Secondly, our delineation of several sources of ethical guidance shows that the catch-cry *sola Scriptura* does not really apply in Christian ethics. "Scripture *alone*," contends Gustafson, "is never the final court of appeal for Christian ethics."[13] By itself the Bible is not enough to tell us what to do. The Bible may be a *necessary* source for Christian ethical reflection, but it is not a *sufficient* resource on its own. Arriving at moral judgments entails a dialectic between scriptural and non-scriptural fac-

---

9. See, for example, John 14:25–31; 15:21—16:15; Acts 15:28; Rom 8:4-6, 14; Gal 5:16, 18, 25; cf. Rom 8:13; Gal 6:8; 1 Cor 2:12.

10. 1 Cor 3:16; 6:19; 12:13; 14:29, 38; 1 Thess 5:19-22; 2 Thess 2:2; 1 John 4:1.

11. Davies, "Paul and the Law," 11.

12. Cf. Kilner, "Pauline Approach," 366-79.

13. Gustafson, "Place of Scripture," 455. Gustafson affirms that the role of Scripture is to inform Christian moral judgments, "but it does not by itself determine what they ought to be. That determination is done by persons and communities as finite moral agents responsible to God." So too, Long, "Use of the Bible," 451; Verhey, "Bible," 57, 60–61.

tors, between considerations based on circumstance and rational inquiry and those that appeal to the biblical witness. The challenge of Christian ethics is to achieve a judicious balance between these considerations in the task of moral deliberation. A dialogical interplay between Scripture and experience is unavoidable, for every claim to understand the Bible presupposes finite human interpretation, and every interpretation is invariably conditioned by a wide range of (extra-biblical) personal and contextual factors.

Having said that, for most Christians, including those who do not subscribe to a "high" doctrine of biblical inspiration, Scripture is still felt to possess a unique authority in Christian ethical reasoning. The essential test of validity for ethical judgments is whether they are consistent with what is perceived to be scriptural teaching. Even if our understanding of that teaching is subject to change, Scripture *per se* has long been accorded, at least in theory,[14] a privileged role in adjudicating Christian moral teaching; indeed, it is precisely as an authority that the Bible has chiefly been employed in Christian ethics.[15]

The Role of Scripture

Much has happened over the past two hundred years to undermine the privileged position traditionally accorded Scripture in determining Christian thought and practice. For many interpreters today, such considerations as the pre-scientific worldview of the biblical authors, their reliance upon primitive mythological language and apocalyptic symbolism, the alleged dependence of New Testament ethics on a discredited

---

14. According to Barnabas Lindars, although the Reformers claimed to transfer authority in ethical matters from the pronouncements of the *Magisterium* of the church to the Bible, their moral traditions "were largely prefabricated, and really only employed the Bible as the authoritative sanction for them," "Bible and Christian Ethics," 181. Yoder similarly urges that "Protestant scholasticism . . . claimed that the Bible was the only moral authority and announced a fundamental suspicion of moral discernment . . . [which] claims rootage in reason, nature, and tradition. Yet when this official Protestantism turned to the problems of administering its own society, there resulted at the time no profound difference between it and Catholicism on any practical moral issues: divorce, usury, war, or truth-telling," Yoder, "Hermeneutics," 45. See also Yoder, "Authority," 265–72.

15. More ink has been spilled asserting the fact that the Bible possesses authority than in reflecting on what is meant by "authority" itself. For helpful discussions on this, see Wright, "Authoritative?," 7–32; Hauerwas, "Moral Authority," 356–70.

imminent eschatology,[16] and the sheer, irreconcilable diversity of ethical perspectives in Scripture, make it impossible to ascribe a normative role to the Bible in ethical deliberations.[17] And yet, as Marshall observes, "there remains a lingering suspicion that the Bible *is* authoritative; sermons are still based on biblical texts, and if a preacher or scholar disagrees with what Scripture says, he usually feels compelled to produce some good reasons for his disagreement."[18] Whatever the problems in appropriating Scripture today—and they are considerable—there continues to be a widespread conviction, across confessional lines, that Scripture can, does, and should shape Christian moral life. And there remain strong historical, theological, and practical arguments for according the Bible such a decisive or normative role.

Historically, the Bible has significantly shaped the moral ethos of Western culture. In the past, considerable knowledge of the Bible was transmitted through general culture, and biblical authority was almost universally accepted in the West. This is no longer the case, so that comparison with the Bible provides one yardstick for measuring changes in the moral values of contemporary society, as well as highlighting the declining power of the Judeo-Christian ethic in shaping our social and cultural life.

Theologically, the Christian community still affirms, with a fair measure of confidence, that the Bible contains or bears witness to divine revelation. Most important in this respect is the fact that it provides our only access to God's self-disclosure in the life, death, and resurrection of Christ, to which Christians are directly accountable. In the final analysis, it is because Christian believers discover themselves to be directly encountered by Christ in the text of Scripture that they continue to listen to Scripture.

Practically, the Bible provides an indispensable framework for understanding the human situation in general, and the task of the Christian community in particular. The biblical story offers a perspective on the

---

16. The particular model used to interpret New Testament eschatology, has been the most decisive consideration in determining how scholars have judged the contemporary relevance of New Testament ethics. See the survey in Scroggs, "New Testament and Ethics," 77-93 (especially 84-89).

17. For brief surveys of those with such views, see I. H. Marshall, "Using the Bible," 45-49; Swartley, *Slavery*, 204-11; Cook, *Moral Maze*, 46-50; Furnish, *Moral Teaching*, 18-23.

18. I H. Marshall, "Using the Bible," 39-40.

human condition that carries the conviction of truth. It attests, as Gustafson observes, both to the limitations and the potentialities of human action in the world.[19] It affirms the existence of moral evil; the temptations to pride and arrogance in human achievements; the capacity for people to rationalize destructive behavior by appealing to noble ends; the finitude of moral judgments. It provides, on the other hand, a vision of the possibilities of human life. It affirms that the unfulfilled future is in the hands of a compassionate and just God; it gives insight into God's ultimate intentions in history; it describes actions and events that are seen to be consistent or inconsistent with God's aspirations for humanity; it gives voice to the longing of oppressed people for peace and justice; and it depicts the creation of a special people to serve as co-workers with God in bringing these about. All this has profound ethical significance.

> This scriptural faith disposes the Christian community toward moral seriousness, toward profound dissatisfaction with those events that are destructive of human life and value, toward aspirations for a future which is more fulfilling for all God's creation; and thus toward negative judgment on events which are not consistent with the possibilities that God is creating for man.[20]

Thus, while Scripture is not, and cannot, be the exclusive source of guidance for Christian ethics (even within the New Testament, written Scripture does not fulfill such an exclusive role),[21] there is good reason to regard it as the primary or normative authority for Christian morality and identity. And, as George Lindbeck notes, the "instinct of the faithful" is still to invest such worth in Scripture, even if popular knowledge of the actual content of Scripture is in noticeable decline, inside as well as outside the church.[22] Despite this, the Christian community is still more ready to accept ethical judgments that run counter to theological tradition or philosophical morality or contemporary scientific judgment or the advice of their clerical leaders than those that are plainly inconsistent with Scripture.

---

19. Gustafson, "Place of Scripture," 448–49.

20. Ibid., 449.

21. In Paul's paraenesis, written Scripture serves primarily to confirm, reinforce or illuminate ethical demands that are derived from other considerations; see Furnish, *Theology and Ethics*, 28–43; Furnish, "Belonging to Christ," 151.

22. Lindbeck, "Scripture," 74–101.

But none of this takes us very far. It is one thing to assert the unique authority of Scripture for Christian morality; it is quite another to demonstrate how the Scriptures can most appropriately function this way, and to decide precisely what Scripture authorizes and denies. The fundamental issue is not whether the Bible is authoritative for ethics but how we move from biblical ethical judgments to present problems. Using an ancient religious text, even an inspired one, for ethical guidance today is fraught with hermeneutical difficulties, and the Bible itself does not give us clear instructions on how to reason from its moral imperatives to their practical application to the problems of real life. Consequently, ways of interpreting both the ethics of Scripture, and the use of Scripture in ethics, vary enormously.[23]

Some Hermeneutical Problems

A great deal could be said about the hermeneutical hurdles that confront the Christian ethicist in turning to Scripture.[24] The most obvious is the problem of historical distance, the fact that we face ethical dilemmas today of which the Bible knows nothing. How can the Bible be a lamp for our feet in matters such as genetic engineering, *in vitro* fertilization, nuclear weapons, world hunger, or free market economics? Even in areas of current concern to which the Bible does apparently speak (for example, politics, war, labor relations, marriage and sexuality), it presupposes a radically different socio-political reality, with a different range of options open to actors. How can advice given in one context be reapplied in another, totally different context, even if the topic under discussion is the same? Just because the topic is the same does not mean the central issues are the same.

Now the problems of historical distance are certainly weighty; to disregard them is to doom the Scriptures to irrelevance. But the dilemma is perhaps not as serious as some allege,[25] since the most pressing ethical

23. Gustafson observes that "the study of the ethics in the Scriptures . . . is a complex task for which few are well prepared; those who are specialists in ethics generally lack the intensive and proper training in biblical studies, and those who are specialists in biblical studies often lack sophistication in ethical thought" ("Place of Scripture," 430).

24. See, for example, the eleven problems briefly surveyed by C. D. Marshall, "Use of the Bible," 131–33. See also Rodd, "Use of Old Testament," 101–2. A more technical discussion of hermeneutical dilemmas is found in Cahill, *Between the Sexes*, 15–44.

25. There is truth in Fowl and Jones' assertion that "the most important

issues human beings face, even those peculiar to modern life, usually turn on perennial questions of power, wealth, violence, class, or gender, and about such matters the Bible speaks extensively.[26] Although the Bible cannot function as a direct guide with respect to many modern problems, particular courses of action can still be evaluated in light of the central commitments of the biblical text on matters of power, wealth, justice, and the like.

More serious than the problem of cultural distance is the many-sided phenomenon of pluralism that confronts us in the interpretation of Scripture. There is, first, the pluralism in the content and expression of biblical morality itself. There is no shortage of ethical material in Scripture. But it comes in a huge diversity of literary forms—commands, laws, warnings, exhortations, prohibitions, wisdom teaching, proverbs, allegories, prayers, parables, visions of the future, narratives, living examples, dialogues, vice and virtue lists, and more. Different forms of moral discourse require different modes of interpretation. More than this, there is diversity in the ethical perspectives presented on particular themes, such as the handling of wealth. In some places, the biblical writers endorse a prudential morality accessible to everyone; in other places, they propose an ethical absolutism that defies every canon of common sense or social pragmatism.[27] As the record of God's interaction with people over a long historical period, and in a wide range of cultural and social situations, there is development as well as variety in biblical ethics. Scripture is a historical document, not a legal constitution in which all parts can be treated as equally important for all generations. There is both intracanonical dialogue, with one part of Scripture interpreting and complementing another; and intracanonical critique, with some perspectives being relegated to preparatory and accommodating roles.[28]

Now the sheer quantity, variety and historical conditionedness of ethical material in the Bible makes sustaining any "objective" authority

---

discontinuities are not historical, but moral and theological. That is, the important discontinuities between Scripture and our contemporary settings are more likely found within us, specifically in our inability and unwillingness to provide and embody wise readings of the texts, than in gaps of historical time." Fowl and Jones, *Reading*, 61, also 81. See also Hauerwas, "Moral Authority," 369–70.

26. I. H. Marshall, "Interpret the Bible," 10; Packer, "Infallible Scripture," 331–32.

27. For a recent discussion of this with respect to the ethics of Jesus, see Harvey, *Strenuous Commands*.

28. Swartley, *Slavery*, 217–18.

for Scripture problematic. It poses the question of how we do justice to the variety of perspectives Scripture offers without imposing our own agenda. How do we determine the continuities and moral priorities of Scripture? How do we bring some degree of organization and integration to biblical teaching? Is such secondary organization legitimate, or is it an arbitrary imposition on a heterogeneous range of texts? Is it admissible to set up a canon within a canon? Can we in fact avoid doing so?[29]

Such internal canonical pluralism is matched, secondly, by a pluralism of historical and theological reconstructions of the biblical message. There has always been a diversity of ways of construing the overall unity of biblical teaching—be it in terms of covenant, nature and grace, law and gospel, sequential dispensations, the kingdom of God, and so on. To this diversity have been added the results of modern historical criticism. Invaluable light has been shed on the biblical world by historical criticism, but it has also spawned an enormous diversity of explanations for the origin and meaning of the text, all of which are tentative and constantly changing. One result of historical criticism has been to convince the educated laity that biblical interpretation is a technical enterprise that requires prolonged specialized training, so that "it is now the scholarly rather than the hierarchical clerical elite which holds the Bible captive and makes it inaccessible to ordinary folk."[30]

Third, there is a pluralism of modern idioms and conceptions that the biblical message is translated into, some philosophical, some political, some mystical. How do we decide what is, and what is not, a

---

29. The practice of setting up a canon within a canon is usually rejected in principle by most interpreters. But in practice it seems unavoidable, for the moment we favor New Testament over Old Testament teaching, or differentiate between what is culturally relative and what is abiding revelation, we are effectively setting up a canon within a canon (so Scroggs, *Text and the Times*, 273–75; also Dunn, *Living Word*, 44–64, 141–74). In relation to this, Fowl and Jones, *Reading*, make a helpful distinction between a normative and functional canon within a canon. A *normative* canon within a canon is where certain texts are excluded from consideration on *a priori* grounds. This is to be rejected outright, for "no text—no matter how 'difficult'—should be excluded from the ongoing processes of communal discernment in relation to the whole witness of Scripture." A *functional* canon within a canon is where certain texts are discerned by certain communities at certain times to be more appropriate than others. This is quite acceptable. "Within a canon as diverse as the one Christians recognize, there is no reason to think that all of its texts will be equally relevant in any given situation. Some texts will be more appropriate than others in any given situation. This sets up a 'functional' canon within a canon." Fowl and Jones, *Reading*, 53n23.

30. Lindbeck, "Scripture," 90. So too Francis Schüssler Fiorenza, "Crisis," 356–57.

faithful reinterpretation of the biblical message? The conscious attempt of modern interpreters to re-express biblical thought in the language of the day, while both helpful and necessary, has resulted in a "pluralistic cacophony" of diverse and variable accounts that are often mutually unintelligible.[31] Indeed such is the diversity of modern approaches to biblical interpretation that it has become increasingly problematic to speak of the "meaning" of the text at all. For a text can mean different things to different people, depending on the interpretive interests pursued by the reader, and there is no impartial way of determining the text's "real" or "true" meaning.[32]

Modern (more so, postmodern) readers of Scripture are more aware than ever before in history of the hermeneutical dilemmas posed by this threefold pluralism. Sadly, for many ordinary Christians the Bible has become a closed book. Yet there is no magical way of avoiding such pluralism. The problem exists, it is real, and it has to be faced whenever we turn to Scripture for guidance in ethical decisions. What Richard Hays calls "bumper sticker hermeneutics"—"God said it, I believe it, that settles it"—is clearly no solution, since it ignores rather than solves the problem.[33]

But the alternative need not be total relativism or skepticism. Written texts always retain a certain independence of voice over against those of their interpreters, a capacity to challenge readings based on inappropriate or alien assumptions. If this is true of texts in general, it is even more true of Scripture, which, Christians confess, is used by the Spirit-in-community to convey the mind of God to God's people. As long as we are prepared to consent to biblical authority, to be self-critical of our own handling of the text, to allow Scripture to be a "two-edged sword" that can challenge our presuppositions and expose the interpretive filters of our social location, and be open to the possibility, even the necessity, of diverse yet equally faithful appropriations of the text today, the hermeneutical problems of using Scripture for ethics are not insuperable.

---

31. Lindbeck, "Scripture," 88–90.
32. See Fowl and Jones, *Reading*, 14–21.
33. Hays, "Scripture-Shaped Community," 43; Hays, *Moral Vision*, 3.

The Search for a Method

If then the Bible should, and, despite the above hurdles, can be used as a normative reference point in ethical decision-making, it seems self-evident that a method must be devised for exploring the moral implications of Scripture in a systematic and not in a haphazard way.[34] Most biblical interpreters have agreed on this for a long time. Yet despite their very best efforts, none have succeeded in devising a comprehensive method for moving from the text of Scripture to the current situation.[35]

In view of this, there is a growing recognition that the quest for a single definitive method is misguided. It is misguided for at least two reasons. The first is that no single method can cope with the pluriformity of Scripture itself. Since there is a variety of materials in Scripture, there needs to be a variety of ways of construing its moral application. "To reduce Scripture's moral requirements to any single category is to distort both morality and Scripture."[36] Second, there is no one method that can straddle the diversity of contemporary contexts readers find themselves in. Fowl and Jones argue that past attempts to specify a clear and precise method have rested on the false assumption that ethical decisions are made by isolated individuals, who ought to follow a rationally-defensible method, the validity of which is independent of social and historical circumstances. But individuals learn to make moral judgments in particular historical communities; moral descriptions employ the categories and commitments of distinct social traditions; and even if it were possible to identify generalizable methodological principles, every attempt to apply them is context-dependent. Accordingly, "the search for a context-independent method is bound to fail."[37]

This is not to deny the value of systematic methodological reflection, nor to advocate a complete relativism where every interpretation is equally valid. It is simply to recognize the variety of ways Scripture can be used in ethics, and to insist that there is no neutral, transcendent, fail-safe method for evaluating specific appropriations of the text. Moral reasoning and justification are still of critical importance, but such evaluations can only be made by particular communities in particular situations,

---

34. So Sleeper, "Ethics," 460; Gustafson, "Place of Scripture," 439; Birch and Rasmussen, *Bible and Ethics*, 166–67.

35. Cf. Scroggs, "Ethics," 90–91.

36. Childress, "Scripture," 378. So too Spohn, *Scripture and Ethics*, 3–5, 90.

37. Fowl and Jones, *Reading*, 13.

under the guidance of the Spirit and drawing on all the resources available to them at the time. These resources will include methodological controls appropriate to the character and vision of the community.

Various typologies have been suggested to describe how the Scriptures have been used in ethics. In what follows, I will employ a tripartite classification, with various sub-categories. It must be stressed that these categories are not distinct, mutually exclusive methods pursued in opposition to each other; in practice, most biblical scholars and ethicists blend elements of all three (though often with one or the other occupying the driving seat). It is not my intention to suggest that the three broad approaches form a methodological hierarchy, with the third approach superseding the earlier two. Each method has a valid and irreducible contribution to make. Therefore, after analyzing the strengths and weaknesses inherent in each way of using Scripture, we will reaffirm the merits of a methodological pluralism. But there is still value in teasing out the different assumptions and priorities at work in each distinct way of employing Scripture in ethics so that we have some basis for understanding competing evaluations of the moral witness of Scripture in particular issues.

THE PRESCRIPTIVE USE OF SCRIPTURE

In this method, the Bible is understood as prescribing moral rules, ordinances, commands, principles, or ideals, which are to be faithfully observed in current situations. This approach has a very long history,[38] and is perhaps still the most common way the ethical authority of the Bible is understood by Christians. The prescriptive use gives maximum value to the sizeable collections of moral imperatives in the Bible—the laws of the Pentateuch, the moral precepts of Proverbs, the criticisms of the prophets, the ethical teaching of Jesus, the moral codes of the epistles. Together these constitute a "revealed morality" that demands obedience; deontological reasoning prevails over teleological or consequentialist considerations.[39] There are two main expressions of the prescriptive use of the Bible, though each has many possible permutations.

---

38. Cf. Long, "Use of the Bible," 150–52.

39. For the distinction between a revealed morality and a revealed reality, see Gustafson, "Place of Scripture," 430–55.

Biblical Moralism

One expression is a straightforward biblicism that treats the Bible as a rule book and insists on literalistic adherence to the letter of the law. Actions are deemed morally wrong if they violate the rules and regulations specified in any of the biblical texts, and morally right if some explicit biblical warrant, contrived or otherwise, can be cited. The merit of this approach is the attention it gives to the numerous divine imperatives and sanctions in the biblical text, and to some New Testament depictions of Jesus as, in some sense, a new Lawgiver (e.g., by Matthew). But there are also severe methodological flaws in the approach.

(1) It is inherently selective in the way it uses the biblical evidence; it accepts as binding certain imperatives and not others.[40] There is a preunderstanding at work that governs the choice of texts to be applied to particular situations and that provides ways of explaining away other texts that would, on the surface of it, contravene the moral stance being adopted. The diversity of biblical ethical teaching is reduced to a predetermined uniformity.

(2) Advocates of this approach are often guilty of inadequate exegesis. They tend to gloss over the exegetical difficulties tied up with appeals to particular texts and assume that their application today is relatively straightforward. They also fail to take the historical character of biblical teaching seriously wherein certain moral prescriptions are rendered obsolete by later developments. Instead the Bible is treated as a flat-text, with each part potentially carrying the same moral authority today as any other. As Birch and Rasmussen warn,

> The church must constantly guard against those who would declare moral imperatives in areas where the biblical witness does not warrant this. The history of the church is filled with examples of those who endowed some limited portion of Scripture with absolute moral authority. Careful exegesis in the context of the entire canon is a safeguard . . . Only those concerns consistently identified throughout Scripture as moral imperatives necessary to the authentic self-understanding of God's people can be claimed as necessary marks of faith on biblical grounds.[41]

---

40. Of course, this is true of every use of the Bible in ethics; we always relate equivocally or ambiguously to the text, accepting certain parts, rejecting some, and qualifying others. The literalist refuses to admit to doing so, however.

41. Birch and Rasmussen, *Bible and Ethics*, 184.

(3) There is a tendency to legalism or superstition. The paradigm of "law" governs interpretation of ethics in general, so that the words of Jesus or Paul are taken, at least in intent,[42] as legal prescriptions in the same way as Old Testament commands. Emphasis falls on external conformity to pre-set rules, with little attention being paid to the motivations, intentions or consequences of ethical decisions. As a result, obedience to biblical injunctions ceases to be genuinely moral, since moral decision-making requires a free choosing of the good in light of particular circumstances, not a mechanical adherence to rules. Human morality is too complex to define simply in terms of adhering to a law code.

(4) In treating the Bible as a source of moral rules, the method distorts the kind of book the Bible is. Certainly, the Bible includes laws and imperatives. But such material constitutes a very small proportion of the total text; the dominant literary genre is narrative, not law.[43] This is even the case in the Pentateuch, where most of the legal material of the Old Testament is found. Even in interpreting the legal and moral prescriptions, it needs to be recognized that they were never formulated as timeless truths but as timely applications of God's will in specific situations. The very fact that they were intended to be relevant to *that* situation implies they are not *directly* applicable to *our* situation.[44] To treat all biblical prescriptions as eternally valid rules of conduct begs the question of the intention behind their original formulation.

(5) Direct enforcement of biblical injunctions, regardless of circumstances, can end up with ethical results out of harmony with the spirit of biblical teaching or the moral wisdom of the church's tradition. The logic of the position is either a reversal of cultural development and a freezing

---

42. The problem is that when one attempts to take all of Jesus's words this way, one soon discovers many are impossible to keep, so that even the most serious Christian is forced to accept an ethically unsatisfactory compromise. For a brief survey of interpretive options, see Davies and Allison, "Reflections," 283–309. According to Furnish, "Paul nowhere lays down a rigid, legalistic code of Christian conduct" (*Moral Teaching*, 17).

43. Cf. Goldingay, "Models for Scripture," 19–37; Goldingay, "Theological Reflection," 181–88.

44. Furnish has termed this "the law of varying relevancy"—the more specifically relevant any given moral instruction is to a particular biblical situation, the less specifically relevant it is to other particular situations, *Moral Teaching*, 16. In a more recent article, Furnish renamed this "the law of *diminishing* relevancy"—insofar as counsels were *specifically* applicable in the situations to which they were originally addressed, they *cannot be specifically* applicable in other situations; idem, "Belonging to Christ," 146.

of life in a past age, or the elaboration of an accompanying body of oral or written interpretations to apply the laws to changing situations, such as found in Rabbinic Judaism.[45] Neither option has been generally adopted by the Church.

(6) Finally, biblical moralism works best in matters of personal morality, but has little to offer Christian social ethics, since the New Testament has little in the way of explicit social legislation.[46] It may be possible to govern one's personal conduct according to a check-list of biblical prescriptions; it is impossible to organize complex social interrelationships, which invariably entail conflict and the need for compromise, on such a basis.

Biblical Casuistry

The other main expression of the prescriptive approach is a more sophisticated casuistry that seeks to discern underlying principles and ideals behind biblical teaching, then reapply them in contemporary situations. This method overcomes the problems of biblicism by positing a distinction between two main forms of ethical guidance (though the terminology used to identify each varies).[47] On the one hand, there are ethical directives, specific ethical instructions or rules that summon obedience to particular demands. The key thing about such directives is that they are addressed to, and are to be obeyed within, a specific cultural setting. Rules do not make sense in a cultural vacuum. On the other hand, there are ethical principles, general statements of conduct that do not tell us what to do in detail but point us in a particular direction or advocate a particular quality of conduct. Such principles or ideals are trans-situational; once identified they can be applied authoritatively in a variety of contexts. Sometimes these moral or theological principles are stated explicitly in the text;[48] at other times they lie buried beneath

---

45. Cf. Gustafson, "Place of Scripture," 439-40; Longenecker, *Social Ethics*, 3.

46. For an excellent discussion on how the New Testament can be used for social ethics, see Mott, "Social Ethics I, Part I," 11-20; Mott, "Social Ethics I, Part II," 19-26.

47. Cf. Childress, "Scripture," 378-80; Mathieson, "Principles and Rules," 8-16; Bloesch, *Freedom*, 55-56; Longenecker, *Social Ethics*, 14-15; Ramm, *Interpretation*, 179-80.

48. For example, "Do not do anything that causes your brother or sister to stumble" (1 Cor 8:13; Rom 14:13-21); "Keep your life free from the love of money and be content with what you have" (Heb 13:5); "Do not be unequally yoked together with

specific teaching or narrative and need to be excavated.[49] The supreme norm, around which all such principles orbit, is that of Christ-like love: "love one another as I have loved you" (John 14:15).

Thus, the job of Christian ethics is to extract fundamental ethical principles from Scripture, then find culturally appropriate ways (or binding prescriptions) to translate these principles into our situation. "The task of the biblical moralist," says Marshall, "is to extrapolate from Scripture to the particular ethical exhortations appropriate in different situations."[50] Such applications will vary from place to place and time to time. Consequently, the task of deriving new rules from old principles is an on-going one. Both sides of this ethical task are important. If we simply stress ethical rules in Scripture, we end up in rigid legalism. If we stop at the level of identifying general principles without granting specific application, (e.g., "do what love requires in each unique situation"), we end up in total subjectivism.

Now this method of using Scripture for ethics has several strengths.

(1) It takes biblical authority seriously; all biblical teaching, not just specific ethical injunctions, is treated with respect, since ethical principles relevant to some contemporary situation may be locked up in material that at first sight has little resemblance to the modern problem. Even the sternest, most uncompromising demands, such as the "hard sayings" of Jesus, can receive a genuine hearing when one is searching for underlying ideals and principles.

(2) We are not forced to take literally commands that are no longer applicable in changed circumstances. Instead of a wooden literalism, we are free to find creative re-applications of underlying principles, without minimizing the importance of concrete prescriptions. Our task is to follow the biblical message faithfully rather than literally.

(3) It enables us to cope better with diversity in biblical morality. The existence of such diversity is explained by the fact that the same principles may find quite different expressions in different situations.

---

unbelievers" (2 Cor 6:14); "Do all things decently and in order; for God is not a God of confusion but peace" (1 Cor 14:35).

49. For example, the ban on charging interest in Old Testament law (Exod 22:25; Lev 25:36; Deut 23:19), in the context of primitive agrarian society, expresses the principle that *it is wrong to exploit the poor*. In our modern, commercial, inflationary economic system, charging interest may be acceptable as long as it does not violate this principle.

50. I. H. Marshall, "Using," 51; I. H. Marshall, "Use," 133, 135–36.

Conversely, the extant variety of concrete ethical advice in Scripture all but requires some attempt to discern guiding convictions behind it.

(4) When the norm of agape is given a governing role, as it is in the New Testament itself, harsh legalism is ruled out. For love, by its very nature, requires that situational factors are taken into account in applying biblical teaching, so that in a given instance it may be the most loving application of a principle to do the very opposite of a specific biblical injunction (e.g., refusing to give freely to an alcoholic [cf. Luke 6:30], or to pay taxes where they will be used to prepare for nuclear genocide [cf. Rom 13:6]).

(5) It allows for continuing progress in ethical application beyond the canonical boundaries.[51] Slavery is tolerated in the Bible, but there are other principles in biblical morality that ultimately render it unacceptable. Patriarchy is presupposed in biblical teaching, but the principle of equality, enunciated most clearly in Gal 3:28, heralds its eventual transcendence, while subverting its oppressive character in the meantime. Capital punishment is explicitly sanctioned in the Old Testament and challenged only by implication in the New. But there was good reason to make the implied challenge explicit at a subsequent period, in light of the broader concerns of the gospel.

The positive features of this casuistic approach are therefore considerable. But the method is also open to abuse and criticism:

(1) It can easily become too rationalistic and abstract. It begins with concrete examples, then moves up the ladder of abstraction to general principles or ideals. In so doing, it can verge on an ahistorical idealism or intellectual reductionism that wrenches biblical statements out of their social, historical, and covenantal context and converts them into timeless ethical norms. This is particularly apparent in attempts to isolate timeless, supracultural principles in scriptural teaching.[52] But did the biblical authors intend their specific statements to be abstracted into abiding, universal principles? One further temptation of this method is to blunt the radical edge of specific commands in Scripture, such as those of the Sermon on the Mount, by transposing them into bland principles or ideal dispositions.[53] Clearly there are "ideals" in Scripture, though they are not

---

51. See especially Longenecker's "developmental" hermeneutic in *Social Ethics*; also Fuller, "Paul and Galatians," 9-13.

52. For a recent example, see Tiessen, "Toward a Hermeneutic," 189-207.

53. Harvey points out that although it has been generally recognized to have made a distinctive contribution to the moral development of the West, Jesus's ethic has been

timeless metaphysical values but visions of a concrete state of affairs in the future toward which the historical community is beckoned (e.g., Isa 11:6-7). In short, a concern for divining prescriptive principles and ideals can divorce biblical ethics from the exigencies of specific contexts and persons.[54]

(2) The procedure of deriving principles becomes a very subjective exercise, too easily reflecting the bias of the interpreter.[55] Different interpreters may derive different principles from the same text. What criteria exist for deciding who is right? Rules of thumb can be suggested for isolating key principles (e.g., differentiating between what the Bible records and what it commends; seeking the intention or goal of a particular instruction; ensuring consistency with overarching themes; etc.), but such guidelines can still yield diverse results. The distinction between "rules" and "principles" is also rather fluid. Is "thou shalt not kill" an underlying principle of the value of human life, or a specific rule forbidding murder within the context of the covenantal community?

(3) As an ethical method, it is too vague and atomistic. Sometimes the principles deduced are so general or banal as to be virtually useless in granting specific direction in contemporary reflection.[56] Moreover, there is more to ethical life than applying a series of isolated principles. Especially in social ethics, some overall model or social theory is needed to show how the principles interrelate and promote a particular way of life.[57] What happens, for example, when two principles conflict (e.g., the principle of private property and the principle of economic justice; or the principles of justice and mercy)? How are the principles to be related to each other in an overall framework?

(4) The mode of application of biblical principles or ideals in different circumstances is more complex than often assumed. Where

---

greatly neglected, both in everyday practice and in Christian moral philosophy. Harvey, *Strenuous Commands*, especially chapters 1, 2, 9.

54. Horsley, "Ethics," 4; cf. Yoder, "Hermeneutics," 59-61.

55. Schluter and Clements, "Jubilee," 49.

56. For instance, Mathieson suggests that many items of Paul's teaching (on gender, on work, on disputes between believers) imply the principle of doing nothing to bring church into avoidable public contempt by deliberately flouting conventional secular morality; "Principles and Rules," 10

57. So Schluter and Clements, "Jubilee," 49. Such a pattern is often sought either in the social life of ancient Israel or Jesus's proclamation of the kingdom of God. See, for example, C. Wright, *Use of the Bible*; Kaye, *Using the Bible*; Barclay and Sugden, "Biblical Social Ethics," 5-18; Barclay, "Theology," 6-23.

present reality does not wholly conform to the ideal or principle, some compromises or approximations are necessary. How do we decide how much compromise is required or justified, if indeed compromises, even unavoidable compromises, can strictly be "justified"?[58] Furthermore, a principle derived from a biblical command or text related to a specific socio-political context should ideally be reapplied in a contemporary context that is analogous to the biblical context. How are these analogies to be identified?

Now such cautions as these do not render the prescriptive appeal to the Bible wholly illegitimate. By no means. Moral rules *do* have an indispensable role in ethical life, and it *is* possible to identify important concerns or principles within biblical morality. According to James Childress, biblical authority is distorted if the rules and principles contained in Scripture are ignored or down-played.[59] But equally the nature and function of Scripture are also distorted if the Bible is reduced to a collection of ahistorical moral prescriptions, and Christian moral experience is impoverished if it is equated with the intellectual application of a norm-based system of rules.

THE ILLUMINATIVE USE OF SCRIPTURE

In this approach, the Bible is viewed not as a source book of moral norms or prescriptions but as a resource for basic values and perspectives that can inform contemporary decision-making. It sets forth a moral and theological framework, or symbolic universe, that provides the context for considering ethical decisions. Recent scholarship has tended to reject the prescriptive in favor of an illuminative use of Scripture, for both theological and practical reasons. Theologically, there is, especially in Protestant scholarship, a dread of legalism, a fear of substituting genuine obedience to the sovereign Word of God with a rationally devised system of ethics, which might then become a ground for commending ourselves to God.[60] Practically, the plurality of literary forms in the Bible, the cultural distance that separates the "then" of the biblical text from the "now" of today, and the sheer complexity of the moral questions we face today, mean that biblical prescriptions are inadequate to the task of moral

---

58. See Boston, "Moral Dilemmas," 2–12; Boston, "Sinning Boldly," 7–17.
59. Childress, "Scripture," 380; Spohn, *Scripture and Ethics*, 135.
60. Cf. Spohn, *Scripture and Ethics*, 19–35.

guidance. But ethical decisions can still need to be *illuminated* by, and must be consonant with, the central concerns and commitments of the Bible. Scripture thus provides a kind of "revealed reality" that determines the basic direction and orientation of Christian morality.

The illuminative or perspectival use of Scripture can take many forms. To illustrate, we shall consider two methodological procedures that seek to allow Scripture to elucidate contemporary moral situations.

Reasoning from Biblical Images

Earlier we noted how Scripture provides both a compelling portrait of the human condition and an account of a God who acts and speaks in particular historical events. If history is the arena of divine revelation, then Christian ethical decision-making needs to be based on a "reading of the times," on a decision about what God is saying or doing in contemporary events. To determine this, Scripture should be consulted. The answer will come not from the prescriptive commandments or moral norms of Scripture but by a process of discernment guided by the central images of the text. Since God is not capricious, the patterns central to biblical revelation and theological generalizations about the character of God can be used to detect the continuing manifestation of God in current affairs. Just as the exilic prophets used the exodus to interpret release from Babylonian captivity, so modern Christians can use the images and symbols of Scripture, and supremely the way of the Cross, to uncover God's actions in the present, and hence decide an appropriate ethical response.

The strength of this approach is its movement away from isolated proof-texts and principles toward a holistic application of biblical revelation. The concern to root ethics in a theologically sound image of God, and God's definitive manifestation in the Crucified One, is also important. This makes Christian morality distinctive, not merely as a result of accumulated moral judgments about particular matters, but because of the theological worldview that gives meaning, direction, and content to ethical conduct.

But there are also problems with this approach.

(1) The key problem in an appeal to the guiding images of Scripture is knowing the right ones to select. "Some current writers," observes Spohn, "seem to have abandoned proof-texting for 'proof-theming'—selecting

biblical images that support moral conclusions they have reached on other grounds."[61] History has witnessed many times the tragic results of Christians choosing the conquest of Canaan or Samson's destruction of the Philistines as the central paradigm for discerning God's present will. Some criteria (or "rules"?) are needed to avoid such distortions.[62]

(2) Even if such negative images are excluded, there remains a wide diversity of positive images that might be used to grant perspective on contemporary events, each potentially yielding a different conclusion. It is too easy to make a moral judgment on the basis of personal or political values, and then find some biblical image to support it from the variety available. Indeed, the same image can produce diverse judgments; the exodus has been used, for example, to justify both violent liberation movements and to commend nonviolent resistance to oppressive regimes.[63] In short, whether we allow a single privileged image or set of images to guide discernment, or if we seek to do justice to the variety of images in Scripture, the result may well be ambiguous.

(3) While biblical images and themes provide an important framework for approaching specific decisions, surely Scripture can also offer a little more normative clarity on specific concerns. The exclusion of any normative authority for Scriptural commands, laws or principles threatens to undermine the distinctively Christian character of Christian ethics, and allow too much place for subjective judgment. While the Bible's ethical function should not be reduced to that of a prescriptive code, there are matters about which the Bible speaks to us in the form of direct moral address, and does so repeatedly and consistently. This suggests that there are certain moral imperatives, such as care for the poor and oppressed, that are not optional for those who claim allegiance to the God of the Bible.

---

61. Spohn, *Scripture and Ethics*, 82.

62. Spohn identifies several criteria implicit in Niebuhr's use of Scripture: (1) Those biblical images that function as continuing sources of revelation for the biblical tradition (e.g., the exodus) are most appropriate; (2) guiding images should be consistent with a theologically sound image of God; (3) images should be consistent with God's definitive revelation in Jesus Christ; images from both testaments must be gauged against the story of Jesus; (4) images should be appropriate to the situation addressed and shed light upon it; (5) the images used should indicate courses of action that concur with the standards of ordinary human morality. *Scripture and Ethics*, 83f.

63. See Yoder, "Withdrawal," 76–84.

Reasoning by Analogy

The second methodological procedure seeks to establish a connection between the current situation and appropriate biblical teaching by a process of analogical and dialectical reasoning. Biblical texts may be accepted as relevant for today if there is a significant similarity between the situation addressed in Scripture and the situation that pertains now. Conversely, contemporary actions may be evaluated by a comparison to similar actions under similar circumstances recorded in the Bible. In this way, the Bible becomes a collection of models or paradigms that can be mobilized when a significant parallel exists between circumstances then and now.

The principle of analogy can operate in a prescriptive fashion, with the pattern of the biblical model having binding authority in comparable circumstances today. The illuminative use of analogy is somewhat looser. Its aim is to learn from biblical examples, not necessarily to duplicate them in particulars. The function of biblical paradigms is neither to provide an external goal toward which we work, nor a timeless ideal that we strive to apply, nor a legal rule that we obey. Instead it serves to inform and influence present actions. The present community is free to make the paradigm its own, to adapt it into the texture and fabric of its own historically conditioned setting.[64] Schüssler-Fiorenza captures this distinction by suggesting that Scripture provides not fixed *archetypes* that later Christians must conform to in particulars, but open-ended *prototypes*, dynamic models of structural transformation that are exemplary but may be reshaped under current circumstances. Scriptural prototypes are initial models that can be reformed, refined, even improved on, although future designs should retain some recognizable resemblance to the original.[65]

Three points can be made in favor of such analogical reasoning. The first is that it presupposes a dialogical rather than a unidirectional relationship between text and interpreter. Instead of first attempting to discern from a neutral standpoint, what the text "meant" in the past, then asking about its contemporary relevance, past and present are brought into dialectical relationship. The past illuminates the present, while the

---

64. Cf. Gustafson, "Relation of the Gospels," 111–16.

65. Schüssler Fiorenza, *In Memory of Her*, 33–34. As Pheme Perkins observes, "The interrelationship between our experiences of the demands of justice and love in our context and the exhortations of the Bible are quite different if we perceive the latter as structuring prototype rather than definitive archetype" ("New Testament Ethics," 325).

needs of the present raise new questions and cast new light on the past. Instead of being paralyzed, as some interpreters are, by the historical and cultural discontinuities between then and now, analogical reasoning presumes there are legitimate connections between the patterns of human action in the biblical world and today.[66] Secondly, the biblical writers themselves often discern analogical or typological relationships between past and present events, using the "type" to grant insight or revelation into the later "anti-type."[67] The New Testament writers do not engage in historical exegesis for its own sake, but make illuminating connections between events recorded in the canon and their own present situation. Thirdly, such an approach honors the dynamic and historical character of biblical revelation. Rather than providing a fixed deposit of static, ahistorical truths, the Bible points beyond itself to a God who remains active in human history and who calls for faithful responses from his people in contemporary situations not envisaged in Scripture, but nonetheless analogous to previous situations faced by the people of God in biblical times.

At the same time, the use of analogy encounters several difficulties. (1) Some critics would suggest that the value of seeking analogies is vitiated by the fact that every ethical situation is *sui generis*. "The hard fact of the matter is," says Robin Scroggs, "that historical situations in which

---

66. See Fowl and Jones, *Reading*, 57–65.

67. It is generally accepted that "typology" best expresses the way the New Testament writers handle Old Testament Scripture. It is worth noting, however, that typology is employed throughout the Old Testament as well as in the New Testament. For example, the exodus is the supreme example of God's saving activity in the Old Testament, and thus is frequently treated as a typical event by other biblical writers, both in Old Testament (e.g., Pss 66, 77, 135, 136; Hos 11; Isa 63:11–14) and New Testament (1 Cor 10:1–11; Rev 15:1–8). Sometimes David serves as a type of how other believers should live (1 Kgs 3:14; 15:3, 11; cf. Ezek 34:24; Zech 12:8; Matt 12:3–4; Heb 11:32). On the other hand, *Cain* (1 John 3:12; Jude 11) and the stubborn Israelites in the wilderness (Ps 95:8–11; Heb 3:7—4:11) are examples not to be imitated. Again, Zion is sometimes used to refer to the holy city built on the hill of Zion (Ps 97:8; Isa 28:16), and thence becomes a type of the spiritual home of all who belong to true Israel (Isa 60:14; Mic 4:1–2; Heb 12:22; 1 Pet 2:5–6; Rev 14:1). For other typological connections, cf. Num 21:4–9 with 2 Kgs 18:4; Jn 3:14–16. The Old Testament prophets, rather than giving a photographic outline of the future, usually describe the future in terms of what happened in the past (e.g., Isa 44–66 describes the deliverance from Babylon in terms of a second exodus, and even employs imagery drawn from creation, Noahic stories, the flood narrative and Abraham's call). This means that the prophets used past history typologically—historical events were a type of how God would act eschatologically.

ethical/theological judgments emerge are unique. Unique situations cannot be superimposed on one another. Thus the principle of analogy must seriously be called into question."[68] There is some truth in this. Decision-making situations *are* unique; actions followed in one setting cannot be replicated in another. But what is learned in one unique situation can be adapted and *re*-applied (not duplicated) in another. The principle of analogy requires a significant correspondence between situations in the text and today, not an absolute identity.

(2) But there is still difficulty in determining the scope of the correspondence. Biblical texts derive their meaning from the total cultural-linguistic system to which they belong. In using a biblical example for analogical elucidation, to what extent should there be a correspondence between the wider environment of the text and that of today? (If a comprehensive analogy were drawn between the New Testament world and modern society, biblical scholars and professional ethicists would correspond to the scribes and Pharisees, whom Jesus condemned as bereft of genuine ethical insight!).[69]

(3) This highlights the complexity of determining what is entailed in following biblical paradigms in our modern setting. The modern world is so different from the world of the biblical text that contemporary equivalents to biblical paradigms may require strategies so different that there will be little resemblance to the alleged paradigm. Jesus enjoins his followers to do good and lend without interest, to share what little they had with those in need. A modern analogy would probably require a complex and sophisticated socio-economic response to the needy, within the framework of an international trading economy where buying bananas at the local supermarket has an impact on the poor in the Third World.[70] Biblical paradigms that embody concern for the poor ought to lead to discussions of the possible shape of contemporary analogies.

(4) The most significant problem lies in the area of the "control" of analogy, that is, of determining how a legitimate connection is made between biblical text and contemporary circumstance.[71] If present events are in control, there is the danger of selecting biblical analogies that merely confirm prior ethical commitments or personal interest on the

---

68. Scroggs, *Text and the Times*, 276; cf. his earlier, more positive appeal to analogy in "New Testament and Ethics," 93.

69. Horsley, "Ethics," 4.

70. Ibid., 26.

71. So Gustafson, "Place of Scripture," 443; Horsley, "Ethics," 4, 25–26.

part of the decision maker. If one believes, for example, that liberation from oppression is the chief need of the present situation, one might select events such as the exodus or Jesus's inaugural address in Luke for the purposes of analogical elucidation. The danger here is one of exploiting the Bible as simply a rhetorical support for strategies that have actually been derived from secular sources. If, on the other hand, one starts with biblical models then seeks contemporary applications, there is the danger of imposing biblical models arbitrarily on current situations on the basis of rather superficial resemblances. What constitutes sufficient evidence that the circumstances in our time are similar enough to those of biblical times to justify application of the biblical model?

Again, these concerns are real. But the problem of control, of avoiding a merely decorative use of the Bible to embellish pre-established moral judgments, is common to all interpretive strategies. In reality one never "starts" with either the biblical text or the contemporary situation; both are always present, and there is a constant dialectic between them. This mutual interrogation of readers by the text, and the text in light of the readers' present situation, permits a progressive refinement in faithful appropriation of the text. The only ultimate controls are the checks and balances offered by the wider community of God's people honestly seeking to live faithfully before God in light of Scripture. This leads directly to our third way of appreciating the moral import of the Bible.

THE FORMATIVE USE OF SCRIPTURE

Common to both prescriptive and illuminative handlings of Scripture is the assumption that ethical decision-making is predominantly an individual affair guided by rational and theological analysis. The key questions are methodological: Which interpretive strategies are most effective for apprehending the moral role of Scripture? And the test of validity is the universalizability of the method for all contexts and situations.

Little has been said so far about two matters that fundamentally influence both ethical decision-making and biblical interpretation, whatever the method employed. They are the personal character of the moral agent, and the location of decision makers within a wider community of discourse. When these considerations are addressed, a third way of thinking about the moral use of Scripture comes into view, namely its formative role in shaping character and building Christian community.

Recently, there has been a definite shift of interest among biblical scholars and ethicists from "trying to assimilate biblical morality to the model of deductive argumentation to an interest in Scripture as foundational to the formation of communities of moral agency."[72]

In the formative approach the relevance of the Bible for ethics goes beyond providing appropriate verses, principles, images, or analogies for resolving specific ethical dilemmas. It also lies in its role of transforming the character, vision, values, motivations, and intentions of moral agents, both individually and collectively. Scripture affects the decision maker as well as informs the decisions to be made. Of course, the importance of personal moral virtues has long been stressed in Christian ethics, but increasing attention is now being given to the interconnection between character formation, community building, and Scripture reading. In their recent excellent book on the topic, Fowl and Jones insist that,

> because there is no way to talk about moral decisions apart from people's contexts, convictions, and commitments, a preoccupation with decisions made by isolated individuals distorts our conception of ethics in general and the relation of Scripture to Christian ethics in particular. An adequate conception of ethics requires attention to issues of character and formation of character in and through socially-embodied traditions.[73]

In what follows we will comment on these aspects sequentially, though it is their interrelationship that is most significant.

Scripture and Character-Formation

One of the clear presumptions of New Testament ethics is that personal conversion and transformation in self-understanding lies at the root of ethical behavior.[74] For Paul, the work of grace serves to liberate us from our bondage to "the works of the flesh," to impart new motivation for ethical obedience energized by gratitude for God's undeserved love and mercy, to give new content to ethical life (patterned on the self-giving love of Christ), to enable moral discernment no longer dependent on the "letter" of the law, and to empower a new level of ethical attainment that spontaneously produces "the fruit of the Spirit" and thus "fulfills" (not

---

72. Cahill, "Communities," 384.
73. Fowl and Jones, *Reading*, 9.
74. Cf. Scroggs, *Text and the Times*, 280–85.

simply obeys)[75] the just requirements of the law. Moral conversion and on-going character-formation are considered crucial by Paul to engender a true obedience. Indicative and imperative are inseparable; believers are called "to be" what they have already "become" in Christ. Accordingly, "the starting point of an authentically Christian ethics is the recognition that the conversion of the individual leads to a new obedience, a new lifestyle, a new ethic."[76]

Scripture stands in a two-fold relation to this process. On the one hand, the disciplined reading of the biblical account promotes and nurtures character-transformation.[77] And it is the biblical account in its entirety, not just its explicitly ethical content, that nourishes character development. It names and helps to form virtues and values, it identifies and encourages obligations, and it fosters and renews moral vision. It engenders a new orientation toward God, the world, and others; it affects what sort of persons we are; it functions to "renew our minds" so that we may "discern what is the will of God" (Rom 12:2); it evokes attitudes and affections of the heart by disclosing to us what God is like and what God has accomplished for us. In other words, the Scriptures have the capacity, when illumined by the Spirit, to touch "the concrete regions of the heart" from whence true moral conduct emerges.[78] As we are shaped and reshaped by the concerns of Scripture, we are equipped to think and act in relation to ethical questions in a way consistent with the biblical account of God's will.[79]

On the other hand, as the lifelong process of character-formation and transformation continues, believers are increasingly enabled to interpret Scripture wisely. The goal of biblical interpretation is not just correct understanding, but the faithful embodiment of Scripture in life. Christians are required to "present their bodies" in obedience, not just their minds, if they are to discern God's will and be transformed in character (Rom 12:1–2). This is one of the most consistent and recurring themes of biblical teaching. Well-formed character does not guarantee proper discernment, but the discernment of God's will in Scripture cannot be evaluated apart from the virtues of Christ-like character it produces in the interpreter.

75. For this distinction, see Westerholm, *Israel's Law*, 201–5.
76. McGrath, "Doctrine," 152.
77. See Birch and Rasmussen, *Bible and Ethics*, 62–65, 189–94.
78. Spohn, *Scripture and Ethics*, 127.
79. Cf. Thompson, "Ethics of Jesus," 58.

Scripture and Community-Formation

The formation of individual character always occurs in and through participation in communities. Individuals do not exist prior to or apart from community but always in relation to others. We are taught to make moral judgments and to exercise approved qualities in the context of particular historical communities. We learn to be virtuous by observing and copying others in the community; their example inspires us to be virtuous. Ethics, then, is not just the history of abstract ideas but the history of communities.[80] This insight has significant implications for appreciating the moral role of Scripture, not least because Scripture itself is the product of, and charter document for, a faith community with its own particular history.

It means, in the first place, that the fundamental "analogy" between the biblical text and the current context lies not in some ethical situation or event but in the believing community itself. The distinctive social reality of the Christian community is the primary form of continuity with the biblical world. And it is within this community that the Scriptures assume their authority; "the church is the community defined by its allegiance to the Scriptures or as shaped by scriptural witness."[81]

From this it follows, second, that the ethical discernment of Scripture is a communal task. Scripture was originally addressed not to individuals but to specific communities called into being by God to embody a particular way of life.[82] The texts fulfilled a social function in promoting a lifestyle of non-conformity to the world. Similar, in some respects counter-cultural, communities are therefore the most appropriate context for their interpretation today. Discernment of the moral import of Scripture is not just the job of specialists; it is a communal responsibility involving every member of the congregation (1 Cor 14:26, 29). The role of specialists is to contribute to the communal process. Yoder discusses, for instance, the distinctive contributions to be made by "agents of direction" (prophets, 1 Cor 14:3, 29), "agents of memory" (scribes, or scholars, Matt 13:52), "agents of linguistic self-consciousness" (teachers, Jas 3:18; 2 Tim

---

80. Cf. Meeks, "Understanding," 4–6.

81. Cahill, "Communities," 384–85. Schüssler Fiorenza proposes that the Scriptures provide the basic constitution of the community, consisting not of a set of laws but "a set of interpretive principles that provide basic paradigms of Christian identity" ("Crisis," 364).

82. In his important study, Hays stresses the "ecclesiocentric" as well as christocentric nature of Paul's interpretation of Scripture, *Echoes of Scripture*.

1:13; 2:16), and "agents of order and due process" (overseers/bishops/elders, Acts 15:13, 28).[83]

Third, the goal of interpretation must be the faithful embodiment or re-socialization of the moral vision of Scripture, visually, the formation of a common life that reflects the values, convictions and practices related in the text. This is what the "authority" of Scripture means—the capacity of Scripture to form a people who live in a way that continues the story of God in the world.[84] The normative authority of the text lies in the concrete social strategies it uses to engender such a radical community. Consequently, in Meeks' words, "a hermeneutical strategy entails a social strategy," and at both ends of the interpretive task. At one end, the social function of the text for the biblical community must be uncovered. Sociological and historical tools can be used to discover that the impact the earliest Christian communities had in their socio-political contexts. At the other end, the text can be used to suggest comparable social configurations today; and "the hermeneutical circle is not completed until the text finds a fitting social embodiment."[85] The modern community ought to be analogous to the first Christian communities by its conformity to the paradigmatic social challenges they presented in their own socio-political contexts. The moral authority of Scripture thus lies in the social identities and social relationships it calls forth in the believing community. Accordingly, "moral norms are justified not as transcriptions of biblical rules, or even as references to key narrative themes, but as coherent social embodiments of a community formed by Scripture."[86]

Fourth, the commitment to embody the witness of Scripture in a common life is essential in order to adjudicate interpretive disputes. Moral ratification is not principally a matter of deductive reasoning or individualistic intuitivism, though rules, principles, analogies and individual judgment may all play a role; it is the outcome of a communal process of discernment in congregations committed to the "hermeneutics of obedience."[87] The interpretive options chosen can only be confirmed in the praxis or lived-discipleship of the community.

83. Yoder, "Hermeneutics," 50–56; cf. Birch and Rasmussen, *Bible and Ethics*, 108–11.

84. Cf. Hauerwas, "Moral Authority," 356–63; Birch and Rasmussen, *Bible and Ethics*, 145–51.

85. Meeks, "Social Embodiment," 183–84.

86. Cahill, "Communities," 393.

87. Cf. Ollenburger, "Hermeneutics of Obedience," 45–61.

> The aim of Scriptural interpretation is to shape our common life in the situations in which we find ourselves according to the characters, convictions, and practices related in Scripture. Because no one interpretive strategy can deliver *the* meaning of a text, there is no hard and fast method that will ensure faithful interpretation. No particular community of believers can be sure of what a faithful interpretation of Scripture will entail in any specific situation until it actually engages in the hard process of conversation, argument, discussion, prayer and practice.[88]

Finally, interpreters who stress the formative role of Scripture often (but not always) give maximum value to the narrative quality of Scripture for ethics. Not only is "story" the dominant genre in the Bible, but the completed canon tells one narrationally unified story (or meta-story) that starts with "in the beginning" and closes with "come Lord Jesus." Current scholarship sees great significance in both these facts. The story-mode of Scripture is believed to be crucial to its moral authority because stories signify characteristic ways of thinking and acting that shape the self-understanding of their hearers. All good stories have the effect of drawing the audience into the action, engaging our emotions, encouraging identification with the narrative figures, so that we experience what the characters experience in the story.[89] In this way, stories create a basic orientation to the world; they foster convictions and commitments, sharpen sensitivities, and inspire virtues and values. Stories are self-involving and self-revealing, in a way that moral philosophy, rules and principles are not. Stories are also fundamental to communal solidarity and identity. "We are story-telling creatures," Birch and Rasmussen observe, "compelled to make sense of our experience through recollection and narrative. Narration . . . gives form and meaning to our experience."[90] Shared stories express the common origins, history, memories and values of a people, while religious stories relate such experience to matters of ultimate significance. Accordingly, the story of Scripture, and in particular the stories of Jesus, have a character- and community-constituting power. The story imparts a distinctive way of life that inculcates certain character-virtues and moral dispositions in its recipients.

There is, then, a growing conviction that the contribution of the Bible to ethics lies at the level of character- and community-formation,

---

88. Fowl and Jones, *Reading*, 20.
89. C. D. Marshall, *Faith*, 27.
90. Birch and Rasmussen, *Bible and Ethics*, 127; cf. 105–7.

not primarily at the level of rules or principles. Scripture serves as a reminder of the kind of people we are to become and the kind of way we are to be present in the world.[91] Its moral authority lies in the socially revolutionary strategies it commends for handling wealth, power, violence and social prejudice.[92] The connection between what the text "meant" and what it "means" today is the concrete community that seeks analogous expressions of social life. Praxis is the criterion of verification of ethical claims and injunctions. As Hays explains,

> knowledge of God's will *follows* the community's submission and transformation. Why? because until we see the text lived, we cannot begin to conceive what it means. Until we see God's power at work among us we do not know what we are reading. Thus the most crucial hermeneutical task is the formation of communities seeking to live under the word.[93]

With the demise of Constantinian Christendom, this emphasis on the social embodiment of Scripture's moral witness in distinctive communities of faith and witness is of strategic importance. It is not an entirely new emphasis; the "believers church" tradition of the radical Reformation, where voluntary communities of dissent embodied an alternative to both the authoritarianism of the Catholic *Magisterium* on the one hand, and the arbitrary individualism of later Protestantism on the other, has something important to offer the contemporary church. The work of John Howard Yoder is becoming very influential in this respect.[94] The model of the "Scripture-shaped community" of discernment does not "solve" the issue of how we use Scripture for specific ethical direction, but it does put the question in a different light. The primary question is not "what should I do," but "what distinctive *form of life* does Scripture call *us* to?"

At the same time, this emphasis on the formative role of Scripture involves its own range of quandaries.

(1) Some critics level a charge of "fideism" or "sectarianism" against it. They detect an elaboration of ethics from a self-enclosed religious

---

91. For examples of such an approach, see Lischer, "Sermon," 157–69; Hauerwas, "Sermon," 36–43.

92. See C. D. Marshall, *Kingdom Come*, 76–93.

93. Hays, "Scripture-Shaped Community," 51.

94. For a recent evaluation of Yoder's contribution, see Zimbelman, "Contribution," 367–99.

standpoint that is not accessible or accountable to the broader secular community. They also fear the loss of an intelligible Christian contribution to the public discourse of the wider community. However, in response it must be said that there is an inescapable tension in Christian ethics between commonality and distinctiveness, between universality and particularity, a tension present in the New Testament itself. There is something unavoidably alien about the values derived from the way of Christ that cannot be universalized or validated by the wider community of discourse.[95] On the other hand, insofar as Christians live simultaneously in both Christian and non-Christian communities, and are fully involved in both, they will remain open to cultural challenge, receptive to the wisdom and perspectives of outsiders, and ready to contribute Christian perspectives to communal discourse and social ethics.[96] Indeed, a willingness to be interrogated by the world, to be open to outsiders, and to be committed to the well-being and transformation of the wider world, are essential ingredients of healthy Christian communities.[97] Such features were characteristic of New Testament communities.[98]

(2) The use of communities and their praxis as the basic analogy with the biblical texts raises the question of what is meant by "Christian community." The term may be used today to refer to realities very different from the tightly knit and disciplined local churches of the first-century. It includes the larger institutional church, with elaborate power structures and longstanding traditions. The notion of analogous social strategies works best if the *form* as well as the commitments of the contemporary community are analogous to those of the "household" churches on the New Testament, visually, intimate in fellowship, inclusive in social make-up, egalitarian in relationships, and charismatic in operation. But, as Fowl and Jones lament, there is a distressing paucity of vital Christian communities in the contemporary Western world; and such common life as we do experience is often impoverished.[99] In some

---

95. See the discussion in Yoder, "Hermeneutics," 61–64.
96. See Cahill, "Communities," 384.
97. Fowl and Jones, *Reading*, 44–49, 110–34.
98. It would be a mistake to divorce the distinctive communal character of early Christian faith from its eschatological or apocalyptic character. When both features are seen as inseparable, it becomes impossible to use the New Testament to justify a sectarian retreat from the world. See Wilder, "Kerygma," 509–36; Henley, "Eschatology," 24–44; and especially Duff, "Significance," 279–96.
99. Fowl and Jones, *Reading*, 64.

respects, the "base" Christian communities of Latin America, Africa, and Asia offer much closer analogies to those of New Testament times.

(3) Aside from the need to rehabilitate authentic Christian community in the West, "a huge remaining question for ethicists is how to guarantee the truth of the interpretations *by* the community."[100] Corrupt character and self-serving falsehood can become as embedded in the fabric of a community's life as readily as in an individual's, as demonstrated by the German Church of the Nazi era and the Dutch Reformed Church of South Africa during the days of apartheid. How is communal deception to be prevented or exposed? What should guide individuals in standing against disobedient or misinformed communities? If social embodiment is the *sine qua non* of ethical verification, how does one evaluate communal experience? Are there any broader norms of community and praxis to which local communities remain accountable? How do communities know whether certain features of New Testament practice, such as nonviolence or economic redistribution, are to be reproduced in their own situation in order to remain faithful? Are not certain criteria that transcend a community's partial perspective on truth necessary? Are not rationally defensible methods of moral analysis open to cross-communal testing and validation still essential?

(4) Several queries also attach to the central place some give to "story" or narrative in the educative role of Scripture. Story is only one element in the communicating structure of culture, along with customs, rituals, laws, sacred symbols, and the like, and is only one among several genres in the canon. Why then should narrative be made the governing pattern of moral formation and normative ethics?[101] There is also no need for story to be set in tension with moral rules and principles. As long as the moral imperatives of Scripture are allowed to function initially within the story-world of the text and not be abstracted into universal rules, they have an indispensable role in facilitating the contemporary embodi-

---

100. Cahill, "Communities," 394.

101. According to Meeks, "The judgment that the controlling pattern is, or ought to be, narrative does not emerge either from a tabulation of actual uses or from a compilation of the different genres found within the canon" ("Social Embodiment," 185). For Hauerwas, however, the fact that Scripture contains much material that is not narrative in character does not undermine the priority of story, since such material, so far as it is Scripture, gains its intelligibility by being a product of and contribution to the wider story, which the community lives through remembering. Also, "one of the virtues of calling attention to the narrative nature of Scripture is the way it releases us from making unsupportable claims about the unity of Scripture or the centrality of the 'biblical view of X or Y'" ("Moral Authority of Scripture," 366).

ment of the text. There is, in fact, danger of a different kind of abstraction in the narrative method, with the historical particularity of Abraham, Moses and Jesus being reduced to specimens of a new kind of universal, namely "narrative forms."[102] Then there are the questions of how we avoid reading the story in highly selective fashion. Is it possible for people in positions of privilege and power to "hear" stories oriented toward the poor and judgmental toward the rich? The social location of the modern faith community decisively influences, and can easily determine, how the text is understood.

CONCLUDING COMMENTS

The preceding discussion demonstrates that while there is general agreement *that* the Bible is to be used as an authority in Christian ethics, there is disagreement about *how* the Bible's witness is best actualized. Traditionally most attention has centered on the need for a universal, rationally-defensible hermeneutical method that individual believers may employ in any situation. Individualism (what individuals, divested of their local traditions and parochial attachments, have in common as rational human beings) and universalism (what is categorically applicable to all situations) have been the guiding beacons of moral philosophy since the Enlightenment.[103] Recent discussion however has shifted the focus from "proper" methodology to the role of the church as a hermeneutical community committed to the social embodiment of the text it reveres. This "formative" emphasis reminds us that personal character and communal process are absolutely indispensable to a faithful handling of the text.

This implies that before, and as well as, calling on the state to seek social justice, churches themselves must be practicing what they preach. Whether denominations and their individual congregations may be justly regarded as eschatological colonies of peace and justice is a moot point. But insofar as the Church leaders seek to use Scripture to educate and sensitize their members to the need for social justice in the wider community, a commitment to become such counter-cultural communities is crucial.

This is not to suggest that Christians have no right to offer social and political critique *until* they have put their own house in order first; that

---

102. Yoder, "Hermeneutics," 57.
103. Birch and Rasmussen, *Bible and Ethics*, 204n3; cf. 114–17.

is a recipe for political quietism that would compromise the church's responsibility in society. Nor am I proposing that the churches meekly accept that it is their responsibility *rather* than the state's to meet the needs of the socially disadvantaged, and so cease criticizing the government for failing to do so; that the church is God's primary agent of redeeming love and justice does not mean that the state is exempt from its own responsibilities in these areas. What I am saying is that unless Christian congregations are as vigorously committed to embodying in their own common life the values they commend to the government, they are devaluing the primary moral function of Scripture, its role in creating alternative communities of Christ-like character.

As such communities seek to apply Scripture to their historical situation, the full storehouse of the biblical witness should be appropriated. This will require attention to themes and analogies ("illuminative use") as well as rules and principles ("prescriptive use") of relevance. Methodological dichotomies that set one approach against another should be avoided; "the task of the teacher will rather be to contribute to the community's awareness that every decision includes elements of principle, elements of character and of due process, and elements of utility."[104]

A methodological pluralism is demanded, not only by the inherent limitations of each method in isolation, as explored above, but by the evidence of Scripture itself. The New Testament writers appeal to written Scripture in several different modes. Scripture is treated as a source of *moral rules or laws,* as, for example, in New Testament appeals to the Decalogue (e.g., Matt 5:21-48; Mark 10:17-22; Rom 7:7; Eph 6:2; Jas 2:11);[105] as a source of *ideals or principles,* as in Jesus's appeal to creation norms (e.g., Mark 10:6),[106] or his linking of Deut 6:4-5 with Leviticus 19:18 to form the double love command (Mark 12:28-31/Matt 22:34-40/Luke 10:25-28); as a source of *analogies or precedents for action,* as undergirds the entire argument of Hebrews and biblical typology in general; as a collection of *narratives* that characterize appropriate actions and self-understanding, such as in Jesus's appeal to the stories of Noah and Lot (Luke 17:26-37); as a source of *images and themes* that help pinpoint God's action in present history, as in Stephen's apology (Acts 7:2-53) or

---

104. Yoder, "Hermeneutics," 58. Cf. the synthesis of the traditional juridical style of ethical reasoning and koinonia ethics advocated by Birch and Rasmussen, *Bible and Ethics,* 108-19.

105. See R. H. Fuller, "Decalogue," 243-55.

106. See Davies, "Relevance," 35-38.

Paul's sermon in Pisidian Antioch (Acts 14:14-43); and as supplying a *symbolic universe* that illuminates both the human condition and the character of God, as in the diagnosis of the fallen human condition in Romans 1:18-32, or the characterization of God in Matthew 5:43-48.

This multiplicity of ways in which the Scriptural text is appropriated suggests that all of them are potentially legitimate modes for reflection on the normative role of Scripture today, and that no one mode (such as law or narrative or principle) should be allowed to overrule all others.[107] The need for methodological discipline does not imply methodological uniformity. The key issue is deciding which method of appropriation is most suitable to particular texts. Initially effort should be made to correlate the mode of interpretation with the mode of moral discourse employed by the text itself, so that narratives are not read as rules, or analogies turned into laws or timeless principles.

Of course, treating laws as laws and principles as principles still leaves open the question of how they apply to particular ethical debates today. The indispensable context for making such interpretive judgments is the shared life of the worshipping community itself. For the supreme calling of the Christian community is not merely to be a biblically tuned critic of trends in secular society but to embody a distinctive pattern of life, foreshadowed in Scripture, that challenges society with an alternative vision of life under God's reign of peace and restorative justice and that enables Christians to become ever wiser in their reading of the biblical text.

---

107. So also Hays, "Scripture-Shaped Community," 49; Childress, "Scripture," 378.

2

Re-engaging the Bible in a Postmodern World*

As virtually a brand new theological student, I was invited to teach one or two courses at the small Wellington Bible College, established in 1980 by Dr. Clyde Vautier. I well remember Dr. Vautier's passionate enthusiasm for expositing the biblical text, energized by his deep commitment to the so-called "Old Princeton" theory of the "full verbal and plenary inspiration of Scripture." This is the belief that the Spirit of God has consciously selected every single word of the scriptural text for the purpose of imparting infallible, propositional truth.[1] While such a conception of biblical origins raises more problems than it solves, there is no denying that, as in Dr. Vautier's case, it engenders an appropriate reverence for, and delight in, the text of Holy Scripture.

Such reverence and delight are increasingly rare in the modern church. Indeed some critics have suggested that the contemporary church is virtually operating in a post-biblical environment. There is an alarming lack of sustained biblical engagement in most Sunday sermons and a diminishing expectation that congregations are interested in a serious encounter with Scripture. Some commentators speak of the "crisis of biblical authority" that confronts the modern church and of the need to "reclaim" the Bible for the church.[2] Whether the word "crisis" is helpful in

---

* The 2006 Clyde Vautier Memorial Lecture, Wellington, October 11, 2006.

1. For a useful summary of old Princeton scholasticism and its fundamentalist step-children, see McKim, *Bible*, 52–75.

2. See, for example, the collection of essays edited by Jenson and Braaten, *Reclaiming the Bible for the Church*.

this connection is debatable. It has a panicky ring to it, as if an unforeseen danger has fallen upon us, and implies that unless we take remedial action urgently, disaster will follow. But the phenomenon these commentators discern has not come suddenly upon us. It is a result of a progressive ebbing away of biblical consciousness over several generations, even over several centuries, and there is no quick-fix solution. So if there is a crisis, it is a very gradual and quiet kind of crisis. On the other hand, we should not minimize the problem. "Crisis" does capture the importance of the issues at stake, and it is worth remembering that the biblical prophets often announced crises that nobody else saw coming. So perhaps the term is worth retaining simply for its prophetic punch.

What, then, is this crisis of biblical proportions (!) to which people refer? Put simply, it is the way in which the Christian community is becoming increasingly estranged from its sacred text, the Bible, increasingly deaf to its witness, bewildered by its contents, unsure of how best to read it or apply it responsibly to life, and unable to explain just why the Bible ought to be esteemed so highly. This is true even of the most conservative evangelical and Pentecostal churches that make the loudest claims about the divine dignity, authority, even inerrancy, of the Bible, yet who, in some respects, are the most adept at distorting the text. They describe the Bible in grandiose terms, but the depth and breadth of their engagement with Scripture remains superficial at best, and downright manipulative at worst. There may even be a direct correlation between how emphatically people insist on the inspiration and infallibility of the Bible and how little they wrestle with its meaning and its complexity.

Yet it is not enough to make big claims about the Bible's uniqueness and authority. The authority that any text possesses is not measured by what we *say* about the text, but by what we *do* with the text, by the way we permit the text to function in our life and thought. If it is true (as I believe it is) that Scripture possesses supreme authority in faith and life, then what ought to be evident in our congregations is serious, sustained, and intelligent attention to the actual meaning of the text. After all, the church universal has always confessed that when the faithful listen attentively and humbly to Scripture, they can hear the very voice of God addressing them, instructing them, comforting them, and transforming them—which, when one stops to think about it, is an awesome thing to contemplate!

So what further can be said about the problem of biblical disengagement that afflicts us today, and what can be done about it? For the sake of analysis, I want to tease out four distinct, but interrelated dimensions of the problem, and sketch out some possible remedies. My goal is simply to open up the conversation rather than offer definitive answers, because I am as much affected by the predicament as anyone else and claim no special insight into the way ahead. But I share the concern of others that, without a serious and sustained engagement with Scripture, the church's voice on important issues, including those to do with crime and justice, will likely fall victim to capture by conventional wisdom or political interests.

A Crisis of Acquaintance

Perhaps the most obvious symptom of biblical disengagement is the diminishing level of biblical knowledge that the average Christian possesses today. Despite the fact that we have more Bibles available to us, in more translations, versions, languages, and dialects than ever before, the current cohort of churchgoers simply knows less of the actual content of Scripture than was true of previous generations, while for those outside the church, the Bible is now an almost wholly unknown book. In my long career as a theological educator, I have found that each generation of students comes to study with less and less prior knowledge of biblical material, and with only the slimmest awareness of the single large story the canonical text narrates. They may be familiar with a smattering of biblical facts or know a few favorite verses. But what is lacking is any extensive acquaintance with the stories, teachings, genres, themes, actors, and key narrative moments of the biblical record.

As already indicated, this is not due to some sudden memory lapse; it is the result rather of a gradual deterioration that has taken place over generations. I have often pondered how my own father knew much more of the content of Scripture than I do (notwithstanding my professional training), while I know a great deal more than my own children do. Gregory Jones, a prominent American ethicist, tells of once asking a class of sixty Christian undergraduates where the words, "Let justice roll down like waters and righteousness like an ever-flowing stream," which Martin Luther King uttered in his famous *I Have a Dream* speech, came from. Some students thought that King had composed them himself; others nominated Shakespeare or "somewhere in the Bible" as possible sources. Not a single student was able to identify the allusion to the OT prophet

Amos, although in *his* day Martin Luther King could simply assume his hearers would pick up this powerful intertextual echo.[3]

Why has the average level of biblical knowledge declined in this way? No doubt there are many contributing factors. One is the increasing secularization of society, so that citizens today hear little of the Bible quoted in public settings, such as in school assemblies, at weddings or funerals or civic ceremonies, or in the mass media. Another reason is that we live in an increasingly visual or multi-media environment, so that people read less in general than they used to and are less patient with memorization. But a substantial part of the blame must be laid at the door of the church. The level of biblical enquiry in most Sunday sermons is lamentable, while Sunday schools and youth groups often struggle to attract members, let alone train them in the Scriptures.

The shift of preference in some congregations towards cell groups or home groups, or the informal gatherings characteristic of the so-called emerging church, is probably not helping things either. In 1994, sociologist Robert Wuthnow estimated that as many as two-thirds of all small group meetings in America gathered specifically as Bible study groups. But what Wuthnow found was that, in practice, these groups focused more on providing pastoral support for participants than on learning from the Bible. When they did consult the text, they often produced wooden interpretations, and achieved little actual increase in knowledge of biblical teaching.[4]

Lutheran theologian Robert Jenson blames American clergy for the growing level of biblical illiteracy in their congregations. He notes that, in contrast to what prevailed in earlier generations, clergy today give much less attention to catechizing young believers, teaching them how to access the Scriptures and stocking their minds with biblical stories, language and themes.[5] If this is true of more liturgical traditions, such as Lutheranism, how much more true must it be of evangelical, Pentecostal, and other free-church traditions that usually lack any formal apparatus for the catechesis or instruction of young believers? Indeed, one sometimes wonders whether, ironically, it is the relative strength of so-called "Bible believing" churches compared to the declining mainstream congregations that partially accounts for falling levels of biblical knowledge. At least in

---

3. Jones, "Formed and Transformed," 18–19.

4. Cited in ibid., 19. For a method of theological reflection in small groups that makes no mention of Scripture at all, see Johnson, "Theological Reflection."

5. Jenson, "Hermeneutics," 91.

liturgical worship, the congregation every week hears the public reading of Scripture on the basis of the lectionary, a time-honored practice stemming back to the earliest days of the church. In most looser evangelical church services, by contrast, the only time Scripture is publicly read is to furnish the launching pad for some sermonic excursion that focuses more on the experiential or therapeutic needs of the listeners than on the meaning of the text itself.

The same is true of the music repertoire found in our most popular churches. Although the old "Scripture in Song" genre had distinct limitations, at least it served as a vehicle for inculcating our minds with biblical imagery and language. By comparison, it is striking how lacking in biblical allusions many of the most popular worship songs are today. Many say little more than "Jesus is my boyfriend," and a very cool boyfriend too, countless times over! When it is recognized that what people sing in church is today arguably their primary source of theological instruction, this is rather troubling.

But why should it be troubling? Why should diminishing familiarity with Scripture be a cause of concern? Does it really matter? Yes, it does! It matters because what is being lost is an awareness of the Bible's central role in shaping Christian identity and forming Christian character. The church is, to use Richard Hays' phrase, a "Scripture-shaped community."[6] The leading function of the Bible is to tell us who we are as a people, where we fit in the history of God's redemptive activity, and how we should think and act in ways that will enable us to continue living God's story faithfully. Only by attending carefully to Scripture can our imaginations be converted so that we can envision the kind of world God wants to bring about, both in us and through us. Without having our worldview consistently shaped and reshaped by the message of Scripture, without being continually renewed in our minds and hearts as we listen for the word of God, we will, as Paul warns, be irresistibly squeezed into the world's mold, so that we think and act and live according to the seductive wisdom of *this* age rather than the paradoxical wisdom of the *new* age (Rom 12:1–12; 1 Cor 1:18–25). The less we listen to Scripture, the more we will accept the world as we know it as our default setting, and the less we will have to offer the world that is fresh and powerful and redemptive.

So then, one major cause for biblical disengagement in the contemporary church is the diminishing level of acquaintance with the actual

---

6. Hays, "Scripture-Shaped Community," 42–55.

content of the Bible, and this is partly because the traditional media for instruction—preaching, Sunday school classes, Bible study groups, catechetical lessons, the regular public reading of Scripture, and worship songs—no longer serve this purpose very well. But there is a *second*, and even more *serious*, reason for biblical disengagement—a general loss of confidence by many in the church in the credibility and relevance of the Bible.

A Crisis of Confidence

Since the Enlightenment, the Bible has been subjected to more critical scrutiny, and generated more secondary literature, than any other document in the world. Whereas the essential truthfulness of the Bible was once taken for granted by almost everyone in Western society, virtually the opposite prevails today. Many people outside the church consider the Bible to be little more than religious propaganda, and the very fact that it is authorized by the institutional church—which is now profoundly disliked and distrusted—simply compounds their cynicism. It is this atmosphere of hostility to religious authority that has allowed the *Da Vinci Code* and similar fantasies to enjoy such phenomenal success.

Even within the church, many harbor profound doubts as to whether the Bible has somehow now been shown to be false or flawed or fictitious, whether by modern scientific research or by historical analysis. Some voice this fear openly and embark on new journeys across the choppy Sea of Faith. Others refuse to face their doubts and simply shout louder about biblical inerrancy. Many remain in a state of flux, painfully aware that the world probably wasn't created in six literal days, or that homosexuality can't simply be wished away by biblical fiat, or that the great bulk of humanity probably isn't going to fry forever in hell, but not quite sure where this leaves the Bible, which they do still want to believe in, but don't feel quite as certain about as they once did.

One of the most regrettable features of this crisis of confidence is that the task of interpreting the Bible has largely been captured by a professional, and often skeptical, scholarly elite. A shift of context has occurred in which the Bible is normatively interpreted from the church to the academy. British theologian Alister McGrath even speaks of the "Babylonian captivity of Scripture," to make the point that the Bible has been exiled from its true homeland in the community of faith and banished to an alien academic society, with its own definite, though often unacknowledged, agenda. Scripture has been made subservient to the interests of a fragmented scholarly community in which originality and innovation are valued above all else, and faithfulness to tradition is denigrated. What Luther called "the papacy of the professors" prevails, wherein the ability of ordinary believers to read the Bible aright is treated with contempt by scholars who insist that the only acceptable way to study the Bible is by means of a sophisticated battery of historical-critical techniques and in a spirit of critical detachment from, if not overt suspicion towards, the theological truth-claims of the text.[7]

This is not to decry the enormous advances in understanding that have accrued from the employment of critical methods over the past two centuries. Nor is it to deny the importance of scholarly enquiry unfettered by the controls of ecclesiastical dogma and politics. But what is easily lost sight of in the academy is that the Bible exists both on account of, and for the sake of, the community of faith, not for the prestige or professional advancement or intellectual stimulation of scholars.[8] Like the church itself, the Bible owes its very existence to what Paul calls "the truth of the gospel" (Gal 2:5, 14), the revelation of God's saving initiative in Jesus Christ, which is to be received with humility and accepted in faith. The primary purpose of the Bible, and of theological reflection on the Bible,[9] is to bring believers into greater knowledge of this God, not to answer the welter of technical questions that modern critics might dream up.

There is nothing wrong, of course, with posing critical questions to the biblical text, and answering many of them is essential to a responsible appropriation of biblical teaching in this age of historical consciousness. But insofar as critical methodology serves to deny ordinary believers

---

7. McGrath, "Reclaiming Our Roots," 63–88 (especially 69–78).

8. Of course, the church needs always to be open to new ways of understanding the Bible, which often emerge out of technical scholarship. But, as N. T. Wright insists, those who propose new interpretations ought never to thumb their noses at cherished points of view: "When a biblical scholar, or any theologian, wishes to propose a new way of looking at a well-known topic, he or she ought to sense an obligation to explain to the wider community the ways in which the fresh insight builds up, rather than threatens, the mission and life of the church" (*Last Word*, 35).

9. For an insightful discussion of how what she calls early "sapiential theology," aimed at the knowledge of God, gave way to the scholastic or speculative theology in the Middle Ages, concerned with intellectual rigor, thence to the post-Enlightenment fragmentation of theology into disconnected disciplines, see Charry, "Walking," 144–69.

rights of access to the text, or to undermine their confidence in consulting the text, or to discredit the church's historic practice of reading the Bible under the conscious guidance of the Holy Spirit and in light of its existing faith-confession, it functions to disengage Scripture from its primary constituency of committed disciples.[10]

Again, let me be clear that the problem is not primarily with the critical methods themselves; it is with the spirit and manner in which they are deployed. Academic study of Scripture in the post-Enlightenment period has been characterized by two things in particular: a pretense to scientific neutrality and a decidedly anti-theological bias. Scholars have asserted that their own use of critical reason is free of confessional assumptions and theological motivations, so that their approach has the status of an objective science, quite unlike the "fundamentalist" approaches they so despise. To prove their objectivity, they have insisted that the only proper subject matter of biblical scholarship is the historical or sociological world *behind* the text, or the literary or narrative world *of* the text itself, or, more recently, the readers' world *in front* of the text—but never the world *above* or *beyond* the text, the world from which God speaks. Never the theological claims the text exerts on its recipients, never the knowledge of God disclosed by the text. Critical scholarship has been content to concentrate all its attention on what the text meant historically, back then, and to defer endlessly the question of the validity of the theological truths that the text declares.

Fortunately, this modernist claim to neutrality has now been exposed for what it is—a fallacy, and a fallacy of the most pernicious kind. To quote Kevin Vanhoozer:

> A host of post-modern thinkers has slain the giant assumption behind much modern biblical scholarship that there can be objective, neutral, and value-free reading of biblical texts. Post-modern thinkers have charged modernity's vaunted historical-critical method with being just one more example of an ideologically motivated approach. The critical approach only

---

10. At least since the time of Irenaeus, and probably before, the church has explicitly affirmed the importance of reading Scripture in light of its antecedent "rule of faith," that is, its understanding of the gospel, as later crystallized in the creeds. This is not necessarily to champion tradition over Scripture; it is simply to recognize that one can only make sense of the Bible in light of some prior conception of its overall meaning and direction, as given in Christ. For a commendation of Irenaeus' interpretive rules, see Jenson, "Hermeneutics," 97–100. For a philosophical defence of bringing to the text prior interpretive convictions, see Wolterstorff, *Divine Discourse*, 206–23.

pretends to be objective, neutral and value-free. Modern biblical critics are as rooted in the contingencies of history and tradition as everyone else. Indeed, biblical criticism is itself a *confessional* tradition that begins with a faith in reason's unprejudiced ability to discover truth. The question post-moderns raise for historical critics is whether, in exorcising the spirit of faith from biblical studies, they have not inadvertently admitted even more ideological demons into the academic house.[11]

By exploding the myth of neutral scientific interpretation, what is sometimes called "the postmodern turn" in human thought has given new legitimacy to an explicitly faith-based or theologically attuned reading of Scripture, an approach that historically has always characterized the church's reception of the text.[12] The hegemony of objectivist historical criticism is now over, and with it the theological liberalism that so heavily dominated the academy over the nineteenth and twentieth centuries.[13]

But this demise, as welcome as it may be to some, has brought with it a new, and even more unsettling, assault on the confidence Christians may have in the truth-value of the Bible. In the current intellectual context, the confidence-question no longer centers on whether biblical teaching agrees with scientific reason; it centers on whether the biblical

---

11. Vanhoozer, "Introduction," 21.

12. Vanhoozer joins those who call for a rehabilitation of theological exegesis. "Theological interpretation of the Bible . . . is biblical interpretation oriented to the knowledge of God . . . This is perhaps the ultimate aim of theological interpretation of the Bible: to know the triune God by participating in the triune life, in the triune mission to creation" (ibid., 24). This includes a recognition that God is not merely the product of a certain community's interpretive interest. God precedes the community and the biblical texts themselves, and only a proper appreciation of God's priority can guard against idolatrous images generated by interpretive communities. Moreover, knowledge of God is more than intellectual acknowledgement; to know God is to love God and to obey God, "for the knowledge of God is both restorative and transformative." While employing scholarly tools and approaches, theological criticism is *confessional* in nature—it proceeds from faith. It is governed by the conviction that God speaks in and through the biblical texts.

13. "But the hegemony of liberalism is over. The embargo on being different has been lifted. Christianity is free to be itself once more, liberated from the stifling paternalism of a 'we're all saying the same thing, really' worldview—a worldview that, I may add, was found just as nauseating by non-Christians as it was by Christians. We are free to rediscover our distinctive identity as Christians in this world. And how are we to do that? By returning to our roots. By rediscovering that we are different. And reclaiming Scripture as the common heritage of all Christian believers is an integral element of this great process of coming to life once more, more that the homogenizing iron curtain has been lifted" (McGrath, "Reclaiming our Roots," 81).

text (or any text for that matter) contains any objective meaning at all, any meaning that is independent of the interpreter. In postmodernity, the playful reader is all-supreme. Meaning is no longer something readers *discover* in a text, a meaning intended by the author and reliably conveyed by the text; rather meaning is something readers themselves *create* from the text, in pursuit of their own private interpretive interests.[14] To quote Vanhoozer again:

> Post-moderns typically deny that we can escape our location in history, culture, class, and gender. Our readings of the biblical text will be shaped, perhaps decisively so, by our particular location and identity. The goal of interpretation is therefore to discover "what it means to my community, to those with my interpretive interest." Post-modern readers come to Scripture with a plurality of interpretive interests . . . though no one interest may claim more authority than another. The post-modern situation of biblical interpretation gives rise to a pluralism of interpretive approaches and hence to a legitimation crisis: Whose interpretation of the Bible counts, and why? Biblical interpretation in post-modernity means that there are no independent standards or universal criteria for determining which of many rival interpretations is the "right" or "true" one.[15]

Anyone who has undertaken formal theological training will be familiar with this dilemma. Once scholars spoke of "exegesis," assuming that there was a single fixed meaning in the text to be ferreted out by sound exegetical method. Then they began speaking of "interpretations," in recognition of the richness or polyvalence of textual meaning, and the extent to which readers are involved in unfolding aspects of meaning. Now it is common to speak of "readings," by which is meant the conscious attempt by specific communities to read the biblical text in light of explicit ideological commitments, such as radical feminism or postcolonialism or queer theory or whatever. So-called advocacy readings—where the text is interpreted to promote overt political agendas—have proliferated over the past generation, and they are usually legitimated by the assertion that, since there is no fixed meaning in the text, we ought to read it a way that will advance our own community's quest for justice

---

14. In the judgment of Karl Donfried, "Many in the professional guild of biblical scholarship are satisfied to offer private ideological speculations, yielding a myriad of conflicting options distant from the canonical witness and alien to its major theological testimonies" ("Alien Hermeneutics," 21–22).

15. Vanhoozer, "Introduction," 20.

and equality. A common feature of such approaches is use of the so-called "hermeneutics of suspicion and retrieval"—where the biblical text is subjected to radical critique to determine which parts fail to conform to the ideological values of the interpreter, and must therefore be rejected, and which parts can be retrieved to reinforce the interpreter's cause.

Now in a real sense it could be said that advocacy interpreters are simply being honest about the pre-understandings and political biases that inevitably guide any appropriation of Scripture. Far better to own these biases than to pretend they do not exist, which is infinitely more dangerous. It also should be conceded that advocacy readings are usually motivated by a genuine commitment to greater justice, which is consistent with the spirit of the gospel. The interpreter's larger political program, in other words, often has moral legitimacy.[16] Advocacy readings also often cast new light on the text and expose the power dynamics hidden behind "received" interpretations. All this is good. But the net result of sustained ideological criticism is often a substantial erosion of confidence in the reliability of biblical meaning. Assuming the indeterminacy and relativity of textual truth, some interpreters feel free to massage textual meaning to their own advantage. Yet to surrender all belief in authorial intention and the relative stability of textual meaning in favor of some version of radical deconstructionism serves, finally, to subordinate the word of Scripture to the manipulative proclivities of human beings. It is perhaps significant that the first biblical character to subject the word of God to a hermeneutic of radical suspicion was the crafty serpent in the Garden of Eden: "Surely God has not said . . . ?"[17]

So then, postmodern sensitivities—that is, our profound awareness of the contextual nature of all human knowledge, of the role of human subjectivity in apprehending knowledge, and of the power of privileged elites in defining reality for the rest of us—bequeath to the current Christian community a fresh reason for faltering confidence in the Bible. What

---

16. This need not be the case, however, such as in past readings that advocated slavery or apartheid or the subordination of women, or in present readings that endorse religious violence or American militarism. So the question arises, if advocacy readings are justified on the grounds that textual meaning is constructed more than given, then on what grounds does one repudiate readings that advocate racial segregation or patriarchal dominance? If this question can only be answered by an appeal to liberal democratic values external to the text, then biblical interpretation falls victim to some higher authority, and Christian faith loses its potential to criticize the world in the name of the divine will.

17. I owe this observation to Dennis Olson, "Truth," 18.

then is to be done about it? How can Christian readers today engage responsibly with the Bible in light of our new consciousness of the seemingly endless capacity of readers to generate diverse readings of the same texts?

I am not sure how to answer this question! Postmodernism is a work in progress, and where it will take us is not entirely clear. It is an intellectual and cultural shift that confronts not just the church but Western thought in general with an epistemological quandary. But let me mention just three things that I think contemporary Christians ought to cultivate in this new context.

The first is a self-critical humility on the part of every reader about the extent to which our understandings of Scripture are always going to be partial, provisional, and invariably tainted with self-interest[18]—and how much, therefore, we need to listen respectfully to all other interpreters of the text if we are to discern the word of God. Determining the meaning of Scripture is often much trickier than we realize, and we must listen with charity to those who see things differently to ourselves.

In their useful book, *Reading in Communion*, Stephen Fowl and Gregory Jones propose that a key feature of healthy Christian communities is the extent to which they are open to the perspective of outsiders, both to the perspective of marginal figures within the community, such as homosexuals, and of those beyond the community.[19] Listening to strangers is not always comfortable of course. But if we are to hear what the Spirit is saying to the church, we must read the Bible "in a wide company of interpreters, who both nurture us and challenge us."[20]

The second thing needed is a courage to resist the interpretive nihilism commended as a virtue by some postmodern interpreters. The critical role of readers in actualizing textual meaning cannot be denied; it must be factored in to our understanding of biblical truth. But it can also be exaggerated out of all proportion. Meaning is not merely generated by readers at a whim. It is the product of a three-way conversation between author, text and recipients, with each party exercising an irreducible

---

18. One of the first things that epistemological self-consciousness does is focus attention on the relativity of all interpretations. But, as Colin Gunton points out, relativity is not the same as absolute relativism. "To acknowledge that all treasure is contained in the earthen vessels of language is not at the same time to concede that no treasure is contained therein" ("Being Used," 248–59).

19. Fowl and Jones, *Reading*.

20. Jones, "Formed and Transformed," 28.

role.[21] Texts are not infinitely malleable. They exert constraints on readers and are capable of resisting alien or misguided interpretations. Try using a cake recipe to fix your computer problems, and you'll see what I mean. If this is true of any text, how much more so is it true of the biblical text, which, Christians confess, is given by God to speak constraining words of grace and judgment to the believing community.

Accessing the meaning of Scripture is certainly not a simple process, and absolute certainty will ever elude us. But neither is it a wholly impossible enterprise in which the text inevitably becomes an echo-chamber of the reader's own prejudices and priorities. There is no point in reading Scripture at all if we doubt its power to speak a true or discomforting word to us. So a second crucial requirement for engaging meaningfully with the Bible today is retention of confidence in Scripture's potential autonomy from human control, as long as this "hermeneutics of trust" is always matched by a sober recognition of our own human propensity to try to exert such control over Scripture.

The third thing needed for reading the Bible in the postmodern era is a fuller and richer understanding of the nature of truth. In his book *The Ethics of Biblical Interpretation,* Daniel Patte highlights the way in which both evangelical fundamentalism and critical biblical scholarship have shared a similar understanding of truth. Both have assumed that texts have a single meaning, and that the truthfulness or otherwise of this meaning resides in its correspondence to external factual reality. The fundamentalist insists that for the Bible to be true, it must be absolutely correct in every chronological and historical detail, such as in six literal days of creation or two separate cleansings of the Temple. The biblical critic shares this conception of truth, but concludes that the Bible cannot be wholly true because it obviously errs in scientific and historical detail. Both camps assume a realist conception of truth, but disagree on the extent to which the biblical text measures up to reality. Over against such modernist realism, Patte proffers a non-realist or constructivist conception of truth, where textual meaning is indeterminate and where the truth of the text resides in the ethical uses to which it is put.[22]

But neither of these alternatives is satisfactory. Instead we ought to be guided by the Bible's own *relational or personalist* view of truth. Jesus said, "I am the truth" (John 14:6), and Jesus is a person, not a proposition.

---

21. For a full-scale defence of this fact, see Tate, *Biblical Interpretation*.
22. Patte, *Ethics*. For a stirring critique, see Malina, "Witness," 82–87.

Scripture speaks of "truth" most often, not as some abstract property that a propositional statement possesses, but as an enduring quality of faithfulness and constancy in relationships. Biblical truth implies fidelity and dependability, in the same sense that we speak of a "true friend" or a "true brother" or a "true commitment." Truth in the Bible, in other words, is more than factual accuracy; it is something that inheres in steadfast relationships.[23] Viewed from this perspective, the truth of the Bible resides primarily in the trustworthiness of its witness to the activity and purposes of God, not in its historical or chronological detail, nor in its utility for constructing endless castles in the sky for postmodernists to inhabit. Scripture is true because it can be counted on to faithfully represent who God is, what God is doing in the world, and what God wants from us.[24]

What, precisely, does God want from us? Nothing less than our ongoing transformation into the image of his Son, in our hearts, minds, and souls, in our thinking, feeling and doing (2 Cor 3:18; Col 3:5–17). And it is here that Scripture has unrivaled power. It is now widely recognized in moral anthropology that the formation of moral character requires the engagement of a person's emotions and imagination, not just their reason and intellect.[25] People are formed morally as much by the stories they hear, the examples they observe and the groups they belong to, as they are by the moral rules or precepts they are taught (something particularly worrying in our celebrity-saturated age). The Bible's stories and examples, as well as its moral commandments and injunctions, have a unique capacity to engage the full panoply of our moral capacities, to transform us at the deep level of our affections, motivations, volitions, and values, so that we measure up more to the stature of Christ. In this respect, the truth of the Bible lies in the way it can be counted on to achieve this purpose, if we willingly submit to it, which brings us to the third dimension of our topic.

A Crisis of Authority

It is with some trepidation that I turn to the matter of authority, since the phrase "biblical authority" has become one of the "stuck" terms in

---

23. It could be said that even in propositional statements, something is deemed true because it bears the requisite *relationship* to reality; it is a *faithful* account of what actually is.

24. For a helpful Christological view of truth, see Padgett, "Truth," 104–14.

25. Cahill, "Christian Character," 3–17.

Christian discourse. The phrase most often crops up today in discussions over controversial moral matters, such as same-sex relationships, with conservatives accusing liberals of spurning the authority of Scripture, and liberals retorting that conservatives misconstrue the Bible. Appeals to biblical authority in such settings usually do more to deepen the antagonism than to resolve the disagreement. Moreover, what is frequently touted as an issue of authority is, more often, an issue of hermeneutics. Even those who offer fresh or revisionist readings of biblical texts do so precisely because they implicitly recognize the authority of the text and want its teachings to justify their stance.

I would propose that the issue the church faces today is not so much to do with the *fact* of biblical authority, as it is to do with the *theory and practice* of biblical authority. It is not that believers are increasingly rejecting the authority of Scripture, but rather that they don't know *why* Scripture ought to be authoritative, nor *how* the Bible should function in practice with respect to other sources of Christian guidance, such as reason, tradition, and experience.[26]

The reason why the fact of biblical authority is not really the issue is because, since its inception, Christianity has always been a religion of the book. There has never been a single moment in Christian history, going back to the time of Jesus himself, where there did not exist a scriptural text to make recourse to. Initially it was the text of the Jewish Bible, later supplemented with the twenty-seven documents of the New Testament canon. Christianity, in other words, has always acknowledged the authority of Scripture, though how this authority has functioned in practice has varied considerably.

As is well known, the sixteenth-century Protestant Reformers made the authority of Scripture their *cause célèbre*, calling on the church to subject its sometimes-corrupt practices to biblical scrutiny. The three great watchwords of the Protestant Reformation were *sola fide* (faith alone), *sola gratia* (grace alone) and *sola scriptura* (Scripture alone). For all their differences, Lutheran, Calvinist and Anabaptist Reformers all agreed on four basic truths: the Bible possesses supreme authority in the life of the church; the Bible is meant to be understandable, even if some parts are

---

26. Richard Hays helpfully observes that whereas the fundamental question of the sixteenth century was the authority of Scripture with respect to *tradition*, and the fundamental challenge of the Enlightenment period was the authority of Scripture with respect to *reason*, in the postmodern period the issue is the authority of Scripture with respect to *experience*. See Hays, *Moral Vision*, 209–11.

difficult to grasp and require special techniques; the Bible's interpretation should not be restricted to the ecclesiastical authorities; and the Bible's teaching must be heeded.[27] These four principles remain foundational to any adequate theology of Scripture, and virtually all Christian traditions still subscribe to them.

But why does the Bible possess supreme authority? Is this just an arbitrary claim made about one book among many? Or is there good reason to accord supremacy to *this* book rather than any other? One of the assumptions behind the *Da Vinci Code*, and similar books such as *The Jesus Papers*, as well as behind some of the scholarship that emanated from the Jesus Seminar during its time, is that the New Testament canon is a somewhat random collection of documents, assembled for largely political purposes, and accorded authority primarily as a means of suppressing dissident (and allegedly more interesting) theological voices in the early church. This increasingly common assertion presses home the question of why should we accord authority to the Gospel of Mark or the Gospel of John, but not the Gospel of Mary (which, after all, allegedly speaks of the woman in Jesus's life) or the Gospel of Thomas, or the Gospel of Peter, or the Gospel of Judas?

To answer this question adequately would require a long detour into the history of the canonical process, the criteria of canonicity, and the merits of the New Testament documents vis-à-vis other early Christian writings. For our purposes, it is enough to note that the reason why the church accords authority to its canonical documents is because it believes that God has chosen these documents to be the primary medium for exercising *his* authority in the community of faith. As N. T. Wright points out, the phrase "authority of Scripture" is really a shorthand way of saying "the authority of *God* exercised *through* Scripture."[28] This is important, for according to biblical teaching itself supreme authority is possessed by God alone (e.g., Rom 13:1)—which means, incidentally, that when the New Testament writers ascribe "all authority in heaven and earth" to the risen Jesus,[29] they are necessarily allocating to him a divine status. That being so, the only legitimate reason the church could possibly have for attributing supreme authority to some human book is because it believes that this book bears a unique relationship to God. Put simply, the *authority* of Scripture depends, ultimately, on the *authorship* of God

---

27. See McKim, *Bible*, 38–39.
28. Wright, "How Can the Bible," 7–32; see also Wright, *Last Word*.
29. Matt 28:18; John 19:11; Phil 2:9–11.

("authority" and "authorship" belonging to the same semantic field). This is not to say that God personally wrote the Bible in some direct sense; or that he dictated its contents, word for word, to human scribes (which is more a Qu'ranic than a biblical conception of inspiration). Rather it is to say, as Nicholas Wolterstorff spells out in his exacting philosophical analysis *Divine Discourse*, that God has *appropriated* human speech as a vehicle of divine speech, so that in attending to the human speech of the biblical authors, we can hear the voice of God.[30]

So one reason why the church grants authority to Scripture is because it believes in the Bible's divine origins (or its divine-human origins, to be more accurate), that God, in some unfathomable way, has been involved in the writing, preserving, and canonizing of these documents. The other main reason why the Bible is accorded authority is because it bears unique witness to Jesus Christ. The central truth-claim of the Christian religion is that the only true God is made most fully known in the person and work of Jesus Christ, who is the Word of God made flesh (John 1:14). Christians believe that Jesus is the human face of God, which means, in turn, that God's own identity must be fundamentally Jesus-like in character.[31] Without this foundational conviction, the Christian movement would never have gotten started in the first place. Yet this claim would have no material content whatsoever were it not for Scripture, for without the canonical gospels we would know virtually nothing of the life, teaching, death, and resurrection of Jesus or of his larger significance for the story of Israel. Extra-canonical sources do exist, but they are of questionable authenticity or add nothing substantial to the historical information afforded by the New Testament writings.

So, then, if the person of Jesus Christ is indispensable to the Christian religion, so too must Scripture be indispensable. And if Scripture is indispensable because it bears unique witness to Jesus Christ, then it must be Jesus Christ himself who furnishes the indispensable key for making sense of Scripture. This brings us to the fourth dimension of our theme.

---

30. Wolterstorff, *Divine Discourse*. More briefly, Wolterstorff, "True Words," 34–43. Cf. Ollenburger, "Pursuing the Truth," 44–65.

31. Alister McGrath cites former Archbishop of Canterbury Michael Ramsey (*God, Christ*, 98) as observing that "the importance of the confession 'Jesus is Lord' is not only that Jesus is divine but that God is Christ-like." McGrath, "Reclaiming Our Roots," 67.

A Crisis of Interpretation

Earlier I commented on the "Babylonian captivity" of Scripture—the fact that interpretation of the Bible has been commandeered by an academic community that insists on an allegedly disinterested employment of critical methodology as the only legitimate method for understanding the text. This metaphor implies that what is needed is for the Bible to be returned from exile to find its true homeland once again in the confessing Christian community. This is not, I have emphasized, to repudiate the value of critical methodology itself, only the pre-understandings and skeptical spirit with which it is often employed in many parts of the academy.

Lest this point be missed, it is important to stress that any serious engagement with Scripture, even within the worshipping congregation, *must be critical in nature*—critical in the sense that it is guided by sound interpretive procedures and informed by self-conscious hermeneutical reflection. For arguably what is the most concerning feature of the contemporary church's disengagement from Scripture is not the declining level of biblical acquaintance, nor mounting qualms about biblical truthfulness and authority, but the sheer lack of hermeneutical competence shown by our preachers and teachers, as well as by ordinary readers.

Some will bridle at this charge, resisting any inference that it is only those with theology degrees who can properly interpret the Bible. And, in the spirit of the Reformation, and the spirit of the New Testament itself, it is absolutely right to resist any suggestion of clerical control over biblical exposition. But the alternative to clerical monopoly cannot be the hermeneutical free-for-all that prevails in some church settings, where every reader is deemed equally skilled in judging the meaning and implications of the text. After all, Jesus himself highlighted the importance of correct interpretive procedure for apprehending Scripture's true meaning: "You search the Scriptures because you think that in them you have eternal life; and it is they that testify on my behalf. Yet you refuse to come to me to have life" (John 5:39–40). On the road to Emmaus Jesus needed to "open the Scriptures" for his companions so they could rightly understand them, as "beginning with Moses and all the prophets, he interpreted to them the things about himself in all the Scriptures" (Luke 24:27). In similar vein, the apostle Paul accuses his Jewish compatriots of misunderstanding Moses because they read him with hardened hearts and through a veil of ignorance. "Indeed, to this very day, when they hear the reading of the old covenant, that same veil is still there, since only in Christ is it set aside" (2 Cor 3:14).

In each of these instances, the problem is not a failure to *read* the Scriptures, or *trust* the Scriptures, or even to *learn* the Scriptures in detail; it is a failure to *understand* them. Why such a failure? Because the message of Scripture can only be understood properly when viewed through the correct hermeneutical lens, the lens that is Jesus Christ himself.

Yet what often prevails in fundamentalist, evangelical and Pentecostal churches, as well as in mainline congregations, is a "flat text" approach, where verses are taken at random from this or that part of the Bible to support some theological or moral viewpoint. In such settings, the oft-heard assertion that a particular position is "biblical" simply means that some verses can be found somewhere in the Bible that seem to say what one already believes. This is what I meant by the charge that so-called "Bible-believing" churches are often guilty of trivial and manipulative mishandling of the text. The Bible is treated in a quasi-magical fashion, where each isolated component is imbued with some mysterious potency quite independent of its larger literary, historical, canonical or theological context. What Richard Hays calls "bumper sticker hermeneutics" is practiced—"the Bible says it, I believe it, that settles it."[32]

But such naïve biblicism is not to honor Scripture as the written Word of God. It is, in fact, to manipulate Scripture to suit our own preconceptions—every bit as much as postmodern ideologues do, but without the self-critical awareness of doing so. If evangelical preachers and teachers really did believe in the uniqueness, authority and inspiration of Scripture as much as they say they do, then the least one would expect is that they learn how to "rightly divide the word of truth" (2 Tim 2:15). This does not necessarily require a full theological training, but it does require some minimal degree of hermeneutical awareness and wisdom.[33] Much could be said about what this hermeneutical awareness should consist of,[34] but space allows me only to flag four of the essential prerequisites for becoming a competent or wise reader of the Bible.

---

32. Hays, "Scripture-Shaped Community," 43; Hays, *Moral Vision*, 3.

33. Wright affirms the need for reading of Scripture that, as well as being thoroughly contextual, liturgically grounded and privately studied, is "refreshed by appropriate scholarship" and taught by "accredited leaders of the church." Wright, *Last Word*, 127–42.

34. For a still very useful discussion of important hermeneutical principles, see Swartley, *Slavery*, especially 229–34.

The first is an appreciation for the *narrative quality of Scripture*. Often in our churches the Bible is treated as a devotional manual or as a doctrinal or moral handbook. But that is to misconstrue the kind of book the Bible is. The Bible is not a collection of timeless truths dropped from heaven by parachute; rather it is, fundamentally, a story book. Not only is narrative the dominant genre within the Bible but the biblical canon itself tells a single, overarching story, beginning in the Garden of Eden and ending in the New Jerusalem. It is a progressively unfolding drama made up of several distinct scenes or narrative moments: creation, fall, Israel, Christ, the church, new creation.

The importance of this narrative progress cannot be over-estimated, for the meaning of individual texts must always be assessed, in the first instance, in terms of that part of the story to which they relate. In several cases, realities that pertain in earlier scenes of the story are superseded by later developments, so that Moses does not have the same relevance for Christian practice as does Christ who follows him in the drama of salvation. "The law indeed was given through Moses," John writes, "grace and truth came through Jesus Christ" (John 1:17).

The narrative quality of the Bible is also crucial to appreciating how biblical authority ought to function. If the Bible is meant to exercise normative authority in the church, and if the Bible is first and foremost a narrative, then the kind of authority the Bible possesses must be a narrative-kind of authority, a story authority more than a legislative or prescriptive type of authority. How then do narratives exercise authority? They do so by providing us with a compelling way of looking at the world, with a way of making sense of experience, of understanding our lives and the purpose of our existence, a way of challenging our priorities and scrutinizing our values. Stories have unique power to crack open our existing frame of reference and afford us fresh ways of conceiving reality, which is precisely why Jesus made such heavy use of parables in his ministry. As a single large story, the Bible exercises its authority not by dictating in detail how we should behave, thus robbing us of all freedom or creativity, but by teaching us how we should understand the world and where it is going, and by inviting us to shape our lives in ways that are consistent with how reality *really* is, from God's point of view.[35]

---

35. Enormously helpful in this respect is Wright's analogy of the Bible to a five act Shakespearean play, with the final act still to be completed. See "How Can the Bible," 18–20; Wright, *Last Word*, 121–27.

A second prerequisite for the wise reading of Scripture is recognition of the *centrality of Jesus to the meaning of the biblical drama*. Each and every part of Scripture must, finally, be assessed in relation to him. This means the Old Testament must be read in light of the New, and the New must be understood against the backdrop of the Old (or, as someone else has put it, the Bible must be read back-to-front, as well as front-to-back).[36] The two Testaments should neither be fused nor separated but read together, for, as Brevard Childs explains, "the goal of the interpretation of Christian Scriptures is to understand both Testaments as witness to the self-same divine reality, who is the God and Father of Jesus Christ."[37]

The Protestant Reformers all agreed on this principle of christocentric interpretation. For the magisterial Reformers, however, it tended to assume a markedly doctrinal character. For Luther it meant the centrality of justification by faith in Christ; for Calvin it meant the centrality of God's elective purposes culminating in the threefold office of Christ.[38] For the radical Reformers, however, such as the Anabaptists, christocentric interpretation took on a more ethical form. For them, it was the entire Gospel story of Jesus's words and deeds, not just his atoning death, that is the key to unlocking Scripture. For Christ is not simply the agent of eternal salvation; he is also the normative ethical paradigm for Christian existence. This means that no interpretation or appropriation of Scripture that fundamentally contradicts the teaching and spirit and example of Jesus can be accepted as a valid interpretation for today. It was on this basis that the Anabaptists rejected, not just sacrifice and circumcision, but also the swearing of oaths and the bearing of the sword.[39] In my view, recovery of such ethical christocentrism, both as a hermeneutical principle and as a form of Christian presence in the world, is an urgent priority for the church in the Postmodern and post-Constantinian world we now live in.

This brings us to a third prerequisite for being a wise interpreter: a *life of discipleship as the* sine qua non *for understanding Scripture*. The radical Reformers insisted that in order to understand what is written *about* Christ in the gospels, and what is consistent with his teaching and spirit elsewhere in Scripture, one must first walk *with* Christ on the path

---

36. Jones, "Formed and Transformed," 31; cf. Hays, *Echoes*.

37. Childs, "Reclaiming the Bible," 15.

38. For a brief comparison between the hermeneutics of Luther and Calvin, see Stacey, *Interpreting the Bible*, 81–97.

39. See briefly Augsburger, *Principles*; Swartley, *Essays*.

of obedience. The sixteenth-century Anabaptist leader Hans Denk put this point memorably: "No one can claim truly to know Christ unless one follows him in life." Modern theologian Jürgen Moltmann glosses this saying in more theological categories: "There is no christology without christopraxis, no knowledge of Christ without the practice of Christ. We cannot grasp Christ merely with our heads or our hearts. We come to understand him through a total, all-embracing practice of living; and that means discipleship."[40]

This basic Anabaptist axiom—that we can only know the truth of Scripture insofar we *live* the truth—has come to the fore in much recent theological scholarship.[41] It is one of the most positive insights of Postmodern epistemology, that knowledge is acquired, not through the exercise of disembodied reason, but through the embodied practices of life, which knowers acquire from their historical contexts. Postmodernist thinkers recognize that people actually "talk their walk"; they conceptualize and verbalize reality in light of their political practice. This is why Jesus called on his hearers to *change* how they walked—by following him—in order to understand his message,[42] and only to talk *of* him in light of their walk *with* him.

The fourth requirement for sound interpretation is *sensitivity to the leading of the Spirit in the interpretive community*. Both elements are essential—conscious openness to the Spirit and the collective discernment of the believing community. Again, this fits well with postmodern instincts, for, as we have seen, Postmodern thinkers highlight the interpretive privilege of specific communities that necessarily read texts in the spirit of their own age and context. The New Testament writers similarly privilege the shared insights of the Spirit-filled community in the task of discerning God's word (e.g., Acts 15:1–35).[43] But the Spirit they speak of is not merely a projection of human ambitions or subjective intuitions. It is the Spirit of God, the giver of Scripture, who is also the Spirit of Truth, whose task it is to guide the community, albeit falteringly, into greater truth (John 16:13). Moreover, the Spirit does this, not least, by bringing to the community's remembrance all that the earthly Jesus said and did (John 14:26). This means that a wise reading of Scripture is one

40. Moltmann, *Today's World*, 47.

41. For just one example, see Meeks, "Social Embodiment," 176–86.

42. E.g., Matt 7:24–27; 11:29; John 7:17.

43. For a discussion of the importance of communal hermeneutics, see Adler, "Community of Interpreters."

that issues in a Christ-like way of life, a life that replicates the values and priorities and redemptive concerns we see evidenced in the gospel stories of Jesus, who is the one to whom the Scriptures bear ultimate witness.

CONCLUSION

In this wide-ranging discussion I have suggested that the phenomenon of biblical disengagement in the church has four main dimensions. It is marked by falling levels of biblical literacy in our congregations; by nagging doubts, though often repressed, about the truthfulness and relevance of the biblical witness; by confusion around how and why the Bible is authoritative for Christian belief; and by low levels of hermeneutical competence in interpreting and applying the text as wise readers. "The Bible is to be the bloodstream of the church's worship," N. T. Wright observes, "but at the moment the bloodstream is looking fairly watery."[44]

The task, then, is one of trying to remedy these problems. And perhaps the place to start, or at least the place to give most emphasis to, is the task of wise interpretation. For there is no good in encouraging people to read the Bible more, or to trust the Bible more, or to submit to the Bible more, unless they can make sense of the Bible, unless they learn to read the Bible as a coherent story of God's redemptive love at work in human history, and unless they can discern in the gospel story of Jesus Christ Scripture's center of gravity, and also the singular paradigm for Christian discipleship. In many respects the church today has, quite literally, lost the plot, and it is only by relearning, and reliving, the story of Jesus that the church has any hope of not simply surviving postmodernity, but even being a blessing to it.

44. Wright, "How Can the Bible," 29.

3

What Language Shall I Borrow?
The Bilingual Dilemma of Public Theology

WHEN CHRISTIANS ENGAGE IN public life or seek to contribute to social or political debate in light of their faith, among the many quandaries they face is deciding on the appropriate language to use. Do they use the language of faith or do they adopt the secular language of mainstream political discourse? Can the Christian ethic be translated, without loss, into a general ethic incumbent on all people, irrespective of personal belief? Or is every attempt at such translation, however well intentioned, already an admission that Christian faith is essentially superfluous to public life? Behind this question lies the much deeper philosophical question of the relationship between religion and morality, and between faith and culture in general.[1] Is there any such thing as a distinctively Christian ethics?[2] Or is every assertion of ethical obligation necessarily universal

---

1. For a helpful discussion, see David Hicks, "Dimensions." Hicks proposes that religion adds a depth dimension to morality, so that for a religious believer both spheres become mutually enriching and validating. Christianity specifically enriches morality by adding a theological dimension (relating morality to God's purposes in history), a spiritual dimension (enhancing the development of character virtues), a Christological dimension (which mediates participation in Christ, the ultimate source of moral goodness) and a doxological dimension (where morality is a response of worship).

2. Nicholas Harvey argues, for example, that given the diversity present in Scripture and the irreducible role of human interpretation of both scripture and doctrine, it is impossible to speak of any Christian basis for morality, although there are Christian resources available for assisting in moral decision-making. Harvey, "Christian Morality," 106–15. For a different view, see Cosden, "Pluralistic Society," 337–45.

in scope?³ These are all very difficult matters, but before offering some reflections on them, let me set the scene with some general observations on the task and complexities of public theology.

WHAT IS PUBLIC THEOLOGY?

At its simplest, public theology is the attempt to address matters of common or public concern in the community in light of the special truth-claims and insights of Christian belief. Duncan Forrester offers a more detailed definition:

> Public theology, as I understand it . . . is theology which seeks the welfare of the city before protecting the interests of the Church . . . [It] seeks to offer distinctive and constructive insights from the treasury of faith to help in the building of a decent society, the restraint of evil, the curbing of violence, nation-building, and reconciliation in the public arena, and so forth. It strives to offer something that is distinctive, and that is gospel, rather than simply adding the voice of theology to what everyone is saying already. Thus it seeks to deploy theology in public debate, rather than a vague and optimistic idealism which tends to disintegrate in the face of radical evil.⁴

Public theology, then, is theology employed for public ends. It aims to construct "a theologically sound, publicly accessible, and practically viable social ethic . . ."⁵ Yet the label itself is a somewhat unhappy one. The term could imply, for instance, that only one part of Christian theology is public in nature and that the rest is somehow private. That of course is impossible, for all theology, by its very nature as talk about the one true

---

3. Marion Deckert offers an unusual but instructive orientation on this question. He proposes that there is no such thing as distinctive Christian ethics, but there is still a distinctive Christian lifestyle and code of conduct focused on love. As the systematic presentation of moral obligation, ethical standards are obligatory for all people, irrespective of faith commitment. At times, the use of lethal violence may be ethically justifiable by the state. Pacifist Christians, instead of trying to argue that nonviolence is always ethically superior, should accept the necessity of violence in certain circumstances. At the same time, pacifist believers should still not make recourse to violence themselves on the grounds that Christian life requires one to go beyond the moral requirement in the interests of love, which is a supererogatory rather than moral requirement. See further "One Ethic."

4. Forrester, "Public Theology," 16.

5. This set of phrases is drawn from Stackhouse, "Public Theology," 80.

God, is inescapably public in character. That is to say, it deals in statements that claim universal validity, irrespective of whether particular people or communities subscribe to them. As Jürgen Moltmann rightly states, "From the perspective of its origins and its goal, Christian theology *is* public theology, for it is the theology of the kingdom of God."[6] As such it *must* engage with the political, cultural, educational, economic and ecological spheres of life, not just with the private and ecclesial spheres.

But if that is so, then surely the designator "public" is redundant at best, misleading at worst. Part of the problem is that the word "public" is itself laden with ambiguity. Sometimes it is used in a spatial or sociological sense (to designate institutional or collective life), and sometimes in an epistemological sense (to designate truth that is open or accessible to all reasonable people), and the content of both senses is ideologically and culturally freighted.[7]

Another problem with the term public theology is that it begs the question of what the proper focus of theology as an academic discipline is. In a perceptive essay, Nicholas Wolterstorff takes Moltmann to task for uncritically accepting "the characteristically modern constriction of Christian learning to Christian theology."[8] Like many, Moltmann seems to regard all Christian thinking as an exercise in theology. But this, says Wolterstorff, represents an illegitimate aggrandizement on the part of theology, whose proper academic focus is the study of the sources and grammar of Christian confession, not the details of social, cultural, economic and political life. What is required is not a public *theology*—as though theology has all the answers to society's needs—but *Christian learning* in all areas of life. To engage in Christian learning is to allow faith in God, membership of the Christian community, and acceptance of the canonical scriptures to shape and inform how one investigates and explains the world. Instead of public theology we should speak of Christian scholarship, which is "kingdom-of-God learning, learning pursued in fidelity to the gospel and in light of the coming kingdom."[9] What is

---

6. Moltmann, Wolterstorff, and Charry, *Passion for God's Reign*, 24 (emphasis mine); cf. 51–52.

7. John Flett points out that in attempting to be publicly or politically relevant, the church often tacitly accepts secular modernity's definitions of public and private, and in doing so ironically contributes to its own privatization and irrelevance, "Public Truth."

8. Wolterstorff, "Public Theology," 76.

9. Ibid., 77.

needed then is not "a theology of economics" or a "political theology" or an "ecological theology," but Christian thinking about economics, and politics, and ecology, that is theologically faithful.

Be all that as it may. Whatever the problems with the label "public theology," it is now widely used and we will stick with it here. Its goal is to bring Christian insights to bear on societal issues, and to do so in public space, that is, within the public institutions of civil society. The legitimacy of the whole enterprise rests on two basic convictions, both of them highly contentious in a secular context. The first is that Jesus Christ claims absolute lordship over the whole of life, and is therefore, as Lesslie Newbigin puts it, "licensed to operate in the public square of all nations."[10] Given its premise of Christ's universal lordship, public theology is duty bound to reject the secular limitation of religion to issues of private morality and the cultivation of the inner life. For if Christ is not lord of all, he is not lord at all.

Second, public theology assumes that Christian beliefs about God and about human nature and destiny, and the values that derive from them, are entirely true. They are so true, in fact, that public policy ought to be shaped in light of them, as this is a crucial way of discharging the biblical mandate to love our neighbors as ourselves.[11] Once again, this necessarily entails a repudiation of the secular assumptions of human autonomy and the relativity of all religious claims.[12]

Public theology thus rests on premises that are diametrically opposed to those of post-Enlightenment liberal secularism, which is one reason why it is such a demanding exercise today. But if for Christian believers the legitimacy of public theology derives from the premise of the universal significance of Jesus Christ, for wider society it rests, more

---

10. Newbigin, *Welfare State*, 1.

11. So, for example, Shupack, "Biblical Basis," 4–7.

12. Max Stackhouse warns that inasmuch as religion is always one of the forces that shapes society (no known society has been able to flourish without an overt religious basis), and given that the comparative study of religion shows that different religious traditions have distinctive socio-cultural impacts on civilization, one of the key challenges that faces global society today is to decide what kind of civilization it wants, and therefore what particular religious traditions it wants. Stackhouse knows that this is an explosive question, given that the commonly accepted basis for the study of religion is that all religions are equal. But people make choices and evaluations anyway, and the question is whether such choices can be made wisely. Also, when it is denied that any particular religion's lord can be universal, Caesar often becomes the functional lord. See further Stackhouse, "Public Theology," 63–86.

simply, on the principle of democratic participation. That is to say, Christians have a right to speak on public affairs simply on the grounds that they are members of a society which endorses the free exchange of ideas. Accordingly, in a liberal democracy such as our own Christians do not really need to defend their rights of access to the public square; they only need to defend the credibility of what they wish to say *in situ*. They also need to say it in such a way as to be intelligible to a diverse audience and potentially persuasive. Both these requirements deserve further comment, though I will say more on the issue of intelligibility than on the issue of credibility.

THE CHALLENGE OF CREDIBILITY

Public theology aims to make a plausible and principled Christian contribution to matters of public life and debate. Before doing so however, it must arrive at what counts as a distinctly *Christian* position or perspective on whatever topics are under discussion. This is by no means easy, for several reasons.

To begin with there is the *problem of sources*. Contrary to what many conservative Christians assume, there is more to public theology than the exegesis of relevant biblical texts or the application of so-called biblical principles. It entails, rather, a wide-ranging conversation between the full range of Christian sources—Scripture, reason, tradition and experience—and the insights of philosophy, history, political theory and the panoply of the social sciences. In other words, public theology is necessarily an interdisciplinary enterprise (which is another good reason for querying the tag "theology"), and interdisciplinary work is always enormously difficult, requiring the expertise of skilled specialists. The challenge is to weigh all the available evidence, both theoretical and empirical, and to do so within a self-consciously Christian worldview, conditioned by the witness of Scripture, the history of doctrine, and the lived experience of the church down through the ages and across cultures, all of which are amenable to sundry interpretations.

Given the diversity and complexity of sources, and the irreducible role of human interpretation in appropriating them, it is futile to look for "the" Christian view on anything. On any contentious issue there is usually as much disagreement within the Christian community as there is in wider society. Nor do all Christian traditions share similar theological frameworks. It therefore behooves public theology to exhibit a fair degree of modesty. Public theologians need not set about to construct a comprehensive Christian social theory, however desirable that may be, but simply to make timely and wise contributions to contemporary social debates.

Such is the approach Duncan Forrester advocates in his book on *Christian Justice and Public Policy*. Rather than elaborating a fully-fledged Christian theory of justice, the task of theology, Forrester proposes, is "to offer 'fragments'—insights, convictions, questions, qualifications—some of which may be identified as true and as necessary complements or enlargements of conventional or commonly accepted accounts of justice."[13] Public theology, in short, should see itself as just one participant in a wide-ranging, multi-sided discussion. It should not seek to take charge of the discussion or to claim that Christians have ready-made answers to complex social problems buried somewhere in their revelatory sources.

Yet, for most Christians, these revelatory sources *do* still offer indispensable guidance. Pride of place, of course, belongs to the canonical Scriptures, and to the New Testament in particular, for without the New Testament we would know virtually nothing about Jesus and the origins of Christian theology.[14] But in turning to the New Testament, public theology encounters what could be called *the problem of focus*.[15] The New Testament has very little to say about the role of the state and the functioning of civic institutions. Instead it has a faith-focus, an ecclesial-focus, and an eschatological-focus.

It has a *faith focus* inasmuch as it addresses committed believers, not unbelievers. It has an *ecclesial focus* in that it is concerned primarily with the internal life of tiny, voluntary Christian communities, not with the affairs of wider Jewish or Greco-Roman society. And it has an *eschatological focus* in that it views moral life from the perspective of the eschatological transformation that has occurred with the dawning of God's kingdom and the gift of the Holy Spirit. The New Testament does not merely affirm

---

13. Forrester, *Christian Justice*, 13, 60.

14. Certainly, it is crucial to consider Old Testament teaching as well. It has much to teach us and is also the indispensable backdrop for understanding the New Testament. But public theology must reckon with the significant discontinuity that exists at a social-institutional level between biblical Israel and early Christianity, and there is a theological obligation for Christians to assess the normative value of Old Testament material in light of the distinctive contours of God's self-revelation in Christ, accessible to us only through the pages of the New Testament, and of the Gospels in particular.

15. See C. D. Marshall, *Beyond Retribution*, 9–16.

a set of ethical standards that are incumbent on all people in virtue of their common humanity and achievable by the exercise of good will. It also enjoins standards of conduct and character that go far beyond what is "naturally" possible and presuppose participation in the new creation that has broken redemptively into the present in the person of Christ. It teaches discipleship ethics, not the ethics of public policy.

Many of the so-called hard sayings of Jesus come into this category. Believers are beckoned not simply to respect the rights of their neighbors but to actively love them, including even their enemies.[16] They are not merely called to avoid murder and adultery, but to eschew lust and anger; not simply to forgive those who hurt them but even to bless their persecutors and pray for those who hate them. The peculiar problem for public theology, then, is to decide how the eschatological values of Christian existence can meaningfully inform the common life of wider, non-Christian society.

This brings us, thirdly, to the *problem of determination*. Once all the sources of guidance are consulted and understood, the question remains of what constitutes a truly "Christian" position on the particular issue at hand. An authentically Christian perspective is not simply one that is held by, or is attractive to, practicing Christians, for sincere believers have done all manner of devilish things in the name of religious truth. It is a position that is demonstrably consistent with the central norms and values of the Christian faith in general, and with the gospel narratives of Jesus's life and teaching in particular. As already indicated, it will frequently be the case that several different, even opposing, perspectives will claim such fidelity for themselves (just war theory and pacifism for example). In this case, there is no option but ongoing discussion and dialogue within the Christian family, in a setting of humility and mutual respect.

But even if a Christian consensus on an issue should, perchance, emerge, difficulties remain. There is still the thorny job of determining what pragmatic policy options will produce outcomes that most closely approximate Christian concerns. Christians ought to agree, for example, that care for the weak and needy is a central obligation for every human society. On this biblical teaching is clear and insistent.[17] But determining what social and economic policies will be most effective in protecting and

---

16. This is not to deny that the Bible affirms the existence of what today we call human rights. See C. D. Marshall, *Crowned with Glory*.

17. See C. D. Marshall, *Little Book*.

empowering those on the margins of the community is matter of fallible human judgment.[18] Religious faith guarantees no special expertise for translating principle into effective policy.

A fourth problem confronting public theology is the *problem of reception*. All attempts to articulate a theological perspective today must reckon with the long history of Christian political involvement and its often-baleful legacy. Following the Constantinian settlement, it was expected that Christianity would fulfill the normal task of religion in antiquity of shaping and legitimating political life. Although there were always features in the Christian narrative that served as an impediment to the total co-optation of Christianity by the state,[19] the church still prostituted itself to Caesar, often advancing its own agenda by a combination of flattery and battery—flattery towards the emperor and battery against heretics and dissidents.[20]

It is not surprising, then, that with the Enlightenment came the attempt to restrict and moderate the public role of religion in society.[21] It was decided that the liberal polity should operate on the basis of reason, positive law, and respect for individual rights. Ideas and values deriving from religious belief were to have no normative public role, for religion, of its nature, appeals to revelation rather than reason, and no one religion can ever command universal assent. Theology was still welcome at the

---

18. It is notable that the public Christian voice in New Zealand politics often focuses heavily on what might be called "pelvic politics"—issues of sexuality, reproduction, and abortion. There is little agitation from Christians for New Zealand to lift its assistance to poor countries. In 1975, New Zealand contributed 0.52 percent of gross national income to development assistance, somewhat short of the 0.7 percent recommended by the OECD. But by 2004, New Zealand's level of contribution had fallen to only 0.23 percent, less than half of what it was thirty years earlier. Where is the public Christian protest at this unconscionable development?

19. These include its central narrative of a savior crucified by the legitimate authorities, its pervasive fear of idolatry, and its eschatological expectations that God's own rule would eventually sweep away all earthly rulers, inaugurating a reign of peace and justice.

20. For an excellent brief summary of the religious character of Christendom, see Kreider, *Change*, especially 91–98. See also Kreider, "Beyond Bosch," 59–68.

21. It has been argued, however, that the post-Reformation wars of religion were not engendered by religion at all but "were fought largely for the aggrandizement of the emerging State over the decaying remnants of the medieval ecclesial order . . . what was at issue in these wars was the very creation of religion as a set of privately held beliefs without direct political relevance . . . [which] was necessitated by the new State's need to secure absolute sovereignty over its subjects." Cavanaugh, "Fire," 397–419.

public table, but only as long as its voice conformed to the truths of reason and could be validated by social consensus.

While that consensus remained nominally Christian, theology continued to play a potent public role in Western societies. But with the steady growth of secularization, the final demise of the Christendom settlement, and the marked increase in pluralism in society, the Christian voice no longer enjoys a positive reception in public life. Religion and theology are now viewed as a trivial, if not malign, influence in political life and are largely ignored in political deliberations. It is no longer accepted that Christian theology trades in public truth; it simply articulates "the beliefs of a minority of 'cognitive deviants' in the population."[22] Even if its rights of access to the public forum are protected by democratic principle, the church's voice today is more often tolerated than welcomed, and it is forced to operate under terms dictated by secular rationalism.

This brings us directly to the other major challenge confronting religious believers in the political arena—how to speak intelligibly and persuasively about their convictions in the secular environment of the public square.

THE CHALLENGE OF INTELLIGIBILITY

If Christians conclude they have something important and distinctive to offer public discussion on some issue, the next question is how to articulate and substantiate their position in a setting that does not use or understand the language of Zion, nor accept the presuppositions of faith. This is a surprisingly portentous decision, for habits of speech soon become habits of thought, and habits of thought soon become habits of behavior.

It is possible to distinguish two main strategies Christians have used to contribute to political and ethical discussion in society. One strategy is to seek common ground with other groups in society and to translate Christian insights into the currency of secular discourse. The other is to openly espouse a distinctive ethic and to employ, as appropriate, the vocabulary and grammar of faith and theology to express it. Both approaches have strengths and weaknesses. It is worth spelling these out in detail in order to clarify the larger consequences that flow from the style of discourse believers choose to adopt.

22. Forrester, *Christian Justice*, 9.

The Common-Currency Approach

One time-honored strategy the church has used to exercise its voice in society has been to appeal to a kind of shared public truth derived from rational reflection on nature and human experience, without making explicit recourse to religious language or revelatory claims. In Roman Catholic natural law theory, for example, the exercise of human reason alone is sufficient to know moral truth. Christian revelation can help clarify such truth, and provides unique motivation for obeying it, but it adds nothing substantial to the *content* of morality. On this understanding, public theology becomes a kind of natural religion, whose claims are communicated and validated by reason and common sense alone, not by revelation.

The strength of this approach lies in its recognition of the potential for a common ethical mind to exist across diverse traditions and cultures. Furthermore, in stressing the givenness of moral truth, natural law theology resists moral skepticism and easy relativism on the one hand, and mere utilitarianism and pragmatism on the other. But the approach is also open to several criticisms. Its main weakness lies in its failure to recognize the extent to which reason itself is shaped by contingent historical and cultural circumstances. As postmodernity has discovered, reason does not operate autonomously, nor deliver self-evident, universal truths.

Another serious weakness is the propensity for natural theology to be captured by ascendant political and cultural orthodoxies. It is a small step from seeking common ground with wider secular society to reinforcing and legitimating the prevailing consensus. This is what Karl Barth saw happen in his day: a free-floating natural theology ended up sanctifying an idolatrous Nazi ideology.[23] A concomitant weakness in natural theology is its tendency to dilute the character and distinctiveness of Christian identity. Christian revelation and tradition are removed to a secondary role in moral discernment, and eventually (as in Kant's categorical imperative) become superfluous to public and ethical discourse.

A different, and more typically Protestant, form of the common-currency approach is one that consciously derives moral guidance from scriptural revelation and theological tradition, but then translates it into allegedly neutral secular language and seeks to persuade others of its validity by appealing to utilitarian or prudential considerations, or to shared convictions about human rights and responsibilities. Its central

---

23. For a brief discussion, see Holder, "Karl Barth," 22–37.

strategy is to employ mediating principles that will clothe Christian values in terms that secular authorities can understand and accept. Arguably this style of public advocacy is a dominant trend in contemporary Christian social ethics.[24]

Once again, the obvious strength of this approach is its recognition of the common citizenship and common moral interests of all members in society. It also recognizes the priority of revelation over reason for discerning what is truly good and for empowering obedience. But this insight is quickly lost. For in the process of translating theological insights into the secular categories, what is most distinctive and essential to the Christian worldview is filtered out. The search for secular terminology to convey Christian beliefs inevitably entails reduction and loss. To speak, for example, of human rights and human autonomy is something less than speaking of humanity as bearing the *imago Dei*, with all its relational and spiritual implications.[25]

More tellingly still, such an approach filters out those Christian convictions and values that cannot be verified on prudential or pragmatic grounds. The eschatological radicalism of Christian ethics is soon blunted or compromised—for love of enemy, uncalculating forgiveness, and self-sacrificing servanthood are not easily commended on the basis of rational self-interest. But if the most distinctive features of Christian faith and language are to be left behind because they are disagreeable or offensive or impracticable to general society, is this not tantamount to admitting that Christian faith is irrelevant to public debate? Why bother with faith at all if its insights can equally well be couched in the language of secular modernity and held as common property by all? Is it not already a defeat for Christian truth claims? After all, secularism is not religiously neutral. It is a *de facto* religiosity in its own right, inasmuch as it offers an overarching metaphysical-moral vision of the meaning and purpose of human existence, a vision and an ontology that stand in stark opposition to the Christian conception of life.

Yet another problem with the common-currency approach is that it assumes Christian values and moral principles can be separated from the larger narrative framework of the Christian story without diminishing

---

24. "The effort to divorce theology from public advocacy of Christian moral positions is a dominant trend in modern Christian ethics." Holloway, "Christian Ethics," 11.

25. So, rightly, Holloway, "Christian Ethics," 10; cf. C. D. Marshall, *Crowned with Glory*, 54–63.

either and without substantially altering their meaning. The principles are considered timeless, the story expendable. But Christian values make most sense when seen in light of the overall biblical story, and it is that story that gives even common-sense values a distinctive flavor.[26] Arguably it is the biblical narrative of God's creative love and redemptive or restorative justice made known in the life of Israel and in the person of Christ and the experience of his followers, rather than a set of general moral axioms, that represents the real Christian contribution to public discourse.

This story offers more than a code of morality. It reveals the *character* of God demonstrated in word and deed; it mediates *participation* in the life of God; and has the power to shape *moral character*, both individually and communally, in conformity to the will of God.[27] Moreover, according to the biblical story the moral problems of human existence cannot be solved by autonomous human effort alone but ultimately only by that "fundamental reorientation of life in rightful worship that the gospel occasions."[28] To divorce Christian ethics from the wider theological presuppositions of the Christian story, therefore, is to tear asunder what God has joined together.

Put differently, public theology must needs have a missiological as well as a communicative dimension.[29] Its goal cannot simply be to master the language of the marketplace, but to furnish an alternative cultural vision, a different diagnosis of reality, using different intellectual ideas and categories, and summoning a deep cultural transformation consistent with what St. Paul calls "the truth of the gospel" (Gal 2:5, 15).

One final observation: the attempt by Christian actors to suppress or even deny their Christian identity in order to be heard in the political arena risks the charge of duplicity. They arrive at their policy position in light of their religious beliefs, but then in public deny that their religious beliefs have been the most formative factor in their decision. No wonder critics sniff a Trojan horse! At the same time, and for the same reason, the policy options they propose are themselves removed for

---

26. Duncan Forrester ("Welfare and Human Nature") addresses the same issue as Newbigin does in *Welfare State* but appeals not just to the Christian view of human nature but to the implications of the Christian story as one in which people are neighbors who belong together in community; see also Forrester, "Political Justice," 1–13.

27. See the excellent discussion by Birch, "Moral Agency," 23–41.

28. Holloway, "Christian Ethics," 20.

29. As argued by Flett, "Theology's Responsibility."

ongoing theological scrutiny by the community of faith. For they are not being openly commended on Christian grounds as a Christian contribution, at least not transparently so. So long as there is equivocation about the Christian credentials of the policies being promoted, and the agents promoting them, there is also little opportunity for a further shaping or fraternal challenging of them by fellow believers also drawing on Christian resources.

The Distinctive Discourse Approach

The second main strategy Christians have used to exercise public influence is to appeal explicitly to the unique narrative and symbolic resources of Christian tradition. According to proponents of this approach, rather than seeking to address public life on the basis of some artificial consensus or body of shared insights, Christians should develop their own ethical practices derived from Christian revelatory sources and justified by the distinctive praxis of Christian communities. For Christianity is not simply the religious explication of universal human experience or of objective moral truths that exist prior to or independently of actual traditions. It is an alternative interpretation of reality, a competing story that seeks to "out-narrate" the story of liberal secularism.

Christian truth is "public" in this approach, not because it appeals to human commonalities, but because its truth-claims are publicly visible and accessible. The first task of the church, then, is to be the church, to live openly as a sanctified and worshipping covenant community. Instead of seeking common ground with, or capitulating to, secularism, or striving to exert control over public space, Christians should concentrate on incarnating an alternative social reality that, of its very nature, will serve the common good.[30]

The strength of this approach lies in its concern to preserve the distinctive identity of the Christian community and the special revelatory claims of Christian faith. It affirms postmodernity's rejection of universal reason and tradition-neutral epistemological foundations. It also recognizes the linguistic character of Christian identity. In directing all their energy at attaining fluency in the second language of political discourse,

---

30. "Christian ethics will be Christian to the degree primacy is given to God's formation of a people who in doxological response to his saving actions in Christ provide the primary locus of and witness to God's moral will in the world." Holloway, "Christian Ethics," 28.

Christians (and Christian organizations) have frequently forgotten their first language, the language of Christian confession.[31] But theological language is indispensable for explaining and preserving what is most essential to Christian identity. When Christians cease to speak the language of faith they are no longer being true to themselves; they are like salt that has lost its saltiness (Matt 5:13). The approach also places appropriate emphasis on praxis rather than disembodied rationality as the test of moral legitimacy. Theology becomes public by being lived in public as an implicit critique of the larger order and as a summons to conversion. Those features of Christian praxis, such as love of enemy, that are not readily translatable in second language terms are still to be treasured and commended rather than being marginalized or watered down or left out of consideration entirely.

Yet the distinctive discourse approach is open to at least five major objections. First, it can easily slide into a sectarian withdrawal from the world that places the church's own sectional interests above those of the wider human family. The *centrality* of the church in God's purposes for the world may become confused with the *monopoly* of the church, so that the church is effectively equated with the kingdom.[32]

Second, it exaggerates the extent of Christian distinctiveness and moral achievement. Empirical evidence suggests that, despite their lofty claims, Christian communities are not that different to other bodies in society. Certainly, Christian narrative and dogma include unique features, such as the story of God crucified and the call to cross-bearing discipleship, but these do not necessarily translate into superior levels of moral attainment.

Third, the approach wrongly assumes that Christian tradition is autonomous and self-contained. In point of fact, Christian tradition, from its inception, has existed in dialectical interaction with other religious and intellectual traditions. Christian revelation does not exist in splendid isolation but often draws upon and underwrites insights from other religious and moral streams.

Fourth, it also disregards the degree of common ground that exists among the diverse communities and traditions that comprise modern society. There *are* many issues where it is possible to achieve a moral

31. I am indebted to Ted Koontz for the metaphor of two languages, "Thinking," 93–108. See also Koontz, "Grace," 1–9.

32. This criticism is mounted against the ecclesial focus of Radical Orthodoxy by Boersma, *Violence*, 240–45, 250–51.

consensus in society despite religious differences, where Christian perspectives overlap or coincide with those of others and can be expressed in commonly accessible terminology.

Finally, the distinctive discourse approach obscures the moral and missional imperative for the church to speak of God's ways and of God's truth in the vernacular of the age. Speaking in tongues is all very well for believers, but, as Paul points out, it is of no benefit to outsiders unless it is interpreted (1 Cor 14:20–25)! Given the reality of common grace and the all-inclusive reach of God's love and presence in the world, the church is duty bound to speak on issues of public concern in a manner that commands common understanding, if not assent, across the spectrum of pluralist society. Christian revelation, in other words, is not just for the benefit of the Christian community. It has an incarnational quality to it that demands constant translation and retranslation. It also has a universal dimension to it, for it speaks of the God who created all things and who intends to sum up all things in Christ.

AN INTEGRATED APPROACH

Both what I have called the "common-currency" approach to public theology and the "distinctive discourse" approach have positive features. The former places most emphasis on finding common cause with all citizens in society and speaking a common language, which has to be an essentially secular language. The latter places more stress on preserving the distinctiveness of Christian identity and speaking the language of faith, thus remaining true to the full dimensions of the Christian story, not just those features amenable to secular rendition. But both have significant drawbacks if pursued as exclusive strategies in their own right. The former risks compromising the gospel summons to conversion; the latter risks confining the gospel to the Christian ghetto. This suggests that some mode of operating is needed that combines the strengths of both approaches and compensates for the weaknesses of each.

An initial move in this direction would be for Christians involved in public life to at least recognize the dilemma I have outlined. One gets the impression today in New Zealand that Christians engaged in politics or public policy debates feel driven to employ secular categories and mask their identity as religious actors for purely pragmatic reasons. How else, they ask, will anyone take them seriously? How will their contribution be valued if they are lumped together with fundamentalists? That is an understandable concern. But it needs to be matched with an awareness of how much is put at risk by the deliberate minimizing of Christian distinctiveness and by the marginalizing of the language of religious confession.

In his sophisticated book *The Public Forum and Christian Ethics*, Roman Catholic philosopher Robert Gascoigne argues for a style of Christian action that avoids the pitfalls of both natural theology and communitarianism.[33] His starting point is recognition of the fact that modern liberal societies are marked *both* by pluralism *and* by significant elements of ethical consensus. The existence of such consensus on many issues shows that genuine communication and agreement between diverse traditions *is* possible, not on the basis of some universal rationality but because of the historical interaction and overlap of human traditions and communities.

Gascoigne also argues that although substantial ethical insights usually have their source in religious experience and tradition, the validity and intelligibility of those insights is not necessarily dependent on acceptance of a particular religious worldview. As insights into moral truth, they are validated by common human experience and can be communicated independently of religious discourse (as natural law recognizes). At the same time, the fullest meaning and continued vigor of these insights does still depend upon the larger religious view of life from which they emerged, a worldview which is sustained by concrete historical communities (as communitarian thinkers rightly affirm).

On the basis of this analysis, Gascoigne argues that public theology should consciously derive its perspectives from Christian revelation, not from some objective, ahistorical rational reflection on nature, which is an impossible undertaking anyway. At the same time, it should always be open to disclosures of truth from outside the Christian tradition and be willing to let other traditions modify and enrich Christian insights. Christians have no monopoly on moral wisdom or moral discernment. Priority should also always be given to the church's lived praxis in communicating its message to others. How Christians live is much more important than what they say or how skilled their political lobbyists are.

Most importantly, the Christian public voice should always have two dimensions to it—a *visionary* dimension that retells the larger Christian story in the language of faith and liturgy, and a *normative* dimension that

---

33. Gascoigne, *Public Forum*.

seeks to specify social, political, and legal norms that will attract public agreement, where appeal to religious premises is not usually necessary. When speaking normatively Christians may employ "mediating principles," such as the sanctity of life, the freedom, dignity and responsibility of the human person, the right to equality of access to the necessities of life, and so on. While these principles derive from a particular theological anthropology, they also have a relative independence from specific traditional contexts and can enjoy a fair degree of public intelligibility.

Gascoigne summarizes his proposal by suggesting that the challenge for Christians in the public square is neither to speak of God too early, which will make Christian judgments seem arbitrary and parochial, nor to speak of God too late, which would be a failure to own that fuller religious vision of life that informs and inspires Christian values and that summons openness to the coming kingdom. Christians must employ *both* the language of faith *and* the language of mediation in the public square, but know when each is most appropriate.

CONCLUSION

I have suggested that public theology confronts two major challenges in its endeavors. The first is arriving at an authentic and credible Christian position on whatever issues are under debate in the public arena. The most challenging part of this exercise is determining how Christian values derived from the eschatological experience of God's redemptive activity recorded in Scripture can be or should be applied to a mixed society.

The second challenge is deciding how Christian perspectives are to be expressed in terms that are intelligible in the marketplace, yet faithful to, and explicitly anchored in, the theological claims of the Christian story. Christians must be able to speak the language of political discourse effectively, albeit with a foreign accent.[34] But they must never shrink from justifying and explaining their perspective in light of the faith-story to which they subscribe, a story that furnishes their first language, their heart-language.

This is important, not just to preserve Christian identity but also to remain open to the ongoing critique of others within the family of faith, who may have a different, perhaps deeper, grasp on the public

---

34. I borrow this analogy from Koontz, "Gospel of Peace."

implications of the story, as well as from those outside the family, who ever remain objects of God's love, creatures made in God's image, and possessed of insight that can often enrich and deepen the Christian contribution to public life.

4

Crime, Crucifixion, and the Forgotten Art of Lament

A GREATLY NEGLECTED DIMENSION in contemporary Christian worship is the practice of lament, or God-directed complaint. Most popular worship songs cruise or hip-hop-bop along, with little reference to pain or without any hint of complaint about the state of world. They function almost as a spiritual anesthetic, dulling our senses to the extent of suffering in the world and to the deep paradoxes and ambiguities of human experience. Yet there is so much in the world we need to lament. There is much we need to cry out to God in protest against. War and violence, death and disease, poverty and prejudice, environmental degradation and religious persecution blight the lives of countless millions. We need to recover ways of articulating, in the context of worship, our perplexity and distress over such things.

One feature of modern life deserving of lament is the prevalence of crime. In every developed country in the world (with the exception of Japan),[1] reported crime rates have risen dramatically in the post-war period. Why this has happened is open to debate. But what is beyond dispute is the ruinous impact crime has on all those caught up in it—victims, offenders, and their respective family and community networks.

Victims suffer most. To be the object of some conscious malice or violation by another individual can have a devastating effect on a person's sense of self-worth and psychological well-being. Victims can feel debased, dishonored, disrespected or shamed. They may become irritable

---

1. See Braithwaite, *Crime, Shame, and Reintegration*, 48–49.

or depressed, even suicidal. They may be plagued by fears and anxieties, by anger and bitterness, by hatred and resentment, not only for the offender but also for themselves. Self-loathing and self-blaming are a common legacy of victimization.[2]

Offenders also suffer from the crimes they commit. Their action of deliberately harming another human being brings about a moral and spiritual degradation in them. They often experience shame, guilt and self-disgust. Repeated offending leads to a coarsening of their character and a corrupting of their humanity. The more habitual their behavior becomes, the more damage they do to themselves and the more dangerous they may become to others.

The families and friends of both victims and offenders suffer as well. They have their own feelings of betrayal, anger, grief, resentment, hatred and revenge. Their lives are also indelibly marked by the criminal act. So too is the life of the wider community. Where serious crime is perceived to be increasing and to be largely random in its occurrence, even those who have never been directly victimized can feel their freedom restricted and their lives diminished by the constant worry that they may be next to suffer.

A CAUSE OF LAMENT

The manifold damage done by serious crime and its aftermath is something Christians ought to bring regularly before God in lament. But we have forgotten the art of lament. Lament has all but disappeared from our regular church gatherings. It is almost as if lament has been systematically filtered out of our repertoire of worship resources. This in itself is lamentable, given the rich and varied lament tradition we find in Scripture. In the Psalter—Israel's hymn book—there are numerous "psalms of lament" in which the song writer expresses profound distress at his own condition or at the condition of the nation. Other examples of lament are scattered throughout the Old Testament, and a whole biblical book is entitled "Lamentations."

Most telling however is the fact that Jesus frequently voices lament. John tells of Jesus grieving over the death of Lazarus (John 11:35–37). Luke records Jesus weeping over Jerusalem, mourning the city's resistance to the way of peace (Luke 19:41–44). He bewails its future destruction,

---

2. Lampman and Shattuck, *Victim*.

which would fall most heavily on its women and children (Luke 20:20–31). According to Matthew, Jesus was "grieved and agitated" in Gethsemane, telling his disciples, "I am deeply grieved, even to death" (Matt 26:37–38). Elsewhere, too, we find Jesus moved with compassion for human need,[3] and distressed at his contemporaries' hardness of heart.[4] We see him frustrated at his disciples' obtuseness,[5] warning them they will soon "weep and lament and . . . be sorrowful," though ultimately their "sorrow will turn into joy."[6]

So Jesus knew a lot about lamenting. But arguably the profoundest, most revealing, and most disturbing example of lament in the entire biblical tradition comes from the last three hours of Jesus's life, where, in Mark's account, he dies with a cry of lament on his lips. As his life ebbs away, Jesus avails himself of the Hebrew lament tradition to express the depths of his anguish and grief. In the so-called cry of dereliction, he quotes Psalm 22, the "Lament of the Righteous Sufferer," to voice his feelings of isolation and discouragement.

> It was nine o'clock in the morning when they crucified him. The inscription of the charge against him read, "The King of the Jews." And with him they crucified two bandits, one on his right and one on his left . . . When it was noon, darkness came over the whole land until three in the afternoon. At three o'clock Jesus cried out with a loud voice, "Eloi, Eloi, lema sabachthani?" which means, "My God, my God, why have you forsaken me?" When some of the bystanders heard it, they said, "Listen, he is calling for Elijah." And someone ran, filled a sponge with sour wine, put it on a stick, and gave it to him to drink, saying, "Wait, let us see whether Elijah will come to take him down." Then Jesus gave a loud cry and breathed his last. And the curtain of the temple was torn in two, from top to bottom. Now when the centurion, who stood facing him, saw that in this way he breathed his last, he said, "Truly this man was God's Son!" (Mark 15:25–27, 33–39)

I want to offer some reflections on this episode to help us understand the context and nature of lament, and in particular its relevance to issues of crime and justice.

---

3. For example, Mark 1:41; Matt 15:32; 20:34; Luke 7:13.
4. Mark 3:5; 6:5; 8:12; Luke 7:32.
5. For example, Mark 8:17–21; 9:19; 14:40.
6. John 16:20–22; cf. Mark 2:18–22.

A CRIMINAL'S LAMENT

It is noteworthy, to begin with, that this example of lament occurs in a *criminal context*. Jesus utters the cry of dereliction as a condemned criminal, suffering judicial execution, at hands of state authorities, in order to uphold rule of law. His words give expression to his plight of criminalization and criminal punishment. Nor is this a merely incidental detail. All the Gospel writers seem to emphasize the criminalization of Jesus at the end of his life.[7] In Luke's Gospel, at the Last Supper, Jesus predicts that he will be "counted among the lawless" (Luke 22:37). In Matthew, when Jesus is arrested by the Temple police, he asks: "Have you come out with swords and clubs to arrest me as though I were a criminal?" (26:55). Mark stresses how Jesus's accusers perjured themselves at his trial, thus rendering his conviction illegitimate (Mark 14:55–59; Matt 26:57–68).

Both Matthew and John note it was in interests of maintaining public order that the Jewish and Roman authorities prosecuted Jesus (John 11:49–50; Matt 27:24). In John, the Jewish leaders say to Pilate: "If this man were not a criminal, we would not have handed him over to you" (John 18:30). In all four Gospels, Pilate offers the crowd a choice between releasing Jesus and an infamous criminal called Barabbas, who is under arrest for murder.[8]

In perhaps the most revealing turn of phrase, Luke's Greek text underlines the criminal status of all three men crucified on Golgotha: "Jesus and two *other* criminals *also* were led away to be put to death with him" (Luke 23:32). Jesus dies with the legal charge against him nailed to the cross (John 19:17–22), despite the fact that his innocence has been recognized by a Roman court,[9] by the Roman police (Luke 23:47), and even by the criminal fraternity.[10]

So, in the Gospel accounts a definite stress is placed on the criminalization of Jesus. He is deemed to be a dangerous criminal by his opponents, he is prosecuted according to criminal law, and he suffers a criminal's fate, in the company of two other convicted criminals. His cry of dereliction emerges directly out of this context. It therefore has

---

7. Several different Greek terms are used in these verses to depict Jesus as a lawbreaker, but each term can be legitimately translated by the term "criminal."

8. Mark 15:6–15/Matt 27:16–26/Luke 23:18–19; John 18:39–40.

9. Luke 23:14–15; Matt 27:19.

10. Luke 23:40–41; cf. Matt 27:4.

something special to offer any attempt to link lament with criminal justice concerns.

LESSONS FROM THE LAMENT OF JESUS

In focusing on the experience of Jesus on the cross we are, of course, touching on the profoundest of all mysteries. We will never fully understand what transpired there. We must be careful not to trivialize it into a string of pious platitudes. The crucifixion narratives do, however, afford several insights into the nature of lament.

Lament Is Occasioned by the Pervasiveness of Evil and by the Evident Distance of God

The story of Jesus's passion is the story of his definitive confrontation with the powers of darkness, his apocalyptic struggle to expose and defeat the mystery of evil. Evil comes to its climactic, most undiluted manifestation at the place of Jesus's death.[11] And significantly it does so by exploiting the mechanisms of the criminal justice system. Evil reaches its zenith in securing the legal prosecution and execution of the innocent Jesus. Luke's account of Jesus's arrest makes this connection between the abuse of police-power and power of evil quite explicit:

> Then Jesus said to the chief priests, the officers of the temple police, and the elders who had come for him, "Have you come out with swords and clubs as if I were a criminal? When I was with you day after day in the temple, you did not lay hands on me. But this is your hour, and the power of darkness!" (Luke 22:52-53)

Jesus's reference here to "the power of darkness" suggests that the three hours of darkness that later envelope the place of his execution represent, at least in part, the unique concentration of evil that takes place at this horrific event.[12] It is Jesus's profound awareness of the overwhelm-

---

11. Cf. 1 Cor 2:8; Col 2:15.
12. Darkness is often used as a symbol of sin, ignorance, and death: 1 Sam 2:9; 2 Sam 22:29; Job 3:4; 5:14; 10:21; 11:17; 12:22; 15:2; 16:16; 17:12; 18:18; 20:26; 22:11, 13, 17; 24:17; 30:26; 34:22; 37:19; 38:17; Pss 18:28; 88:12, 18; 91:6; 107:10, 14; 139:11; 143:3; Prov 2:13; 4:19; 20:20; Eccl 5:17; 6:4; 11:8; Isa 5:20; 9:2; 29:18; 42:7, 16; 45:5; 49:9; 50:10; 59:9; Jer 2:6, 31; Matt 4:16; 6:23, 27; Luke 1:79; 11:34; John 1:5; 3:19; 12:35,

ing power and violence of evil, and his own sense of impotence in face of it, that leads to his woeful lament: "My God, my God, why have you forsaken me?"

Christian commentators, since the earliest of times, have resisted the implication that Jesus was *really* separated from God on the cross (considered to be impossible since the Trinity cannot be divided). Or that he *really* accused God of failing to support him (again impossible, since despair is a sin and Christ never sinned). Various ways of softening the implication of his words have therefore been proposed.[13] But surely the most natural reading of the text is that, at the point of his most intense struggle with evil, Jesus felt completely bereft of God's presence and support. Whatever the objective, ontological reality, subjectively Jesus felt totally alienated from any sense of God's love or goodness or strength. Deprived of any awareness of God's presence, and utterly appalled at the magnitude of wickedness, he cries out in agonized lament. That is what lament is. It is an intense grief over the sheer tenacity of evil and the evident distance of God. At the same time, it is an act of identification with those who suffer at the hands of evil.

46; Acts 26:18; Rom 2:19; 13:12; 1 Cor 4:5; 2 Cor 6:14; Eph 5:8, 11; 6:12; Col 1:13; 1 Thess 5:4; 1 Peter 2:4; 1 John 1:5; 2:8, 11.

13. A literal reading of Mark's words has been considered problematic because (1) it fails to harmonize with the demeanor of Jesus in the other Gospel accounts; (2) it implies that Jesus's faith failed and he despaired, which is a sin; and (3) it seems to imply that the ontological unity between Father and Son was broken, which is impossible. Some therefore ascribe the psalm quotation to the Evangelists, rather than to Jesus. Others take Jesus to be expressing the experience of other sinners, rather than his own experience. Still others soften the meaning of the Greek (or underlying Aramaic) verbs used, for instance to depict Jesus resisting a royal role being handing over to him. Perhaps the most common way of evading the literal meaning of Mark's words is to propose that Jesus was evoking the whole of Psalm 22, not just its opening statement, a psalm that ends in victory. After surveying the options, Raymond Brown concludes, "I find no persuasive argument against attributing to the Jesus of Mark/Matt the literal sentiment of feeling forsaken expressed in the psalm quote" (*Death of the Messiah*, 2:1051). Joel Marcus comments, "It is difficult . . . to imagine that the church would have placed Ps 22:1 on the lips of the dying Jesus if the verse had not originally belonged there, since Jesus' use of this psalm verse created major difficulties. It has required considerable theological finesse for Christians down through the centuries to explain why Jesus, whom they have claimed to be the Son of God, complained in his dying moments that God had abandoned him" ("Death of Jesus," 213).

Lament Arises from Solidarity with Victims of Injustice and Evil

Throughout the Passion Narrative, especially in Luke's version, Jesus's legal innocence is repeatedly emphasized.[14] There was no basis for the charges raised against him. But Jesus was not only without any legal guilt, he was entirely "without sin."[15] His criminalization and execution stemmed, therefore, not from his own fault, but from his decision to stand in solidarity with sinful, suffering humanity. He freely chose to participate unreservedly in the universal human experience of brokenness and sinful alienation from God, and suffered the full consequences of doing so.

Again, it is significant how such solidarity was exhibited. It was not just a matter of abstract sympathy for human need. It was not some legal fiction that took place in the mind of God. Christ's solidarity took the form of a concrete, experiential identification with humanity in its most abandoned, forlorn state. It took place through Jesus's assuming the status of a condemned criminal, robbed of all companionship, dying slowly under torture, in the interests of protecting state security,[16] despite his total innocence. No greater experience of human desolation is possible than this.

This costly solidarity with human estrangement explains two striking features of Jesus's lament. First, Jesus addresses God, no longer as "Father" (Abba), as was his usual habit, but simply as "God." His address is more distant, more formal, more reserved than before. In the depths of his suffering, Jesus no longer knows that unique warmth of intimacy he typically enjoyed with God. Instead, he hangs before God as a weak, human creature before its Creator, dependant but distant.[17]

Secondly, Jesus individualizes his experience of human abandonment: "*my* God, *my* God, why have you forsaken *me*?" Not, why have you forsaken *them* (the human race), or why have you forsaken *us* (your own covenant people), but why have you forsaken *me*. So fully did Jesus identify his lot with sinful, dying humanity, so totally did he take our experience of lostness and condemnation into his own being, so utterly

---

14. See Luke 23:14, 22–23, 41, 47–48; John 19:4.

15. John 8:21, 24, 46; 2 Cor 5:21; Heb 4:15; 7:26–27; 1 Pet 3:8.

16. Luke 19:39; John 18:14; Acts 4:23–26.

17. Brown speaks of "this screamed protest against abandonment wrenched from an utterly forlorn Jesus who now is so isolated and estranged that he no longer uses 'Father' language but speaks as the humblest servant" (*Death of the Messiah*, 2:1050).

did he plumb the depths of human wickedness and suffering, that the entire human condition of subjection to evil and separation from God was somehow concentrated into his personal experience. The man who had known the highest degree of intimacy with God available to any human being now experiences the deepest degree of isolation from God imaginable.

Paul reflects on the extent of Jesus's solidarity with sin-dominated humanity when he writes, "For our sake God made him to be sin who knew no sin, so that in him we might become the righteousness of God."[18] In saying, "God made him to be sin who knew no sin," Paul does *not* mean that God made Christ into a sinner. He means rather that God made the sinless one to share in the experience and fate of the sinful race. God allowed Christ to bear the full burden and consequences of participating in our sinful human state.

Again, this was more than some abstract formula in the mind of God. The circumstances of Jesus's death, and the way in which Jesus responded to them, served to expose, and to remedy, the sinful root of the human predicament. That predicament is one in which every human being is both a sinner and one who is sinned against. We are both the perpetrators of evil and the objects of evil. We are all both victims and offenders.

On the one hand, we are all born into a state of subjection to the dominion of sin and death. We become victims of that pre-existing reality at the moment we join the human race. This happens through no fault of our own, for none of us chooses to be conceived. But, on the other hand, once we are part of the human family, we all perpetuate and extend the reign of sin by resisting God's love and by inflicting harm on others. We all become offenders through own actions. We all victimize others, and we are all culpable for doing so.[19]

In his passion, Christ "became sin" by entering fully into our condition of being both the victims of sin and the perpetrators of sin. In his death, Christ became the supreme victim of human depredation and cruelty. As 1 Peter puts it: "He himself bore our sins in his body on the cross" (2:24). In other words, he absorbed *in his own bodily experience* the full impact of our sin, thus standing in solidarity with every other victim of human evil. Yet, in his victimized state, Jesus did *not* perpetuate sin

---

18. 2 Cor 5:21; cf. Rom 8:3.
19. See especially Rom 1:18–32; 3:9–20; 5:12–21.

himself. He did not extend the reach of sin. He did not retaliate against his abusers. He did not respond to violence with violence; he refused Peter's offer of a sword to defend him (Matt 26:52). He did not respond to hatred with counter-hatred. "When he was abused, he did not return abuse; when he suffered, he did not threaten; but he entrusted himself to the one who judges justly."[20] He did not respond to victimization with vengeance. Instead he prayed for his offenders: "Father, forgive them for they do not know what they are doing" (Luke 23:34).

In short, Jesus broke the power of evil by absorbing its full consequences into himself as a victim without victimizing others in return. He stood with, not against, those who sinned against him. In so doing he freed humanity from the clutches of evil by deconstructing the "pay-back" mechanism through which evil perpetuates itself. And it is out of his immense struggle to do so that Jesus cries out, "Why such godforsakeness"?

All this provides a pattern for our lamenting. Genuine lamenting only emerges when we strive to stand with those who suffer and "weep with those who weep" (Rom 12:15). Our lamenting should be directed at two things—at the pain caused to innocent victims of injustice and evil, and at the distorted state of world that produces offenders who violate others so cruelly. Such lamenting is thereby an act of solidarity with both the victims of crime and with the perpetrators of crime—perpetrators who are caught up in, and shaped by, a sinful reality larger than themselves. It is a reality that has victimized them before they have victimized others. This is not to excuse their offending, nor to minimize their moral responsibility, nor to trivialize the wrongs they have done. It is simply to recognize the fallenness of the world in which we all live, and our common human capacity to hurt and be hurt, to victimize and to be victimized.

The power of restorative justice lies in this insight. It brings victims and offenders together so they can recognize their mutual involvement in the harm inflicted and can work together to bring about healing. In such a setting, offenders can see directly the pain of their victims, which is as real as their own pain, and can seek to make amends. Victims can see the humanity of their abuser, which is as weak and prone to evil as their own, and sometimes even confer forgiveness. The miracle of restoration emerges out of a shared lament by victims and offenders, a lament for the pain caused and the pain suffered, on both sides.

20. 1 Pet 2:23; cf. Heb 12:2.

Lament Requires Us to Feel Emotional Pain

Lament is not just an intellectual objection to innocent suffering. It is a gut-wrenching participation in pain, and especially the pain of victimization. We see this in Jesus. In identifying with our human plight, Jesus embraced pain. He endured an unjust trial, with hostile judges and lying witnesses. He underwent brutal and prolonged torture. He suffered personal rejection, even from his closest friends and followers, even from a fellow crucifixion victim. He encountered continual mockery and taunting, and a cruel attempt to prolong his suffering when vinegary wine was offered to him. On top of all this, he felt repudiated by God. Twice Mark tells us that Jesus "cried out with *loud* voice."[21] There was nothing clinical or detached about it. He *felt* the pain of human estrangement as his own pain, and he cried out in vocal protest to God.

Paradoxically, it is the fear of experiencing vicarious pain that leads us to rely so heavily on inflicting punitive pain as the answer to crime. Rather than entering fully into the sufferings of victims, we focus on hurting the offender in return. It is much costlier for us to walk with victims through the dark valley of their grief and despair and to address their long-term emotional and material needs. Rather than accepting offenders as fellow human beings in need of correction and help, we ostracize and isolate them in prisons. It is much costlier to enter into the darkness of the offender's world, to feel the pain he has known and the evil she has suffered, and to call him or her to genuine repentance and renewal.

But if the story of the cross shows us anything, it shows that redemption involves experiencing pain, and especially the pain of our enemy. For offenders, this means confronting the pain of their victims, whom they have treated as enemies, and seeking to make amends. For victims, it means accepting the pain and the worth of their abuser, who has become their enemy by his actions, and allowing him the opportunity to change. Forgiveness and restoration are born out of their shared lament—a lament over the pain each has known and inflicted.

Lament Is Both a Protest and a Proclamation of Faith

Jesus's lament is a protest. It is a protest at the persistence of evil and at God's apparent distance from the struggle. Jesus feels overwhelmed by

---

21. Mark 15:34, 37; cf. 1:27; 5:7.

the godforsakenness he experiences, and he asks, "Why?" Why have you abandoned me? But his lament still occurs in the context of his ongoing relationship with God, albeit now distant and strained. His protest is not a bitter rejection of God, nor a denial of God's goodness or power. Jesus still speaks of "my God." He still trusts in God, despite the perplexity he feels. He still allows God to be God, since appearances can be deceptive.

God does not answer Jesus's question. No voice from heaven replies to his "why?" There is only silence. Only the darkness of evil. Only continued suffering and powerlessness. Not even Elijah comes to the rescue. But this does not mean that God remains aloof, untouched by pain, absent from the battle, passive in the face of evil. God's response is not to give satisfying answers to the "why" question, but to enter into the situation personally, so as to remedy the problem from within.

At one level, as we have seen, Jesus enters totally into our sinful human condition of estrangement from God, and he feels God's absence. But in so doing he brings God's presence with him into this bleakness and desolation. In and through Jesus, God journeys into "the far country of our estrangement and despair,"[22] in order to bring healing deliverance to us.

God's personal presence in the death of Jesus is signaled in two main ways in Mark's crucifixion narrative. The first is by the three hours of darkness (15:33). I have already suggested that this darkness symbolizes the presence of evil engineering Jesus's demise. But at the same time, it symbolizes God's judgment on that evil. Divine judgment is often accompanied by darkness in Scripture.[23]

The fact that the biblical writers use darkness to represent both evil and God's judgment on evil is striking. Perhaps it is because divine judgment often works itself out, in practice, by God allowing evil to flourish to the extent that it finally consumes those who have promoted the evil.[24] In Isaiah 10, for example, God allows the brutality of Assyrian conquest to discipline "godless" Israel (v. 6). But the depravity that Assyria inflicts on Israel eventually rebounds on her, bringing about her own destruction

---

22. Fiddes, *Past Event*, 109.

23. God is often said himself to dwell in darkness or thick darkness (Gen 15:12; Exod 20:21; Deut 5:22; 2 Chron 6:1; Ps 18:9, 11; 97:2; 2 Sam 22:10, 12 [cf. 1 John 1:5] and divine judgment is frequently accompanied by darkness: Exod 10:21-22; Deut 28:9; Job 19:8; Pss 44:19; 105:28; Isa 5:30; 8:22; Jer 13:16; 23:16; Lam 3:2, 6; Ezek 34:12; Joel 2:2, 31; Amos 5:18; Mic 3:6; Nah 1:8; Zeph 1:15; Matt 2:13; 25:30; Acts 2:20; 13:11; 2 Pet 2:17; Jude 13; Rev 16:10; cf. Josh 24:7).

24. The classical discussion of this is Rom 1:18-32.

in return (vv. 12–27). Something similar happens at the cross. God allows the power of sin to reach its zenith in the diabolical violence of Jesus's crucifixion, so that it may finally exhaust itself. Its power is broken when it fails to reproduce itself through provoking counter-violence and revenge from Jesus. He alone does not succumb to its authority.

The second indication of God's presence in the death of Jesus is the tearing of the temple veil from top to bottom, from heaven to earth (Mark 15:38). This dramatic event indicates that here, in the suffering and death of Jesus, God stands most fully revealed. God is never more truly God than he is in the dying of Jesus. Even the centurion acknowledges that true divinity is displayed here, in the manner of Jesus's death (15:39).

Lament, then, is both a protest at the senselessness of evil and a proclamation that God remains God, and that God is actively involved behind the scenes in the conquest of evil. When we are confronted with the ravages of evil, such as crime, we cannot help but ask God "why?" Why do such bad things happen? Where the hell is God in the tragedy of criminal offending and innocent victimization? There are, however, no satisfying answers to this question. God's response is not to *explain* the problem of evil, but to *participate* in its suffering and to suffer himself for its ultimate undoing.

Lament Summons Action to Make Things New

When Jesus laments the virulence of evil, he doesn't do so from a safe distance. He does not stand on the sidelines bemoaning how terrible things are. Instead he suffers *with* us as he actively takes up *for* us the struggle against evil. He gives his life-blood to defeat the power of sin, to heal its victims and to reconcile its perpetrators to God (2 Cor 5:17–21; Rom 5:6–11).

If we are to join with Jesus in lamenting the impact of evil, we must also join with him in working to overcome evil. And we must do so in the same way Jesus did, not by deploying coercive power to wipe out evildoers but by trusting in the power of reconciling love to restore relationships and to make things new.

With respect to crime, this means resisting the noisy demand for harsher penalties as the answer to serious crime. Violence cannot be defeated by better violence; evil cannot be overcome by further evil. A better way to combat crime is to work harder at sustaining and strengthening human relationships. When crime is committed, relationships are damaged. If we do not invest ourselves in restoring the damage, evil has the final word.

We must seek to restore victims by sharing their pain and lending them strength to deal with what has occurred. We must also seek to restore offenders, condemning their deeds yet affirming their intrinsic worth, while clarifying the moral obligation they have to put things right. Formal punishment may still be necessary. But retribution itself is not the solution to crime, and it is not the essence of justice.[25] True justice is only achieved when healthy relationships are created, and it is only healthy relationships that effectively deter further crime.

CONCLUSION

In Mark's Gospel, Jesus dies as a condemned criminal, with words of lament on his lips. His acceptance of a criminal status stems from his voluntary identification with the lostness of the human race. His lament is occasioned by the pervasiveness and power of evil and by the desolation and sense of godforsakeness that accompanies it.

Yet his lament is still directed to God and manifests his continuing trust in God, despite present experience. He trusts that, behind the scenes, God is working through him to destroy evil. This can only happen if he refuses to succumb to the logic of evil by striking back at those who hate and abuse him. Instead he loves and forgives his enemies, giving his life to reconcile estranged humanity to right relationship with God and with each other.

In all this, Jesus provides us with a pattern both for lamenting evil and for combating it. Crime is one such evil. We must do more in our regular worship services to lament the prevalence of crime in our community. We may need to forge our own psalms of lament to do so. We must also do more to combat crime. Rather than simply demanding more police on the streets and greater punishment for criminals, we must not allow crime and punitive violence to have the final word. Trusting in the strength of love, we must work for the healing of victims, the transformation of offenders, and the restoration of relationships. For it was for these things, the work of restorative justice, that Jesus lived, died and rose again.

---

25. For a defence of the role of punishment within restorative justice, see C. D. Marshall *Beyond Retribution*, 97–144.

5

Prison, Prisoners, and the Bible

THERE ARE FEW ISSUES that evoke such powerful emotional responses in people as crime and its consequences. For many people, fear of crime is second only to fear of death. In many ways crime *is* a kind of death. Like death, crime can enter a person's life at any time, destroy forever their sense of safety and security, and leave a legacy of anxiety and mistrust. This legacy is bequeathed not only to the immediate victims of crime and their loved ones, but also to wider society. Where criminal offending is perceived to be increasing or to be largely random in its occurrence, whole communities can be traumatized by it. Even those who have never been directly victimized can feel their freedom restricted and lives diminished by the constant worry that they may be the next to suffer.

Such worry is magnified out of all proportion by selective and sensationalist coverage of crime in the mass media. Even though reported crime rates in New Zealand have fallen steadily in recent years, even though our murder rate has been largely static over the last decade, even though much more violence occurs in the family home than on the streets, media concentration on a few high profile and particularly nasty crimes feeds a general perception that crime is spiraling out of all control and that one's chances of being attacked, raped, or murdered are much greater today than ever before.[1] In many ways, then, we live in an age of

---

1. See Welch, "Fear and Loathing." The New Zealand murder rate has hovered around fifty per year for the past ten years, peaking at seventy-three in 1992 but falling to forty-five in 2001. After rising inexorably for many years, even reported violent crime has fallen since 1996, except for 2001 when it rose by 5 percent, and then mostly because of minor rather than major assaults.

anxiety. Despite the fact that average living standards have never been higher, life expectancy has never been longer, and individual freedoms have never been more protected than they are today, a general climate of insecurity pervades much of society.

The flow-on effects of this pervasive culture of fear are many. But the most obvious and disturbing effect is the burgeoning of our prison population. To our shame, New Zealand now boasts the second highest rate of imprisonment in the developed world (after the United States). Several things have helped to drive up our rates of incarceration, including the willingness of politicians cynically to exaggerate the problem of crime. Yet, contrary to what most people think, our exploding prison population is *not* a symptom of increasing crime rates. There is not a one-to-one relationship between general crime rates and rates of imprisonment (although there is a closer relationship between rates of *violent* crime and rates of imprisonment.) It is not crime rates so much as the community's general perception *about* crime, as reflected in social and political policy, that accounts for the prison boom. The Republic of Ireland, with a population the same size as New Zealand's, has around half our prison population. This is surely not because New Zealand has twice as much crime as Ireland. Perhaps it is because we are a more punitive society, or have less imaginative judges and politicians, or more pronounced social and economic injustices, or more restrictive sentencing laws.

Yet despite the flourishing prison sector, for most people, including most Christians, prisons are "out of sight, out of mind." We know prisons exist (although hopefully in someone else's backyard). We're glad they exist, because they remove dangerous criminals from the streets. But what goes on in prisons, and whether they do any good, are not questions that concern us much. All we really want to know is that bad people will end up in prison, because that helps us feel safe. All the rest is someone else's problem.

But this "out of sight, out of mind" attitude is *not* an option for Christians. Why not? Because of what the Bible has to say about prison and prisoners, and our responsibilities towards them, not to mention what it says about justice, repentance, forgiveness and restoration. Those who claim to take the witness of Scripture seriously in shaping their beliefs and practice ought to find themselves increasingly out of step with the "lock 'em up and throw away the key" brigade that is becoming increasingly noisy in society. In my book *Beyond Retribution*, I set out a thorough biblical grounding for a Christian position on justice, crime and punishment.² Here I want to focus more specifically on what the Bible has to say about prison and prisoners, and draw some lessons for a Christian response today.³ Before doing so, let me comment briefly on how prisons have come to play such a dominant role in modern society.

A BRIEF HISTORICAL OVERVIEW

We are so familiar with imprisonment as a criminal sanction that we don't often realize just how recent an innovation judicial imprisonment is. Prisons as such have existed since antiquity. As Lee Griffith observes, "The power of the sword and the power of the cage have been perennial tools of human governance."⁴ But for most of human history, imprisonment has *not* been used as a way of punishing common criminals. Instead, prisons have served principally as holding tanks where offenders could be detained prior to trial or to the carrying out of the sentence of the court, such as execution, exile, or enslavement, or until debts or fines had been paid.⁵ The use of long-term incarceration as a method of legal punishment is a relatively modern idea, stemming only from the late eighteenth century.

The emergence of an institutionalized prison system at that time was intended as a humanitarian improvement to the existing penal system. Prison was considered a more humane alternative to capital punishment or banishment or public humiliation, as well as a potential means for reforming criminals so they could be returned to society as upright citizens. Prior to this time, the system of punishment was largely arbitrary and often brutal. There was little proportionate gradation of penalties. The sanctions imposed upon offenders depended largely on the whim of the magistrate or prince, and there was a much stronger emphasis on hurting the body, by torture, mutilation, the stocks or the gallows, than on reforming the mind or changing the character of the offender. But as

---

2. C. D. Marshall, *Beyond Retribution*.

3. For a more theological approach to prisons, see Forrester, *Christian Justice*, 63–85.

4. Griffith, *Fall of the Prison*, 89.

5. Long-term incarceration did sometimes happen. King Jehoiachin spent thirty-seven years in a Babylonian prison (2 Kgs 24:15; 25:2–7; Jer 52:31–34). King Jehoahaz died in an Egyptian prison, and there is no trace of King Zedekiah after he was jailed in Babylon (2 Kgs 25:2–7; Jer 39:1–7; 52:3–11). But such cases were the exception rather than the rule.

the idea of rehabilitation took hold, it contributed considerably to mitigating the severity of criminal law.

The function of imprisonment changed from being a system for detaining people before trial or sentence to becoming a mode of punishment in its own right. "The age of sobriety in punishment had begun," Michel Foucault observes, even if the intention was "not to punish less but to punish better"—better because now the mind or soul of the criminal was being targeted, not just the body, and it was being done away from the public gaze behind prison walls.[6] Prisons were built throughout Western Europe and America with the intention not only of incarcerating but also of improving prisoners through a mixture of work, discipline and personal reflection.

It is worth noting that Christianity provided a significant impetus in this direction; in one sense, the modern prison system could be called a Christian invention. "Penitentiaries" were devised by American Quakers to provide a means of encouraging "penance" by offenders. Prisoners were to spend long periods in isolation, to give them time to reflect on their misdeeds and come to contrition. The use of single cells and solitary confinement in these prisons drew upon practices employed in medieval monasteries for disciplining wayward monks. And undergirding the whole regime was a Christian theology that believed in the power of penitence, and the potential for harsh treatment to encourage it.

But what began as a humanitarian gesture has since become one of the most violent and inhumane institutions in modern society. Twice as many rapes, for example, take place inside United States prisons as are inflicted on women outside prison.[7] Caging people for long periods of time, depriving them of autonomy and responsibility and self-respect, tearing apart their families, so that the innocent relatives and children of inmates suffer, throwing together dysfunctional and damaged people into a huge zoo, and all in the name of "correcting" them, is both

---

6. Foucault, *Discipline and Punish*, 14, 82.

7. "Despite the comments one hears about some prisons being country clubs, there is nothing pleasant, humane, or welcoming about most prisons in the United States. Prison life is composed of small sterile cells open to public view, double and triple bunking in cells designed for one person, crowded dormitories, regimented schedules, sometimes brutal treatment, frequent sexual violations—including twice as many rapes as of women nationwide—limited opportunities for self-expression and self-improvement, body counts, strip searches, identification by number rather than by name, impenetrable walls topped by razor wire, and guards with sticks and guns. It could hardly be more inhumane." Snyder, *Protestant Ethic*, 135.

inhumane and counter-productive. As Mark Olson observes, "to think that slamming people behind bars, breaking their spirits, and destroying their souls could do anything other than lead to more evil is the ultimate naiveté."[8] Nor is it a response to crime that can claim any biblical support whatsoever.

PRISONS AND PRISONERS IN THE BIBLE

There are dozens of references to prisons and prisoners in the Bible—from Joseph's imprisonment in Genesis 39 to Satan's imprisonment in Revelation 20.[9] Many of the characters of the biblical story experienced periods of imprisonment—Joseph, Samson, Jeremiah, Micaiah, Zedekiah, Daniel, John the Baptist, Peter, James, John, Silas, Paul, Epaphras, Aristarchus, Junia—and even Jesus himself, who was held in custody between his arrest and execution, and then, in death, was "imprisoned" in a guarded tomb. But probably the most renowned (and recidivist!) prisoner of them all was the apostle Paul, who had a veritable career in the penal system!

Prior to his conversion, Paul was someone who imprisoned other people. He locked up countless Christian believers, both male and female, and on occasions cast his judicial vote for their execution.[10] After his conversion, however, the *imprisoner* became the *imprisoned*, which so stamped his experience that Paul could refer to himself as a "prisoner of Jesus Christ."[11] In 2 Corinthians, he speaks of enduring numerous "afflictions, hardships, calamities beatings, *imprisonments,* riots, labors, sleepless nights, hunger."[12] The book of Acts records Paul being locked up on three occasions—at Philippi, Caesarea, and Rome.[13] Later Christian tradition speaks of him being imprisoned on at least seven occasions.[14] Paul was not alone in this experience. Peter and John were also repeatedly thrown in jail, and, like Paul, they too were sometimes busted out of jail

---

8. Olson, "God Who Dared," 15.
9. For a listing of vocabulary and biblical references, see Knapp, "Prison," 973–75.
10. Acts 8:3; 9:1–2; 22:4–5; 26:10; Phil 3:6.
11. Eph 3:1; Phlm 1, 9; cf. 2 Tim 1:8.
12. 2 Cor 6:5; cf. 11:23–28.
13. Acts 16:19–40; 23:10–21; 24:27; 28:16, 20, 30.
14. *1 Clement* 5:6.

by divine intervention.[15] The early church was actually led by a bunch of jail-birds, and God was primary accomplice in their escape!

Now in examining this biblical material for guidance on a Christian perspective on prisons, we must always keep in mind that imprisonment served a different function in biblical times than it does in modern liberal democracies. Society at this time was also very different, with stronger communal bonds and a different range of punitive options available to those in authority. Yet there are still some significant things we can learn from the Bible pertinent to our situation. Four observations are worth making.

Imprisonment Was a Cause of Great Suffering

In the ancient world prisons were usually underground dungeons, or empty cisterns or wells, or pits in the ground. They were dark and miserable places. Jeremiah was put in "a cistern house" for many days (Jer 37:16). When he was released for interrogation, he begged not to be returned to his cell fearing he would die there.[16] Micaiah was put in prison on starvation rations of bread and water.[17] The psalmist speaks of "prisoners in misery and in irons," captives who "groan" and are "doomed to die."[18] Job considers Sheol to be preferable to imprisonment, for at least there "the prisoners are at ease together [and] do not hear the voice of the taskmaster" (Job 3:18). Things were no better in New Testament times. With few exceptions, prisons in the Roman period were dark, disease-ridden and overcrowded places. It was common for prisoners to die in custody, either from disease or starvation,[19] brutal torture,[20] execution,[21] or suicide.[22] Ancient authors commonly described imprisonment as a fate worse than death; even the thought of it was appalling.[23]

15. Acts 5:19, 22–23; 12:6–11; 16:25–26.
16. Jer 37:20; cf. Ps 79:11.
17. 1 Kgs 22:27; 2 Chron 18:26.
18. Pss 107:10; 79:11; 102:20.
19. Cf. Matt 25:36.
20. Matt 18:34; Heb 13:3; cf. Jer 52:11; 2 Chron 16:10.
21. Cf. Mark 6:14–29.
22. Cf. Phil 1:19–24. Wansink suggests that the imprisoned Paul's reference to voluntary death in Phil 1:23–24 may be an allusion to suicide or to ensuring his own execution by failing to testify or co-operate with the authorities, *Chained in Christ*, 96–125.
23. On prisons in the Roman world, see Wansink, *Chained in Christ*, 27–95.

Modern prisons might appear to be luxury holiday parks in comparison (although this cannot be said of prisons in most non-Western countries). Certainly, our prisons are more humane in terms of physical treatment of inmates. But they are still a source of great suffering. *All prisons*—from the hellholes of Somalia to the enlightened institutions of Scandinavian countries—are warehouses of pain, places where hurt and hurting people are made to suffer further hurt through the forced deprivation of freedom, the loss of autonomy and dignity, and prolonged isolation from the people who care for them most. It is precisely *because* imprisonment hurts that we use it as a punishment in the first place. Punishment is, by definition, pain delivery and locking people up is our favored form of administering punitive pain today. Prison hurts because it contradicts our humanity. We are made as free creatures in the image of a freedom-loving God. To take that freedom away from people is to exercise an awesome responsibility because it strikes at the heart of human dignity and identity. So the first thing the biblical record invites us to recognize is the exquisite pain imposed by imprisonment, and *why* it hurts so much, and thus invites us to use great caution in resorting to it.

Imprisonment in Biblical Times Was an Instrument of Oppression More than an Instrument of Justice

Prison is not prescribed as a criminal sanction in Old Testament law.[24] Prisons were later introduced into Israel under foreign influence.[25] Yet a number of factors deterred Israel from making excessive use of them:[26] For example, historically prison systems have grown up alongside the development of standing armies and military establishments (which also fulfilled police duties). Israel was late in developing a formalized military structure, and so jails were also late in coming. Another factor was the emphasis in biblical law on restitution over retribution. Restitution was a way of setting wrongs right with the victim and expressing repentance towards God, which imprisonment would do little to facilitate. A third factor was Israel's strong sense of communal responsibility for obedience to the covenant and corresponding aversion to scapegoating. When

---

24. There is only one place in the Bible where prison appears as a judicial sanction against illegal activity (Ezra 7:26). Even here prison is merely authorized by the Persian king Artaxerxes.

25. So Griffith, *Fall of the Prison*, 89.

26. Ibid., 91–94.

individuals did wrong, the people as a whole, and even the land itself, bore the consequences. "For Israel, the fullest response to crime was not the isolated punishment of an individual lawbreaker but the repentance of the entire nation."[27]

But perhaps the strongest deterrent was Israel's own experience of imprisonment in Egypt and the indelible mark it left on her national memory, and consequently on her social policy. Israel never forgot the bitterness of slavery, nor God's action of setting her free from servitude. Israel therefore never used enslavement as form of criminal punishment.[28] She *did* still practice a form of slavery, but never felt easy doing so, and covenant law built into the institution several limitations and humanitarian protections.[29] Indeed in many ways Hebrew slavery was a more humane institution than modern imprisonment, for slaves were at least permitted to participate in normal family and community life.

While prolonged imprisonment was not used in biblical times as a form of criminal punishment, it was still used for political and military ends.[30] It was a way of silencing pesky prophets who voiced criticism of the reigning king or gave him unwelcome advice.[31] It was a means of keeping defeated enemies under control,[32] or detaining people accused of disloyalty.[33] It was a way of holding individuals before selling them into slavery or putting prisoners of war to servitude.[34] It could be used to prevent debtors from absconding, with the torments inflicted upon them in custody being an added incentive for their families to ransom them from bondage.[35] In the New Testament, prison often serves as an instrument of religious persecution.[36] Prisoners in the Bible are thus always

---

27. Ibid., 93.

28. Cf. Exod 22:1-3.

29. See C. D. Marshall, *Crowned with Glory*, 79-82.

30. Insofar as the victims of imprisonment disobeyed the ruling authorities, they were technically criminals. But they were not jailed for breaching stipulations of the criminal code that prescribed incarceration as the punishment.

31. See, e.g., Jer 32:2-5; 1 Kgs 22:27; 2 Chron 16:1-10; 18:26; Matt 11:2.

32. See, e.g., Judg 16:21, 25; 2 Kgs 17:4; 24:15; 25:2-7, 27-30; Jer 39:1-7; 52:3-11, 31-34; Luke 23:19.

33. See, e.g., Gen 39:20; 40:1-22; 2 Kgs 17:4.

34. See, e.g., Gen 37:24, 28.

35. See, e.g., Matt 5:23-26; 18:30.

36. See, e.g., Acts 5:18, 21, 23; 16:19-40; 23:10-21; 24:27; 28:16, 20, 30; Col 4:3; 2 Cor 6:5; 11:23-28; Eph 3:1; Phlm 1, 9; 2 Tim 1:8; Rev 2:20.

depicted as the victims of injustice, and stories about prisoners are invariably told from the point of view of the prisoner, not from the perspective of those who did the imprisoning.

In many places today, prison still serves as an instrument of political oppression. There are hundreds of thousands of prisoners of conscience all over the world. The words of Lamentations 3:34–36 capture God's awareness of such abuse, and therefore our responsibility also to be aware of it and protest against it:

> When all the prisoners of the land are crushed under foot, when human rights are perverted in the presence of the Most High, when one's case is subverted—does the Lord not see it?

In democratic countries, prison is used not to silence political or religious opponents but to punish and deter criminal offending. This may be a necessary and legitimate use of prison (at least for the "dangerous few" who are a threat to others). But Scripture's consistently negative perspective on imprisonment should alert us to the inherent tendency of all prison systems to oppress and abuse people in the name of some higher goal. This in turn should caution us against excessive or normative reliance on imprisonment as a means of dealing with wrongdoing, since the power to imprison can so easily become a mechanism of oppression.

The fact that our prisons are overpopulated with the poor and disadvantaged, with Māori and Pacific Islanders, with those at the bottom of the social and economic pile, underscores the fact that criminal justice cannot be neatly separated from social justice. It is no accident that those who are marginalized or disadvantaged or discriminated against in the larger social and economic order tend to be over-represented in the prison system. That being so, to concentrate all our energies on imprisoning people for longer and longer periods as an answer to crime diverts attention from the real causes of crime—which are as much to do with social circumstances as with individual wickedness.

As already noted, biblical Israel placed a strong emphasis on communal responsibility for sin and wrongdoing, and resisted individual scapegoating. The opposite prevails today. We strongly emphasize individual freedom and personal responsibility when it comes to crime. We expel offenders from our midst, as though removing people who do bad things will somehow rid us of vice. It is true, of course, that individuals do *choose* to commit crimes and *are* accountable for their actions. But all choices are constrained by environmental circumstances, and it is naïve, if not dishonest, to speak of crime solely in terms of personal free will. Under certain social conditions people will turn to crime who in other social climates would remain law-abiding. Poverty, unemployment, racial inequality, social prejudice, family dysfunction, and drug and alcohol abuse all have a role in fostering crime. A significant proportion of criminal offenders have been offended against as children, many in state care, before they became offenders. It is crucial therefore to inquire into the societal causes of, and collective responsibility for, crime rather than being content to divide individuals into categories of guilty and innocent, and tossing the guilty into jail. Society's own complicity in the creation of criminals is quickly lost sight of in outpourings of moral indignation at individual offenders.[37]

It is also important to recognize that the law that criminals break is not a neutral transcription of absolute morality. It is an irrefutable fact, Barbara Hudson insists, that the law is predominantly reflective of the standpoint of the powerful, property owning, white male and that the justice system bears down more heavily on the poor and disadvantaged than on the rich and powerful.[38] One study in New Zealand showed how the government puts far more money and resources into cracking down on welfare benefit fraud than on white collar crime, even though the cost of white collar crime and corporate fraud was up to ten times higher than the cost of all other crime combined.[39]

The criminal justice system can oppress as well protect; it can persecute as well as punish. Once again, the alertness of the biblical tradition to this fact should caution against a naïve trust in the capacity of the cage to conquer sin.

---

37. "The reality of covenant is that we are implicated with each other, we are shaped by each other, and each response in this relationship changes us all. We cannot escape the fact that when one is harmed, all are harmed; when one is imprisoned, all are somehow trapped. Similarly, when one is healed, all experience healing; when one is built up, all are stronger; when one is rehabilitated, the society becomes more habitable. The inescapable fact is that we *are* our brothers' and sisters' keepers—and they are ours" (Snyder, *Protestant Ethic*, 116).

38. Hudson, *Understanding Justice*, 149–50.

39. The study is reported by M. Thornton of Victoria University of Wellington, reported in the campus newspaper *Salient* 61/12 (1998).

Imprisonment Is Identified in Scripture with the Spirit and Power of Death

In light of the suffering caused by prisons and their capacity to crush the weak and oppress the poor, it is not surprising that imprisonment is often used in the Bible as a metaphor for various forms of human distress. In fact, according to Lee Griffith there is a close association in Scripture between imprisonment and the spirit of death itself. This perhaps stems from the widespread use of cisterns and pits for jails, which were associated in the popular mind with entrance to the underworld. Prison is not simply seen in the Bible as a social institution or material entity but as a spiritual reality, a kind of living death.

> The Bible identifies the prison with the spirit and power of death. As such, the problem with prisons has nothing to do with the utilitarian criteria of deterrence. As such, the problem is not that prisons have failed to forestall violent criminality and murderous rampages; the problem is that prisons are *identical in spirit* to the violence and murder that they pretend to combat. The biblical discernment of the spirit of the prison demythologizes our pretenses. Whenever we cage people, we are in reality fueling and participating in the same spirit we claim to renounce. In the biblical understanding, the spirit of the prison is the spirit of death.[40]

If Griffith is right, we ought not to be surprised at the failure of the prison system today. Rates of recidivism make a mockery of any claim to be "correcting" people. Plain common sense should tell us that we will never defeat violence by throwing violent people together in a violent environment, especially in light of what has been called "the contagious nature of criminality."[41] Prisons are self-defeating because they foster the very behavior they purport to control. They generate the hatred and hostility they claim to correct. This is why, in the Bible, God's solution is not to refine the prison system but to set prisoners free.

God Wants to Set Prisoners Free

We have seen that prisons in the Bible are usually part of a larger apparatus of injustice and oppression, an extension of the spirit of death. Because of this, biblical reflection on prison is uniformly negative. "Scripture

---

40. Griffith, *Fall of the Prison*, 106.
41. Culbertson, "Perspectives," 221.

records some of the worst crimes and most heinous violence the world has ever known," Olson observes. "But *nowhere* in Scripture do we find a divine endorsement of prisons."[42] "Never, ever, in any part of the Bible are prisons a part of God's way. Always they are used to oppress. Always they are an affront to the divine. There are no good prisons. None."[43]

The flip side of this negative evaluation of prison is a repeated emphasis on God as a God who wants to set the captive free and to break the chains of bondage.[44] The psalmist speaks of a God who "looks down from his holy height, from heaven . . . to hear the groans of the prisoners, to set free those who were doomed to die."[45] The same God who "made heaven and earth, the sea, and all that is in them," the same God who "executes justice for the oppressed [and] gives food to the hungry" is also the God who "sets the prisoners free" (Ps 146:6–7).

As Israel languished in Babylonian exile, then fell under the sway of one pagan power after another, she came to view herself as a nation of prisoners in need of liberation.[46] But they were, as Zechariah puts it, "prisoners of hope," looking forward to the day when God would say to her, "I will set your prisoners free from the waterless pit" (Zech 9:12; 9:9). One of the striking tasks expected of the awaited Messiah was to "to bring out the prisoners from the dungeon, from the prison those who sit in darkness."[47] This is precisely the role Jesus claims for himself at the beginning of his ministry:

> He stood up to read, and the scroll of the prophet Isaiah was given to him. He unrolled the scroll and found the place where it was written: "The Spirit of the Lord is upon me, because he has anointed me to bring good news to the poor. He has sent me *to proclaim release to the captives* and recovery of sight to the blind, to let the oppressed go free, to proclaim the year of the Lord's favor (Luke 4:16–20).

Jesus was not just talking here about a spiritual or psychological liberation for those imprisoned by sin and guilt; he was also talking about

---

42. Olson, "God Who Dared," 14.
43. Olson, "No More Prisons," 24.
44. Deut 7:8; 24:18; Pss 68:6; 79:11; 102:19–20; 107:10–16; 118:5; 146:7; Isa 42:7; 45:13; 49:8–9; 61:1; Mic 6:4; Zech 9:11; Acts 5:19; 16:25–26; 1 Pet 3:19; Rev 2:10.
45. Pss 102:19; cf. 79:11.
46. Cf. Isa 42:22.
47. Isa 42:6–7; cf. 61:1.

freeing people from the material structures and ideological systems that robbed them of freedom and dignity.[48] Jesus's entire ministry of feeding the hungry, healing the sick, forgiving the guilty, embracing the outsider, loving the enemy, and confronting the oppressor was a fleshing out of his proclamation of release to the captives. Ironically, it cost Jesus his own freedom and his own life to do so, with the convicted murderer Barabbas being the first literal prisoner to benefit from it (Mark 15:15/Matt 27:26)! But others followed, such as the inmates at Philippi who also had their chains struck off when Paul and Silas were freed by divine intervention (Acts 16:25–26).

How do those who inhabit our prisons today benefit from God's commitment to set the prisoner free? In my book *Crowned with Glory and Honor: Human Rights in the Biblical Tradition*, I outline how the notion of "freedom" in the Bible has both external and internal dimensions.[49] In the Old Testament, freedom typically means freedom from *external* constraint (from poverty, debt, slavery, oppression, and military oppression). In the New Testament, freedom more often refers to an *interior* moral and spiritual freedom which the Christian gospel brings, a freedom from demons and despair, from sin and selfishness, from guilt and greed. The full experience of God's freedom must embrace *both* external and internal dimensions, although each can be experienced separately and neither is dependent on the other.

What this means in practice is that those behind bars can still experience genuine moral and spiritual liberation even while they remain externally unfree. This is the powerful truth that lies at the heart of the ministry of Prison Fellowship. But the same Lord who brings interior freedom also desires to see prisoners set free from their physical incarceration. This doesn't mean Christian prisoners should be encouraged to escape! But it *does* mean their fellow believers should work hard for their

---

48. Griffith gives three reasons for not spiritualizing Jesus's words: (1) The implied reference to the concrete social programs of the Sabbath and Jubilee years would have been obvious to Jesus's hearers; (2) the material in Isaiah 61 from which Jesus quotes does not support a spiritualizing interpretation, since the "material" element of salvation is prominent in Deutero- and Trito-Isaiah; (3) it was not uncommon in the ancient Near East for the enthronement of a king to be accompanied by a declaration of amnesty for prisoners. Jesus's amnesty is not just a momentary thing but an eschatological deliverance. Jesus unmasks the powers of death and imprisonment and declares that prisoners have a right to liberty (cf. Eph 4:8; Col 2:15). Griffith, *Fall of the Prison*, 109.

49. C. D. Marshall, *Crowned with Glory*, 99–100.

eventual release, and support them through their post-release adjustment, as the consummation of the freedom Christ brings. It also means Christians should oppose the practice of "real life sentences," for in biblical perspective room must always be left room for mercy, repentance, and restoration.

KEY ELEMENTS IN A CHRISTIAN RESPONSE

I have made four observations on the biblical material and tried to draw some lessons for today. To finish, let me propose that a Christian response to the modern prison system should revolve around three key ideas:

Care

The New Testament expressly calls on believers to demonstrate practical care for those in prison.

> Remember those who are in prison, as though you were in prison with them; those who are being tortured, as though you yourselves were being tortured. (Heb 13:3)

In 2 Timothy, Paul expresses gratitude that Onesiphorus was not ashamed of his imprisonment, but eagerly searched him out in Rome to support him. Paul is so grateful for this act of compassion that he prays Onesiphorus "will find mercy from the Lord on that Day" (2 Tim 1:16–17). Jesus also makes a connection between caring for prisoners now and the outcome of Final Judgment.

> Then the king will say to those at his right hand, "Come, you that are blessed by my Father, inherit the kingdom prepared for you from the foundation of the world; for I was hungry and you gave me food, I was thirsty and you gave me something to drink, I was a stranger and you welcomed me, I was naked and you gave me clothing, I was sick and you took care of me, *I was in prison and you visited me.*" Then the righteous will answer him, "Lord, when was it that we saw you hungry and gave you food, or thirsty and gave you something to drink? And when was it that we saw you a stranger and welcomed you, or naked and gave you clothing? And when was it that we saw you *sick or in prison and visited you?*" And the king will answer them, "Truly

> I tell you, just as you did it to one of the least of these who are members of my family, you did it to me. (Matt 25:34–40)

The verb "visiting" (*episkeptomai*) here probably means more than spending time with prisoners; it carries connotations of showing practical care for those in jail and acting, if possible, to redeem them from their plight.[50] But the most striking feature of this passage is the way Jesus identifies himself with those in jail, so that those who care for prisoners actually encounter the anonymous presence of Christ. Griffith makes this point eloquently:

> What Jesus was telling his disciples is that, if you want to meet God face to face, the nearest you are going to come to it on this planet is to look into the faces of your brothers and sisters—and especially your sisters and brothers who have been declared unrighteous, unclean, unacceptable. It is not that we find God there; it is that God finds us there. That is where our faith is nurtured and bears fruit. There where we expect to meet monsters, we meet God instead. The opportunity to serve God lies there among the prisoners who have been reckoned to be least deserving of any service at all.[51]

It is worth noting that the New Testament also displays a concern for the welfare of those who run prisons. When the Philippian jailer was about to commit suicide after thinking his prisoners had escaped, "Paul shouted in a loud voice, 'Do not harm yourself, for we are all here.'" As a result of Paul's concern, the jailer underwent a dramatic conversion, not only receiving Christian baptism but even washing the wounds of his former prisoners and feeding them at his own table (Acts 16:27–34).

Critique

If we to take the Bible's consistently negative valuation of prisons seriously, it is imperative that Christians match their practical concern for those in jail with a vocal critique of society's increasing reliance on prison as a strategy for social control. Even if we cannot subscribe to a complete prison-abolitionist agenda, the direction of biblical teaching, and the logic of God's self-revelation as the One who sets prisoners free, should

---

50. Griffith, *Fall of the Prison*, 117–18.
51. Ibid., 126.

surely drive all Christians to stand against every attempt to expand the prison system.

In his excellent book *The Expanding Prison*, Canadian broadcaster David Cayley traces how the modern prison system has steadily encroached upon many other areas of social life.[52] With the resurgence of retributivism in penal philosophy, the advent of the "prison-industrial complex" in the commercial arena, and the ideological use of prisons to symbolize the authority of the state in the political sphere, prisons have become a self-sustaining growth industry. But, Cayley argues, increasing reliance on prison presents "a real threat to the decency and civility of the countries in which it is occurring."[53] Prisons acclimatize society to relying on totalitarian modes of social control. They foster the very behavior they claim to control, and so actually make society more, rather than less, dangerous. They conceal from public view the pain being inflicted on individuals in the name of communal wellbeing. What is needed, Cayley says, are alternatives to imprisonment, such as restorative justice, which are "rooted in the renewal of an old view of justice as peacemaking rather than retribution."[54] This is where Christians ought to direct their energies, for, as I propose in my book *Beyond Retribution*, biblical justice is supremely a peacemaking justice that looks beyond retribution to restoration and healing.

Community

The third element of a Christian position on prisons must be a commitment to the reintegration of released prisoners into "communities of care." Concern for those behind bars must be accompanied by generous hospitality towards them when they have finished their sentences and face the struggle of re-entering an often suspicious and hostile community.

People often defend prisons as a means by which offenders can "pay their debt to society." But the metaphor fails. Not only does society foot the bill for imprisonment, but ex-prisoners are never really discharged of their debt. They bear a seemingly ineradicable stigma of having been

---

52. Cayley, *Expanding Prison*.

53. Ibid., 4.

54. Ibid., 10. On a similar note, Snyder proposes that "Perhaps the greatest evangelistic task facing the churches today is a conversion from the spirit of punishment to the spirit of healing" (*Protestant Ethic*, 155).

inside. In the eyes of society, a period of imprisonment serves to establish criminality as "an indelible ontological attribute."[55]

What former prisoners need most is a community of people who truly understand both the grace and the discipline of forgiveness, a community that loves its "enemies" and welcomes strangers, a community that breaks down the dividing walls of hostility and preaches "peace to those who were far off" (Eph 2:14–17). This is what Christ did, and this is what those who bear his name in the world should also do.

---

55. Cayley, *Expanding Prison*, 41; cf. C. D. Marshall, *Beyond Retribution*, 117.

6

Satisfying Justice

Victims, Justice, and the Grain of the Universe

IN BIBLICAL AND JEWISH tradition, care for the poor and weak—for those in situations of extreme need or vulnerability, such as widows and orphans, immigrants and prisoners, the sick and the destitute—is one of the primary obligations laid on God's people. The biblical writers repeatedly declare God's unwavering concern for the poor, and God's insistence that those on the margins of the covenant community be afforded special provision and protection. An aspiration for what we call "social justice" permeates biblical law, and its neglect by those in positions of authority provokes enraged protests from the Hebrew prophets.[1]

The obligation to care for the needy also pervades the New Testament. If anything, the emphasis is heightened. Not only does Jesus add to the *Shema* (Deut 6:4–5) an obscure verse from Leviticus about "love of neighbor" (Lev 19:18) to characterize the goal and fulfillment of God's law, he radically expands the scope of neighbor-love.[2] Those outside the covenant community, including even national enemies,[3] as well as the

---

1. For biblical references and commentary, see C. D. Marshall, *Crowned with Glory*, 68–86; see also C. D. Marshall, *Little Book*.

2. Mark 12:28–34/Matt 22:38–40/Luke 10:25–28; cf. also Romans 13:9–10; Matthew 7:12; Luke 6:31. See my subsequent, detailed treatment of this combination in *Compassionate Justice*, 55–81. See further Patrick, "Understanding Distance," 101–29.

3. In the Old Testament, "neighbor" usually designates fellow members of the covenant community, although resident aliens are also owed love and respect (Deut 10:18–19; Lev 19:33). Later Jewish tradition included proselytes in the classification of neighbor. But Jesus universalized the category to include Samaritans and even Gentile enemies (Matt 5:43–44; Luke 6:35; Luke 10:29–37).

most disreputable elements within the community, such as tax collectors, prostitutes and sinners,[4] are counted as neighbors to whom the duty of love is owed. Jesus even suggests that how we respond to the most desperate and the disadvantaged of our neighbors will serve as a criterion of eschatological judgment. "For as much as you have done it to one of the least of these my brothers and sisters," Jesus declares, "you have done it to me" (Matthew 25:31–46).

It is important to note that the standard here is not that of *feeling* care for the needy but of *doing* care—clothing the naked, feeding the hungry, welcoming the stranger, visiting the prisoner, and so on. On a similar note, Jesus's most famous parable on the ethics of care, the Parable of the Good Samaritan, ends with the injunction: "Go and *do* likewise" (Luke 10:37). Interestingly this parable describes varying responses to a victim of serious crime. The Samaritan demonstrates the meaning of neighbor-love when, contrary to his cultural instincts, he acts to rescue and restore the Jewish recipient of a vicious beating. By contrast the two religious characters in the story, the priest and the Levite, put concerns about ritual purity above their social responsibility to care for victims of injustice. The story concludes with Jesus telling the lawyer, who approached him with a question about the real intent of God's law, to emulate the actions of a hated foreigner towards a crime victim rather than espouse the piety of religious professionals in his own community. Practical care for the victims of violence, the lawyer learns, is a better satisfaction of the law's true purpose than is devotion to ceremonial holiness.[5]

The lesson remains applicable today. In many ways, religious communities still struggle to respond appropriately to the plight of victims and the legal community still has much to learn about satisfying justice, in both senses of the phrase—what truly satisfies the demands of justice, and what form of justice brings most satisfaction to the parties involved, particularly to victims. In this chapter, I first offer some reflections on the nature of victimization and on the reasons why the presence of victims poses particular challenges to the faith community. I then turn to consider restorative justice, which is one of the most promising justice alternatives to emerge in recent times. I propose that there are theological as well as practical reasons why restorative justice merits our support and confidence as a satisfactory and satisfying way to address the justice

---

4. Jesus was notorious as a "friend of tax collectors and sinners," e.g., Mark 2:15–17/Matt 9:9–11/Luke 5:27–32; Matt 11:19; Luke 15:1–2; 19:1–10.

5. For a thorough treatment, see C. D. Marshall, *Compassionate Justice*, 50–176.

needs of victims, as well as those of others caught up in the tragedy of crime.

VICTIMS AND THE RELIGIOUS COMMUNITY

Attending to the needs of victims is never easy. This is partly because victims make us feel anxious and unsure. We all need to believe that the world is a safe and predictable place, that we have some measure of control over our lives. But the randomness of crime challenges that perception. Victims remind us of our vulnerability and insecurity. In witnessing their suffering, doubts arise about our own safety. Victims frighten us. This accounts for the widespread tendency to blame victims, especially rape victims, for their predicament. If we can explain the victim's experience in terms of their own foolishness, we reassure ourselves that it might never happen to us—so long as we avoid *their* mistakes.

Because victims evoke such anxieties in others, we try to keep them at a distance. This is why, despite outpourings of vicarious rage on their behalf in the popular media, victims typically feel isolated and alone. One might hope that things are different for victims who belong to faith communities, such as churches, since such communities usually strive to be places of hospitality and support. But this is not always the case. In fact, in some ways victims constitute an even more threatening presence in the religious community than they do in the wider community. For the stark reality of their victimization raises profoundly unsettling questions about faith—questions about the origins of evil and God's presumed control of the world, about the arbitrariness of suffering and the effectiveness of prayer, about the value of spiritual commitment when God seems to fail those who trust in him. The inadequacy of stock answers to such questions is threateningly exposed by the hard facts of the victim's experience.

In their shattered state, victims don't easily feel at home in polite religious company. Nor do other believers find their presence very edifying. Many are uneasy with "the coarse, unedited feelings that spew from deep inside the one who has been victimized—the pain, anger, despair, grief, and desire for revenge."[6] Such raw emotions are hard to hear, and trite responses are common. As Howard Zehr observes, "The Church should be a place of refuge, but often we have not known how to listen, how to be present to victims. We have told them that their anger is wrong, that

---

6. Lampman and Shattuck, "Finding God in the Wake of Crime," 6.

they need to move on, to forgive, to forget. We have denied them their right to mourn and instead have laid new burdens on them. All this is understandable—as part of our effort to distance ourselves from pain and vulnerability—but not at all helpful."[7]

If faith communities are to be more helpful, two things are needed. One is a recognition of how alienating to victims our natural coping mechanisms of detachment, blame and superficial pleasantries really are, and how detrimental are our pat theological answers. The other requirement is a much fuller understanding of the distinctive needs and experiences of crime victims (including their need to lament, something alien to the blandness of so much contemporary Christian worship). The precise configuration of these needs will, of course, vary from person to person and offence to offence. But research shows that victims experience many common reactions and have many similar struggles. The trauma of victimization upsets the normal physical, emotional, mental, social and spiritual equilibrium by which people live their lives, and can cause acute problems in each of these areas. One American victims' organization has identified nine categories where victims require support:[8]

- *Physical problems:* Including bodily injuries, nightmares, insomnia, extreme fatigue, impotence, weight loss or gain, and exaggerated "startle response."
- *Mental problems:* Including flashbacks, anxiety, memory loss, the struggle to make sense of what has happened and to get answers to questions.
- *Spiritual problems:* Including a re-evaluation of religious beliefs, a loss of faith, a sense of guilt and self-blame.
- *Emotional problems:* Including loneliness, depression, sadness, fear, self-pity, helplessness, a sense of purposelessness, a tendency to withdraw from people, or a drive to exact revenge on the culprit.
- *Relational problems:* Including reduced parenting skills, divorce, family violence, over-protectiveness, chemical dependency, and so on.

7. Zehr, "Restoring Justice," 151.
8. Trulear, "Go and Do Likewise," 80–82.

- *Financial problems:* Including the costs of medical treatment, funerals, counselling, replacing lost property, meeting court costs, insurance costs, etc.
- *Employment-related problems:* Ranging from an inability to concentrate at work to severe workaholism.
- *Privacy problems:* Either a loss of privacy due to intense media attention or excessive feelings of isolation and aloneness from a lack of public interest in their experience.
- *Legal problems:* Including the strain associated with judicial processes, unfamiliarity with the criminal justice system, pain and shame at encountering the offender in court, resentment if the crime is not solved by the police, and so on.

Given such wide-ranging problems, the challenge is to provide the kind of services and resources that will help victims cope with their trauma, both in the immediate aftermath of the offence and over the long haul. Organizations like Victim Support, Rape Crisis, and Women's Refuges do excellent work in this respect, despite limited resources and volunteers. There is ample room for the involvement of religious believers in such organizations, as well as for the development of faith-based parallels.

But perhaps even more than practical support and a listening ear, what victims most need is a sense of justice. They want to know that the wrongs they have suffered have been acknowledged and that those responsible for them have been held to account. This allegedly is what the criminal justice system exists for. Yet too often victims' involvement in the justice system turns out to be a damaging, even re-victimizing, ordeal.

VICTIMS AND THE JUSTICE SYSTEM

Historically the Western criminal justice system has given scant attention to the needs of victims. The overwhelming emphasis has been on the punishment of offenders and the preservation of the state's interests. Victims are almost incidental to the judicial process since, technically speaking, the designated "victim" of the offence is the state, not the actual person injured. The role of the injured party is simply to give evidence on behalf of the prosecution. Furthermore, the sanctions imposed on the criminal are not intended to help the victim but to uphold the rule of law and reinforce the state's authority. It should not be surprising, then, that when victims look to the formal justice system to deliver them a sense of justice, they are frequently disappointed. They often end up angry and bewildered, feeling that the system has cheated them of what they need most.

Public sensitivity to this problem has been heightened by the so-called victims movement. The movement emerged in the United States several decades ago, and has since spread around the world. One strand of the victims' movement has been "needs-focused." It has concentrated on rendering practical and emotional support to victims as they deal with the consequences of the offence. Another strand has been "rights-focused." It has agitated for institutional and legislative change to give victims specific legal rights, such as the right to be informed of their case, to participate in hearings, to be consulted about sentences, and even, in some American jurisdictions, to witness capital punishments.[9] In New Zealand the victims' movement has certainly encouraged some positive changes. Victim advisers have been appointed in courts and new legislation, such as the Victims' Rights Act and changes to the Sentencing Act and the Parole Act, have given new entitlements and protections to victims.

Unfortunately, however, there is a temptation in the political arena to play the needs and rights of victims off against those of offenders. In the United States, conservative "law and order" lobbyists have exploited public sympathy for victims as justification for the state coming down harder on offenders. In New Zealand, too, rights-based groups, like Sensible Sentencing Trust, tend to have a markedly punitive orientation, arguing for harsher penalties and the reduction of services to prisoners.

Yet it is a mistake to think that what is given to victims must be taken away from offenders. It need not be a "zero-sum," "I win, you lose" kind of game. After all, one of the primary needs of victims is reassurance about their future safety—a guarantee against repetition—and the best way to provide this is by working to secure the transformation of offenders. It also needs to be remembered that many offenders offend as a direct result of their own prior victimization, especially in childhood. They hurt others because they have first been hurt themselves. They have been victims before becoming victimizers. If, then, we are to deal effectively with

---

9. On this, see Strang, "Crime Victim Movement," 69–82.

their criminal offending, we must address their needs as past victims of human malice, neglect or brutality.

This leads to an important observation. As unwelcome as it may sound, what victims often need most, if they are to deal adequately with the destructive legacy of their experience, is direct engagement with the one who has offended against them. This is not widely recognized in society, and many would deny it is true. But arguably the bitterest feature of victimization is that victims are thrust, against their wills, into a profound *relationship* with the person who has harmed them. It is an uninvited, unhealthy, and deeply resented relationship—but it is still a relationship, one born of the criminal event itself. As well as coping with the impact of the crime, victims also need to cope with the relational bond it has created with the offender.

THE BOND OF VICTIMIZATION

When one person intentionally injures another, both victim and perpetrator are unavoidably bound together by their common experience. Both are chained to the same transgression and its aftermath. One is bound by guilt and shame; the other by bitterness and pain. Because they are bound together to the event, victim and offender need each other to experience liberation and healing from the continuing thrall of the offence. If the offender is to change, he needs the victim to trigger or sharpen his contrition, to hear his confession, to acknowledge his guilt, and to affirm his ability to start afresh. But the victim also needs the offender. To be the victim of some conscious malice or violation by another person can have a profound impact on the person's sense of self-worth and psychological well-being. The deeper the injury or the more violent the transgression, the greater the impact. Victims can feel debased, dishonored, disrespected or shamed. They may become irritable or depressed, even suicidal. They can find their freedom constricted by fears and anxieties, by anger and bitterness, by hatred and resentment, not only for the offender but also for themselves (self-loathing and self-blaming are a common result of victimization). The pain of the offence or the person of the offender thus comes to exercise continuing power over the victim's entire life.

For this situation to change, the victim needs his or her relationship with the offender to be transformed. There are different ways this can happen, such as through counseling or cognitive therapy or healing prayer. But arguably the most effective way for it to happen is through a direct encounter with the offender. For, ironically, it is the person who has most deeply injured us who is most empowered to trigger restoration in us. Frequently, what victims most need is for their abuser to hear of their pain, to answer their questions, to absorb their resentment, and to accept their dignity. We might wish this were not so, and there will always be exceptions. But very often it is an inescapable component of the bond of victimization. Both parties are bound together by their co-participation in the criminal event, and hence both need each other to transform their relationship. Each holds the key to the other's liberation.

This is where restorative justice has something special to offer. Restorative justice seeks to bring together those who have been most affected by an incident of wrongdoing, in a safe and controlled environment (usually with trained facilitators), to name the wrong that has been done, to describe how they have been personally affected by it, to speak about the material and emotional needs it has created, and to resolve together how best to repair the harm and to prevent recurrence. From modest Mennonite origins in the early 1970s, restorative justice has grown into an international social movement for the promotion of collaborative and peacemaking approaches to conflict resolution. It has had an impact on judicial thought and practice in many countries, most notably in New Zealand. In 1989, New Zealand reorganized its youth justice system along restorative lines, becoming the first country in the world to incorporate restorative conferencing into national legislation, with very encouraging results. Over the past 20 years, restorative justice has established itself within the adult justice system as well, and legislation now requires that all eligible cases before the courts should be assessed for restorative justice.

But what actually is "restorative justice"? What distinguishes restorative justice from other theories of justice, and especially from the notion of retributive justice that undergirds much of the conventional criminal justice system?[10] And what warrants us placing confidence in restorative justice as an important complement, and corrective, to current retributive practices?

---

10. On this, see my larger study, *Beyond Retribution*, especially 97–144.

THE CHARACTER OF RESTORATIVE JUSTICE

Restorative justice is known by a variety of names, and takes many different forms. Some call it "transformative justice"; others "relational justice"; still others prefer "community justice" or "collaborative justice," or simply "real justice." Whatever it is called however, advocates of restorative justice insist that it is not simply a minor variation on the current justice system, a way of helping it become more effective or more humane. It is an alternative model, a "third way" between the retributive and rehabilitative models that have dominated penal philosophy in modern times, a distinctive way of thinking about crime and punishment, a different "paradigm," to use Howard Zehr's term, to conceptualize criminal justice.[11]

For some, the distinctiveness of the restorative paradigm lies in its *process or practices*. Restorative justice is a particular process in which all those affected by an incident of wrongdoing come together to share their feelings and resolve together how to deal with its aftermath. For others, the distinctiveness of restorative justice lies in its *values or commitments*. Restorative justice is different because it prioritizes the values of healing and respect, participation, truth-telling, mutual care, reconciliation and peacemaking. Of course, there is no need to set these conceptions of "process" and "values" against each other. Both must be held together, for it is the values that determine the process and the process that makes visible the values.[12] If restorative justice privileges the values of respect and truth, for example, it is crucially important that the practices followed in a restorative-justice meeting exhibit equal respect for all parties and give ample opportunity for everyone present to speak their truth freely. On the other hand, as long as these values are honored, there is room for a diversity of processes and a flexibility of practice.[13]

So, restorative justice is both a distinctive process and a distinctive set of values, with each requiring the other. Having said that, what is most important to the success and the future of restorative justice, especially as it becomes more professionalized and more embedded in the formal justice system, is that restorative values are nurtured and promoted in the

---

11. Zehr, *Changing Lenses*; see also Zehr, *Little Book of Restorative Justice*.

12. Strang and Braithwaite rightly insist that a combination of values and process conceptions should be seen as a "normative ideal" for restorative justice, *Civil Society*, 13.

13. On this, see Bowen, Boyack, and Marshall, "How Does Restorative Justice Ensure Good Practice?"

community. Restorative justice does have much to offer our ailing justice system, and to do so it needs to be embraced by the various components of that system (the police, the courts, the prisons, the legal fraternity, and so on). But there is a real danger that, in the course of becoming respectable, restorative justice will be co-opted by the state, and bit by bit forced to conform to an alien set of values, such as the need to process cases as quickly and cost-efficiently as possible, to employ only paid professionals to handle them, and to bury the magic of restorative justice beneath a mountain of official paper work.

But if restorative justice is to make a difference to the prevailing system, its practitioners must be "in the world but not of the world."[14] They must become trusted participants in the public justice system, yet self-consciously drink from a different stream, and cherish a different set of values. Of course, values do not exist in a vacuum; they are held by flesh and blood people who belong to particular historical communities. If it is to flourish, then, restorative justice must be anchored in alternative "communities of value," that is, in communities of people who accord the highest importance to the values of mutual care and accountability, honesty and compassion, confession and forgiveness and peacemaking.

One such community in which this ought to be the case is the Christian church. After all Christians boast a religion that centers on repentance and forgiveness and reconciliation, convictions that lie at the heart of restorative justice. One would therefore expect Christians to be vigorous supporters of judicial and penal reform in a restorative direction. Sadly, this has not been the case historically (with some notable exceptions), and is not often the case today (again with notable exceptions). Perhaps part of the mission of the restorative-justice movement is to remind the Christian church of what it supposedly believes and ought to practice more consistently.

Restorative justice, then, can be understood as a set of practices that give expression to a set of values, and that the constant articulation and affirmation of these values in communities of support is of supreme importance if restorative justice is to deliver what it promises—namely, a way of handling wrong-doing that brings satisfaction to victims, to offenders, and to the needs of wider society. But perhaps there is even more to it than this. As many participants will attest, the practice of restorative justice, especially within traditional or indigenous communities,

---

14. Cf. John 17:15.

is a profoundly spiritual affair. (Indeed, recognition of the inherent spirituality of doing justice is one of the major contributions indigenous peoples have made to the restorative-justice movement, certainly in New Zealand.)[15] Furthermore many of the key values of restorative justice are deeply rooted in the Judeo-Christian tradition, and can be best appreciated when they are seen in the context of this wider religious worldview.

From a Christian theological perspective, restorative justice can be viewed as much more than an effective democratic process and a laudable system of values. It is a manifestation of something far deeper than that, something that helps explain both the power of restorative justice and its cross-cultural applicability. Restorative justice, theologically understood, is grounded in something beyond human devising. It has an objective, metaphysical basis. It is a practice aligned with the grain of the universe. It is a phenomenon that makes visible the way reality really is, the way God has made human beings, and the wider moral order, to function. This, of course, is an audacious thing to say in a postmodern context. But for those who believe that the Christian story is objectively true, such a conclusion is inescapable.

TWO TRUTH CLAIMS

The Christian story rests on two fundamental claims, which it holds to be objectively or publicly true, not just a matter of personal preference or private taste. First, it claims that the Creator God is made most fully known in the person of Jesus Christ. "If you want to know what God is *really* like," the New Testament authors submit, "then look at Jesus." He is the supreme benchmark for our understanding of the Deity. "He is the image of the invisible God," the apostle Paul writes, the one in whom "all the fullness of God was pleased to dwell."[16] "He is the reflection of God's glory and the exact imprint of God's very being," Hebrews declares. He is also the one "through whom God created the worlds" (Heb 1:2–3). "All things came into being through him," John's Gospel begins, "and without him not one thing came into being. What has come into being in him was life, and the life was the light of all people" (John 1:3–4). "For in him all

---

15. On the indigenous contribution to restorative justice, see Consedine, *Restorative Justice*, e.g., 81–89. See also Church Council on Justice and Corrections, *Satisfying Justice*.

16. Col 1:15, 19; cf. 2 Cor 4:4.

things in heaven and on earth were created, things visible and invisible, whether thrones or dominions or rulers or powers—all things have been created through him and for him" (Col 1:16). Jesus, then, is both the human embodiment of God's very being, and the one through whom and for whom God created the universe.

The second truth claim Christianity makes is that this God has acted uniquely in the life, death, and resurrection of Jesus to restore the world to its originally intended purpose. In Jesus, God has entered fully into the human condition, shackled as it is to the power of sin and subject to the scourge of suffering and death, and has acted through him to defeat the power of evil and reconcile its victims to himself. "He has rescued us from the power of darkness," Paul rejoices, "and transferred us into the kingdom of his beloved Son, in whom we have redemption, the forgiveness of sins . . . For through him God was pleased to reconcile to himself all things, whether on earth or in heaven, by making peace through the blood of his cross" (Col 1:15, 20).

Not only is "the blood of his cross," by which Paul means his violent death on a Roman gallows, the decisive event that defeats evil, it is also the definitive revelation of what God is really like. Christian faith asserts that God is never more truly God than he is in the dying of Jesus. In the cross, as the Gospel writers put it, the veil of the Temple is torn in two and God stands revealed. God's *justice* also stands revealed (Rom 1:16–17; 3:20). The cross shows that God's justice is a peace-making justice (Rom 5:1), a reconciling, restoring and healing justice. The God who is made climactically known in the cross of Christ is a God who secures justice for both the victims and perpetrators of evil by pouring out his own life in suffering love to free them from their predicament and restore them to relationship with himself and with each other.

These, then, are the two mind-boggling assertions the New Testament authors make. They dare to propose that Jesus of Nazareth is the human face of God, and that the true character of this God and the justice of this God are nowhere more evident than in his death and resurrection. But this is not all. From these two claims, they arrive at a critically important deduction—*that what we learn of God in the story of Jesus is the key to understanding the meaning, inter-connectedness and destiny of all created reality.* As Colossians states, "All things have been created through him and for him. He himself is before all things, and in him all things hold together" (Col 1:16–17). In him, God has made known his "plan for the fullness of time, to gather up all things in him, things in heaven and things on earth" (Eph 1:10).

What an astonishing assertion this is! All things have been created for, they are sustained by, and they find their ultimate meaning in, the crucified and risen Christ. From this it follows that the central principle of creation is not naked power or control, or order, or balance, but vulnerable, passionate, reconciling, self-giving love, a love that subverts evil, not by an overwhelming display of coercive force, but by acting in amazing grace to redeem offenders and to heal sin's victims, and at great cost to itself. In short, according to the Christian narrative, *restoring love is the ground of the universe*.[17]

All this seems counter-intuitive, even outrageous, in a world of violence and vengeance. But if we can believe it, it has enormous implications for appreciating restorative justice. If the cross reveals God's redemptive *modus operandi,* and discloses the basis on which creation itself is sustained, this explains why restorative justice "works." And it *does* seem to work. Two researchers have recently noted,

> If we have been waiting for the research to prove restorative practices work, we need wait no longer. Collaborative, problem-solving approaches have a history of success in families, communities, organizations and international relations. The social science research is overwhelming, consistent and clear. In the vast majority of situations, restorative practices work better than punishment or treatment approaches.[18]

But why do they work? Restorative practices work because they accord with the way God has made us; they work because they are consistent with what Ephesians calls "the plan" of the universe. In seeking healing for victims and redemption for offenders, restorative justice reflects the very heart of the Christian God, and it is charged with the power of God. No wonder then, restorative-justice meetings can be so potent. No wonder that grace and truth, mercy and compassion, are so often evident. God is anonymously present whenever people honestly confront the consequences of evil and seek to deal with it in redemptive ways.

Now this attempt to identify a metaphysical grounding for restorative justice may seem far-fetched to some. But we need to remember that traditional notions of retributive justice have also appealed to

---

17. One theologian who takes this seriously is Pinnock, *Most Moved Mover.*
18. Wachtel and McCold, "Restorative Justice in Everyday Life," 123.

metaphysical claims (indeed current postmodern skepticism towards justice having a metaphysical basis is unique in the history of human thought).[19] According to classical retributivism, the moral universe operates on the principle of "just deserts." Justice is about giving people their due, balancing deed and desert, in accordance with the law of nature. When people do wrong, they *deserve* punishment, and it is punishment that vindicates and restores equilibrium to the moral order.

What is bold about my claim is not that restorative justice reflects a transcendent order, but the kind of order it reflects, an order that turns, not on the perfect balance of deed and desert (as in retributivism), but on redeeming, restoring inter-personal love. Retributive justice seeks to check and punish evil, believing that the pain of punishment compensates for the pain of wrongdoing, and that somehow by achieving an equity of suffering the moral order is upheld. Restorative justice focuses on the relational consequences of evil, believing that the moral order turns on relationship, so that when relationships are violated by crime, ultimately it is only healing and reconciliation that can affirm what the world is really all about. Punishment may be necessary in the process (for a variety of good reasons),[20] yet it is not the pain of punishment itself but the restoration of peace to human experience that truly vindicates justice.

SATISFYING THE NEEDS OF VICTIMS

I began this chapter by discussing the needs of victims and the peculiar threat victims pose to the religious community. Victimization upsets the normal equilibrium by which people live their lives and raises profoundly unsettling questions about the meaning of life and the state of the world. I then went on to speak about restorative justice, characterizing it as a democratic process that gives expression to particular restorative values, values that derive their potency from the fact that they reflect moral truth and the character of the God who made us. It is now time to bring these themes together by asking what restorative justice specifically has to offer victims. Is restorative justice any better equipped than conventional justice to help crime victims reorient their lives following the disorientation of victimization? There is good reason to think so. Indeed, many would argue that restorative-justice conferences are better suited than

---

19. See Forrester, *Christian Justice*, 45; cf. 187–88.
20. See C. D. Marshall, *Beyond Retribution*, 97–144.

traditional court room processes to meet at least seven crucial needs of victims.

First, the restorative-justice conference offers victims a safe space to speak of their experience. It is a place of both physical safety and of emotional safety, a place where victims can express their anger and fear without judgment or blame or skepticism. In the normal court process, the victim's story is often subject to hostile interrogation by defence lawyers, and must be narrated within strict legal parameters. Victims feel neither safe nor sound. Yet learning to feel safe again in an unsafe world is one of the most basic needs victims have, something that restorative justice can help to deliver.

Second, restorative conferences offer victims validation and vindication. Contrary to what most people believe, victims usually want vindication more than vengeance or even punishment. They want the wrong they have suffered to be acknowledged and their dignity to be affirmed. They want their offender to admit his or her responsibility for causing them harm, and to be reassured that they did not bring it on their own heads.

Third, restorative-justice conferences afford victims answers to their questions. Victims desperately want to know precisely what happened, and why it happened, and what the offender was thinking about at the time, and whether he will do it again. Victimization invariably raises such questions in the minds of those who have suffered, and answers to these questions are needed for them to restore order and coherence to their lives. Regular court hearings do not usually permit victims to ask all the questions they have.

Fourth, restorative justice offers victims genuine truth-telling. Truthful speech is essential if justice is to be done. Conventional justice works on this basis as well, with the court system existing to establish the "truth, the whole truth, and nothing but the truth." But, in practice, the truth in question is often limited to clarifying facts and establishing guilt. A narrow notion of legal truth supplants the fuller moral, spiritual and experiential truth surrounding crime, and even the legal truth is often obscured by technical language, plea bargaining, sharp lawyering, and legislative loopholes.[21] Restorative justice, by contrast, seeks to make

21. "Throughout the Anglo-American adversarial system and the inquisitorial system of continental Europe as well, victims are consistently reported to be angry and bewildered, expecting to be able to turn to the police, to prosecutors and the courts for assistance and advice, and invariably finding that they are regarded by each of these agencies as outside of their area of responsibility." Strang, *Civil Society*, 72.

space for full truth-telling. Time is given for offenders and victims, and for their friends and supporters, to name the evil done, to describe its impact on them, and to speak about the needs it has created.[22] Truth-telling requires offenders to accept genuine responsibility for the harm they have caused and the obligation it brings to put things right. It also allows victims to be discharged of the self-blame and shame they so often suffer from.

Fifth, restorative justice grants empowerment to victims. Victimization itself is an experience of disempowerment on the one hand (a loss of control over one's life) and of disconnection of the other (a loss of relatedness with other human beings). These feelings are often exacerbated by the court system. Victims can feel that the criminal justice system robs them of their experience, reinterprets it in foreign legal terminology, and turns it over to trained specialists to deal with. They are rendered spectators on their own pain. This is why research shows, all over the world, that crime victims often end up feeling as much hostility toward the judicial system as they do towards their own offenders. By contrast, in restorative-justice processes victims themselves are the central players. Victims are empowered by being fully involved in the disposition of their case. They understand what is taking place, and are able to participate in securing outcomes that meet their needs.

Sixth, restorative justice offers victims restitution or reparation. Conferences usually aim to arrive at outcomes by which the offender agrees to make good, insofar as possible, the harm inflicted. Part of this restitution will be emotional (by way of explanation and apology) and part will be material (by way of financial recompense or practical help). But, whatever form it takes, restitution addresses a fundamental need of victims. As Howard Zehr explains,

> Restitution symbolizes a restoration of equity, and it states implicitly that someone else—not the victim—is responsible. It is a way of denouncing the wrong, absolving the victim, and saying who is responsible. Accordingly, restitution is about responsibility and meaning as much as, or more than, actual repayment of losses."[23]

---

22. Research indicates that the average time taken in court hearings is ten minutes; the average length of a restorative-justice conference is forty-five minutes.

23. Zehr, "Restoring Justice," 145.

Finally, restorative justice offers victims hope, the hope of a better future no longer blighted by bitterness and resentment. Hope is an essential ingredient for a healthy life, and a healthy society needs a shared sense of social hope to remain confident and purposeful. But hope has been deemed the rarest of all modern virtues.[24] A vague sense of hopelessness pervades much of contemporary culture. Nowhere is this more apparent than in the criminal justice system, with prison being perhaps the most hopeless of all modern institutions. We speak euphemistically of a "corrections system," but, as statistics show, it does little to correct offenders and even less to restore victims to a state of well-being. By contrast, restorative-justice conferences, for all their emotional intensity, can be the most hopeful of places, so much so that some sociologists are suggesting that the true social significance of restorative justice lies in its capacity to restore hope to a hopeless society.[25] Because it seeks not simply to penalize past criminal actions but to address present needs and to equip for future life, restorative justice provides hope: the hope of healing for victims, the hope of change for offenders, and the hope of greater civility for society at large.

CONCLUSION

These then are some of the ways in which restorative justice renders assistance to victims of crime. Ill-informed critics sometimes claim that restorative justice is simply a way of being soft on offenders. But this is far from the case. Restorative justice is, first and foremost, a means of empowering victims to confront their abusers, with whom they have been locked into a prison house of pain and shame, and to do so in a way that holds them genuinely accountable for their actions and brings satisfaction to victims' needs. For that reason, restorative justice deserves the full support, as well as ongoing critique, from those dedicated to the plight of victims.[26]

It also deserves the full support of the church community, for restorative justice is profoundly compatible with Christian values, virtues and beliefs about the nature of ultimate reality. These values, virtues and beliefs should not be confused for fuzzy sentiments or romantic ideals.

---

24. See Forrester, *Christian Justice*, 246–59.
25. Strang and Braithwaite, *Civil Society*, 7.
26. For victims' criticisms of restorative justice, see Mika et al., *Listening Project*.

They are costly commitments, fashioned in the furnace of human suffering and attested in full face of the ambiguities and contradictions of human life and of the sheer tenacity of evil. They are also the values and commitments that give human life its meaning and beauty, that put us in touch with the divine, and that inspire us to seek a better world, a world in which we do justice with a restoring face. God's word to the religious community, as to the legal community, remains the same as it was to the lawyer to whom Jesus addressed the parable of the Good Samaritan: "Go and do likewise."

7

The Violence of God and the Hermeneutics of Paul

Wrestling with God's Retributive Violence in the Bible

THE JARRING DISSONANCE BETWEEN the God of vengeance and violence in certain parts of the Old Testament and the God of indiscriminate love and mercy proclaimed by Jesus in the Gospels has long perplexed Christian interpreters. Echoing the verdict of many, Paul Anderson maintains that reconciling these contrasting portraits of God constitutes "the greatest theological and hermeneutical problem in the Bible."[1] It is a theological problem because it challenges the notion of a unitary and self-consistent divine will. It is a hermeneutical problem because it forces the question of how apparently contradictory views of God can exercise authority as equally part of sacred Scripture. It is also a moral problem, for the way believers resolve this tension will have implications for how they live their lives as servants of God, even if the common assertion today that violent religious texts lead directly to violent behavior must be dismissed as simplistic.[2]

These difficulties are not unique to Christians of course. Jewish interpreters too have long wrestled with how the compassionate God of, say, Ezekiel 33 is to be reconciled with the punitive God of, for example,

---

1. Anderson, "Genocide or Jesus," 31.
2. See Kille, "'Bible Made Me Do It,'" 55–73. See also Mabee, "Reflections"; cf. also Armstrong, "Strictures."

Numbers 16.³ But they confront Christian readers in a particularly acute way in light of the theological, moral, and hermeneutical privilege that Christianity accords, at least in theory, to the Jesus-tradition.

One early solution to the dilemma, proposed by Marcion and the Gnostics, was to unhook Jesus entirely from the God of the Jewish Scriptures, who was deemed to be a lesser deity. This option was roundly rejected by the early church. The heresy of ditheism not only leads to theological oblivion, it actually inscribes competitive violence in the nature of ultimate reality, something that biblical monotheism avoids. Christian orthodoxy has therefore always insisted that the God and Father of our Lord Jesus Christ must be none other than the one true God of Israel, the Creator of all that exists.

But what does this identification tell us about God? Has God changed? Did God give up his violent ways with the advent of Christ in favor of nonviolent love? Is God's impressive career as a warrior over? Or does God remain fundamentally unchanged? Is God, by definition, unchangeable: the same yesterday, today, and forever? If so, what does that tell us about God's involvement in violence? Is lethal coercion still an important part of God's repertoire of methods for achieving saving and judging purposes in human affairs today as it was in biblical times?

If the testimony of Christian history and doctrine are anything to go by, an affirmative answer to the last question appears to be the most common conclusion Christians have reached, since God's use of violence has continued to be a notable feature of the Christian story of God as it was in the earlier Israelite story of God. Much atonement theology, for instance, as Denny Weaver spells out so clearly, envisages a patriarchal God who visits punitive violence on his only Son in order to defend his personal dignity or uphold his superior justice.⁴ Similarly the post-Constantinian church's majority endorsement of Christian participation in war has disclosed a willingness, if not an eagerness, to equate the violent shedding of human blood with the work and will of God.

---

3. As Dale Allison notes, "The problem of conflicting theologies was not born with Christianity. The problem was already internal to Judaism . . . If, after Marcion, the issue for Christians became which God to acknowledge, this was only a later variant of the earlier question, Which texts should we sanction?" Allison, "Rejecting Violent Judgment," 478.

4. See Weaver, *Nonviolent Atonement*. I am in general sympathy with the direction of Weaver's argument, though I depart substantially from him on his reading of the New Testament evidence. See chapter 8 below.

Then there is the projected violence of Final Judgment. Even those who feel squeamish about the idea of God using human agents to visit wrath on his enemies in present history still often espouse a concept of eschatological judgment where God, patience finally exhausted, violently destroys the wicked—or, worse, callously consigns them to the everlasting violence of eternal torment. It is not uncommon even for Christian pacifists, who conscientiously renounce lethal violence themselves, keenly to anticipate God's retribution on the ungodly at the end of time. Some even argue that Christian renunciation of violence is materially *dependent* on the reality of God's ultimate retributive justice on evildoers, for only an absolute confidence in God's perfect judgment can free believers from the need to take matters into their own hands in the interim.[5] Put crudely, from this perspective Christian nonviolence is sustainable only if there is a violent God giving ultimate backup.

So Christian belief and practice have not, by and large, done away with the concept of divine violence. Even peace theology has not felt the need to posit a nonviolent God. Of course, retention of a militant deity eases the hermeneutical dilemma mentioned earlier, in that the violent God of early Israel does not *cease* to be violent in the Christian era but merely becomes less *blatantly* so. Instead of regularly deputizing human agents to slay the wicked, God now largely reserves that task for God's self at the end of time (although exceptions may apply in the event of justifiable war). Yet arguably a theology that substitutes a conspicuously violent God with a cautiously violent God remains mired in what Walter Wink famously calls the myth of redemptive violence—the belief that violence saves, that war brings peace, that might makes right.[6] As long as God is understood to rely on lethal force to achieve redemptive goals, whether in present history through appointed human instruments or at the end of time by God's own clenched fist, disturbing implications follow, especially for Christian peace theology.

One such implication is the absolutizing or deifying of violence. To reserve to God the right to use overwhelming violence is to pay violence the ultimate compliment. Violence is dignified by its association with God, and God is diminished by dependence on violence. Indeed, the more that violence is reserved as God's prerogative alone, the more

---

5. See for instance Volf, *Exclusion and Embrace*, especially 275–306; cf. also Chase, "Christian Discourse," 119–34 (especially 128–31); McKanan, "Is God Violent?," 50–68.

6. Wink, *Engaging the Powers*, 13–31; Wink, *Powers That Be*, 63–81.

uniquely and terrifyingly violent God appears. "It is a fearful thing to fall into the hands of the living God" (Heb 10:31). But if frail human beings are expected to feel angry without resorting to violence, why should the same not be expected of God? Is God unable to withstand the temptation to hit back? Is crushing the opposition the only solution left for God?

Again, a willingness to exempt God from the normative requirement of nonviolence sustains the kind of exceptionalism that always leaves the door open for human beings to perpetrate violence on God's behalf or approve of it when done in God's name. As long as God sanctions killing—whether now in times of war or during some future apocalyptic maelstrom—no moral condemnation can apply to those who do the business. But whenever exceptions are permitted, there is a human propensity to expand the loophole endlessly. Each and every act of violence can be defended as a legitimate exception to the rule. Not surprisingly, it is always the perpetrators of violence, not its victims, who appeal to exceptional circumstances to legitimate their actions. Something similar happens with respect to those who cherish the expectation of God's final destruction of sinners. They exempt themselves and their loved ones from the awaited firestorm while insisting that God's justice requires others to be consumed by it.[7]

The grounding of Christian non-retaliation on trust in God's eschatological vengeance also has troubling corollaries. The more one waits for God's violent intervention to rectify the world, the less incentive there is to work for peaceful change now. Indeed, it could be argued (and often has been historically) that since God is clearly not yet riled enough by sin and injustice to intervene to overturn it, the unjust status quo ought to be accepted as something God permits to exist. Christians should not actively oppose it, for that would be to usurp God's work. Pacifism then slides into a passivism that leaves it to God to sort out the mess while keeping its own hands clean.

Although John Howard Yoder rejects such quietism, this could be one way of construing (or misconstruing) his proposal that Christian nonviolence bears witness to the fact that Christians are not in charge of history. Their call is to be faithful to the slain Lamb, not to be "effective" in directing historical processes, a goal that is frequently taken to justify violence and is an illusory ambition at the best of times.[8] Does this then

---

7. I attempt to construct a non-retributive view of final judgment in *Beyond Retribution*, 145–99.

8. Yoder, *Politics*, 228–47.

mean that assuming responsibility for the direction of human history necessarily requires violence, even for God? Perhaps a better grounding for Christian pacifism would be the recognition that, in a real sense, humans *are* in charge of this world, and that it is only by emulating the nonviolent rule of God that we have any real chance of undoing the yokes of oppression and recovering the true purpose of our existence. After noting the vast literature written on theodicy and on whether God can ever be forgiven for the atrocities permitted on his watch, such as the incineration of a five-year-old girl called Esther before the eyes of her parents, or the random assassination carried out by a Palestinian gunman called Omar, J. Harold Ellens comments:

> I have figured out that the question is erroneous. It is not a question of justifying God or of bringing God to justice. It is not a question of forgiving God or holding God accountable. It is a matter of recognizing the limitations of God. God is not in charge of this world. We are. We should have gotten that clue at a more profound level of awareness than we seem to have done, from Genesis 1.28, where the ancient Israelite narrative informs us that God assigned *us* the task of dominion in this world, to bring it to its potential fruitfulness. If we do not take care of beautiful blond and blue-eyed Esther, God cannot. If we do not find reconciliation with Omar, God cannot stop the mass murders. If we do not reach beyond the alienations and transcend the terror of the terrorists, God cannot save us.[9]

But perhaps the biggest problem with continuing to imagine a God who employs violence to advance his cause in the world is that it leads to an incoherent Christian monotheism. On the one hand, Jesus Christ is held to be the perfect revelation of the one true God. On the other hand, the God whom Jesus is said to reveal bears little resemblance to Jesus.

JESUS AS THE NONVIOLENT ICON OF GOD

A proposal made in the preceding chapter, that the New Testament makes two fundamental truth claims that set the Christian story apart from all other religious and ideological systems, bears repeating in full here, since the textual evidence is also foundational to apprehending divine nonviolence. First, it claims that the Creator God is made most fully known in

---

9. Ellens, "Revenge," 235.

the human person of Jesus Christ. If we want to know what God is *really* like, the New Testament authors submit, we must look at Jesus. He is the supreme benchmark for our understanding of Deity. "He is the image of the invisible God," the apostle Paul writes, the one in whom "all the fullness of God was pleased to dwell."[10] "He is the reflection of God's glory and the exact imprint of God's very being," Hebrews declares. He is also the one "through whom God created the worlds" (Heb 1:2-3). "All things came into being through him," John's Gospel begins, "and without him not one thing came into being. What has come into being in him was life, and the life was the light of all people" (John 1:3-4). "For in him all things in heaven and on earth were created, things visible and invisible, whether thrones or dominions or rulers or powers—all things have been created through him and for him" (Col 1:16). Jesus, then, is both the human embodiment of God's very being and the one through whom and for whom God created the universe.

This conviction invests the words and deeds of Jesus of Nazareth with unparalleled revelatory significance. When Jesus teaches and practices nonviolence, therefore, it is not enough to see it as a tactical expedient he employs because revolutionary violence against the Roman superpower was not a viable option at that time.[11] It must be understood as an articulation of what God is like and of how God exercises divine rule. That is why Jesus explicitly grounds his summons to enemy love and non-retaliation on the imitation of the heavenly Father, who "makes his sun to rise on the evil and on the good, and sends rain on the righteous and the unrighteous" (Matt 5:44-48). Jesus instructs his followers to conduct themselves as "children of the Most High, for he is kind to the ungrateful and the wicked." They are to be merciful "just as your Father is merciful" (Luke 6:35-36). Jesus's ethic of nonviolence, in other words, is predicated on the premise of a nonviolent God, a God who, as Raymund Schwager puts it, is "exactly the opposite of violence," a God whose "limitless forgiveness and boundless love are distinct in every respect from the

---

10. Col 1:15, 19; cf. 2 Cor 4:4.

11. Wright offers a powerful presentation of Jesus's nonviolent opposition to Rome in *Victory of God*. But he stops short of grounding it in any distinctive apprehension of God's character by Jesus.

mechanism of violence and the vicious cycle of mutual destructiveness."[12] Those who claim to follow this God must therefore be nonviolent too.[13]

The second truth claim Christianity makes is that God has acted uniquely in the life, death, and resurrection of Jesus to restore the world to its originally intended condition of freedom. In Jesus, God has entered fully into the human condition, shackled as it is to the power of sin and subject to the scourge of suffering and death, and has acted through him to defeat the power of evil and reconcile its victims to himself. "He has rescued us from the power of darkness," Paul rejoices, "and transferred us into the kingdom of his beloved Son, in whom we have redemption, the forgiveness of sins ... For through him God was pleased to reconcile to himself all things, whether on earth or in heaven, by making peace through the blood of his cross" (Col 1:15, 20). Not only is "the blood of his cross," by which Paul means his violent death on Roman gallows, the decisive event that defeats evil and brings about peace, it is also the definitive revelation of what God is really like. Christian faith asserts that God is never more truly God than he is in the dying of Jesus. In the cross, the veil of the Temple is torn in two and God stands revealed. God's justice also stands revealed (Rom 1:16–17; 3:20). The cross shows that God's justice is a peace-making justice (Rom 5:1), a reconciling, restoring, and healing justice. The God who is made climactically known in the cross of Christ is a God who secures justice not by violent imposition of his will on his enemies but by freely subjecting himself in suffering love to the violent impulses of humanity in order to liberate creation from its bondage to violence and to restore people to relationship with God and with each other.

These, then, are the two mind-boggling assertions the New Testament authors make. They dare to propose that Jesus of Nazareth is the human face of God, "the flesh and blood embodiment of the perfections of God,"[14] and that the true character of this God, and the justice of this

12. Schwager, *Scapegoats*, 207. So too Wink, *Powers That Be*, 89. Jack Nelson-Pallmeyer observes that "Jesus was not the first Jew to promote or use nonviolence when resisting injustice ... Jesus may have been the first, however, to specifically reject the violence of God as the foundation for nonviolent resistance. Rather than rooting nonviolence in the assurance of God's ultimate and redeeming violence, Jesus saw nonviolent action as a faithful embodiment of a nonviolent God, that is, as reflective of the very Spirit that is God." Nelson-Pallmeyer, *Jesus Against Christianity*, 320.

13. Cf. Mauser, *Gospel of Peace*, 18–84.

14. Haughey, "Jesus as the Justice," 279. See also C. D. Marshall, *Beyond Retribution*, 259–63.

God are nowhere more evident than in his death and resurrection. From these two claims they arrive at a critically important deduction—that what we learn of God in the story of Jesus is the key to understanding the meaning, inter-connectedness and destiny of all created reality. As Colossians states, "All things have been created through him and for him. He himself is before all things, and in him all things hold together" (Col 1:16–17). In him God has made known his "plan for the fullness of time, to gather up all things in him, things in heaven and things on earth" (Eph 1:10).

What an astonishing assertion this is! All things have been created for, they are sustained by, and they find their ultimate meaning in Jesus Christ. All things are eternally imprinted with the moral character and career of the crucified and risen Lord. From this it follows that the central principle of creation is not naked power, or control, or order, or balance, but vulnerable, passionate, reconciling, self-giving love, a love that subverts evil, not by an overwhelming display of coercive force, but by acting in amazing grace to redeem offenders and to heal sin's victims, and at great cost to itself. In short, the Jesus-story reveals that God's nonviolent love is the ground of the universe.

This is not a wholly new revelation however. It is already evident in the creation narratives of Genesis. It is hugely significant that, notwithstanding the violence ascribed to God in the pages of the Bible, the canonical record opens and closes with surprisingly peaceful scenes—the two accounts of creation (Gen 1–2) and the presentation of the new Jerusalem (Rev 21–22). Peace is both ontologically prior to violence and eschatologically posterior to it. Violence has no role in God's work of creation; it only enters into the picture later as a result of human sin and will eventually end.[15] This is quite different from other ancient Near Eastern creation myths, such as the Babylonian *Emuna Elish*, where creation is the result of a violent act of deicide and humans are created from the blood of the murdered god. There evil precedes good, chaos is conquered by violence, and the king serves as Marduk's representative on earth, ruling by means of holy war. By contrast, as Walter Wink observes:

> The Bible portrays a good God who creates a good creation. Chaos does not resist order. Good is prior to evil. Neither evil nor violence is a part of the creation, but enter later, as a result of the first couple's sin and the connivance of the serpent (Gen

---

15. Gen 4:8; Rev 21:3–4, 24; 22:2.

3). A basically good reality is thus corrupted by free decisions reached by creatures. In this far more complex and subtle explanation of the origins of things, violence emerges for the first time as a problem requiring a solution.[16]

The creation narratives, in other words, presuppose a divine ontology of peace. They portray a nonviolent God who speaks the world into existence and who makes human beings in the divine image and likeness in order to cultivate creation as devoted gardeners, not to pillage it as rapacious warriors. Things go badly wrong however and violence invades this peaceable reality (Gen 4:1–16). This is no minor problem that can be easily fixed. It not only escalates out of all control in the human community,[17] it even provokes God to an act of massive counter-violence, something God apparently later regrets.[18] Thus begins the long canonical story of divinely-induced violence, a story that stands in stark contrast to what we have seen of God in the story of Jesus and cries out for some theological explanation.

It is important that this explanation is *theological* in character, not just traditio-historical or psycho-cultural or phenomenological, because the canonical text is principally intended to exercise a theological role in the community that created and preserves it. The biblical traditions, for all their diversity, once gathered together as canonical Scripture combine to tell a single overarching story about God, Israel, and the world. The texts constitute a narrative world into which readers enter, with its own plot, its own cast of characters (including God) and its own universe of meanings, a story that serves authoritatively to interpret God to Israel and Israel to itself.[19]

In this connection it matters little whether the biblical accounts are historically reliable in all their details; of primary importance is the theological claim they make to narrate the story of God. This means that

---

16. Wink, *Powers That Be*, 44–48, at 46. Also McDonald, *God and Violence*, 35–49.

17. Gen 4:23–24; 6:5–7, 11–13.

18. Gen 7:1–24; 8:21–22; 9:11–17.

19. This is not to deny that the canonical tradition is full of tensions, disagreements, contradictions and revisions. Later biblical authors and tradents felt free to disagree with the perspective of their predecessors on certain theological positions even while accepting the authority of the tradition they bequeathed. Indeed, the authority of the tradition is shown precisely in the commitment of later recipients to engage in radical rethinking of its meaning and implications. See further Davis, "Critical Traditioning," 733–51.

the problem of divine violence cannot be dealt with adequately simply by deeming this or that episode to be legendary or fictitious.[20] Whether or not God *actually* killed the children of Egypt, the biblical story *says* God did. This is how the biblical writers understand the involvement of God in the world, and it is their interpretation of God that has normatively shaped and conditioned how the subsequent community of faith (including Jesus) has apprehended God.

What is needed, then, is some explanation for God's violence that both accords with the inner logic of the plotted narrative and that accounts for why it is that God is characterized in this way, especially when there are strong indications at the outset of the story that the Creator God works by peaceable means. Given the many incidents of divine violence that follow, it is also worth pondering how Jesus could possibly have conceived of God as being unfailingly kind to the ungrateful and wicked when he knew full well that within the biblical drama God discriminates in favor of friends, bears grudges against opponents for generations, and visits retribution on sinners.

THE VIOLENCE OF GOD IN SCRIPTURE

The Hebrew Bible has a reputation for being one of the bloodiest works in existence. Firmly fixed in the popular mind is the image of the "Old Testament God" as a God of war and destruction, a brutal, reactive, and ruthless deity who brooks no rivals and leaves no infraction unpunished. Whether this menacing reputation is fully deserved is debatable. Patricia McDonald argues that there is far less violence in the Hebrew Scriptures than is generally supposed and that the deepest concern of the biblical authors is to encourage ways of living that overcome violence and foster compassion. The problem with any textual portrayal of violence, she suggests, is that it tends to have a disproportionate impact on readers. Violent language and imagery take over our imagination and absorb our interest, so that we "find" more violence than is actually there. This rhetorical impact of the violence also diverts attention away from other themes in the text that are often of more fundamental importance to the author. The peripheral thus becomes central and the central peripheral. Nor,

---

20. Of course, legendary elements may exist in the tradition. As De Vries notes, "Battle and war passages in the Old Testament range from the legendary to the mythical, to the realistic and immediate, from the schematic and ideological, to the bizarre and apocalyptic" ("Human Sacrifice," 120).

McDonald adds, does all the violent imagery used in the Bible function to endorse actual violence. The specifically military imagery for God, for example, is plainly metaphorical. God's defeat of Egypt may be spoken of as a triumph of war (Exod 15:1–3), but in practice it was achieved by non-military terms. Although Yahweh uses "weapons" to overthrow his enemies, his weapons are the forces of the natural order. The language is analogical, not literal, although, as McDonald concedes, this choice of military analogies did encourage dangerous perceptions about God to emerge.

As helpful as these considerations are, the fact remains that the biblical narrative attests to a deep and pervasive association between God and deadly violence. The connection between them is varied and complex. Sometimes God resolutely opposes the use of violence and identifies wholly with the victim. At other times God is portrayed as the perpetrator of violence, either by direct fiat or by organizing and sanctioning others to visit judgment on a disobedient people. Often it is precisely God's capacity for superior violence that serves to establish Yahweh's credentials as the only true God. Violence thus emerges as the most frequently mentioned activity in the Hebrew Bible. Schwager has counted some six hundred passages where violence is recorded and at least one thousand verses where God's violence is described. There are one hundred passages where God expressly commands people to kill others, and some stories where God tries to kill people for no apparent reason.[21]

God's violence is particularly evident in the wilderness stories. It has been calculated that in the 40-year period between Israel's exodus from Egypt and their entry to Canaan, the Lord executes at least 30,000 of his own people.[22] Three times Yahweh threatens to annihilate them entirely,[23] and on a number of occasions strikes them with plagues as he did the Egyptians.[24] Even greater in number than such narrative acts of violence are the potential acts of violence commanded in the enforcement of the laws of the Sinai covenant.[25]

When it comes to Israel's enemies, blood runs even more freely. Yahweh smites innocent Egyptian children in Exodus 12, drowns the Egyptian army in the sea in Exodus 14–15, opens up the ground to swallow

---

21. Schwager, *Scapegoats*, 47–71.
22. Miles, "Disarmament of God," 147.
23. Num 11:1–6; 14:10–12; Deut 1:34–40.
24. Num 12:1–16; 14:10–12; 16:41–50; 25:6–9; cf. Exod 11:4–5; 12:12, 13, 23, 27.
25. McEntire, *Blood of Abel*, 61–62.

the Korahites in Numbers 16, orders the impaling of Baal worshippers in Numbers 25, calls for reprisal on the Midianites in Numbers 31, and orders the conquest of Canaan in Joshua 1. The most chilling of all biblical texts to do with war and violence are those that refer to the *herem* or "ban," under which all human beings among the defeated are "devoted to destruction," sometimes at God's explicit command.[26] Emotions of pity are expressly forbidden in such cases.[27] Susan Niditch identifies two main ideologies undergirding and justifying this practice of genocide. In one, the ban is understood as a sacrificial offering to God, which presupposes a God who appreciates human sacrifice. In the other, the ban is viewed as an act of divine justice upon idolatry, which was thought to threaten Israel's own purity and survival. In both cases, mass slaughter is a means of gaining God's favor.[28]

It is possible to identify certain ameliorating features in the institution of *herem*. McDonald mentions, for example, its role in discouraging the use of war purely for plunder since all captured possessions were to be destroyed.[29] Niditch detects a paradoxically high view of human dignity implicit in the ban. The "terrifying completeness and fairness" of the ban's indiscriminate massacre "may be viewed as admitting more respect for the value of human life than other war ideologies that allow for arbitrary killing of soldiers and civilians."[30] This sounds like special pleading. But even if it were true, God is still cast in the role as author or condoner of immense brutality, the instigator of repeated episodes of ethnic cleansing, the perpetrator of what today would be termed crimes against humanity.

According to one critic, the God of Exodus, Deuteronomy, and Joshua is little better than a violent, murderous, genocidal land thief. "Troubling images of God cascade from biblical texts like waterfalls after a violent storm. God's repugnant words and pathological behavior are

---

26. Relevant texts include Exod 17:8-13; Num 21:1-3, 23-24; Deut 2:30-35; 7:2-6; Josh 6:1-16, 7:1, 24-26a; Judg 3:16-25; 4:6-7, 9-10, 13-15, 17, 21-22; 15:4-8; 1 Sam 17:12—18:2; 31:1-13; 2 Sam 18:6-9, 14-15; 1 Kgs 22:31-38; 2 Kgs 9:30-35; Isa 2:4; Mic 4:3; Ezek 38:14-23; Joel 3:9-10; 2 Chron 14:9-15.

27. For example, Deut 7:2; Josh 11:20.

28. Niditch, *War*, 28-29. See also Collins, "Zeal of Phineas," 13-17.

29. McDonald, *God and Violence*, 123, 126; cf. 127, 128, 131.

30. Niditch, *War*, 50. Collins ("Zeal of Phineas," 14) is unconvinced. "Rather than respect for human life, the practice bespeaks a totalistic attitude, which is common to armies and warfare, where the individual is completely subordinated to the interests of the group."

so widespread as to be considered normative behavior for God!"[31] This judgment may be one-sided. But the fact that it can seriously be made at all is testimony to the extent to which God is deeply embroiled in gut-wrenching brutality in many parts of the biblical narrative.

The most graphic accounts of divinely approved violence are set in the context of Israel's early history, even if they were composed at a later stage. With the establishment of the monarchy, the pure ideal of holy war comes to an end and Israel learns to rely on conventional military might. War still carries a sacral element to some extent, but, as Mark McEntire explains "God is removed from the battlefield and eventually closed off in the temple along with the ark . . . the presence of God is no longer an essential element of a battle."[32] In later prophetic and apocalyptic literature, emphasis shifts from the mediation of divine violence through historical agents to the expectation of God's eschatological victory, which is portrayed in language no less violent than is found in Deuteronomy and Joshua. The Psalms, too, celebrate and anticipate the coming of the "God of salvation" who will "shatter the heads of his enemies" and will enable his own people to "bathe their feet in blood" and to feed their enemies to their dogs.[33]

Not that God ever deserts the cut and thrust of present history. McEntire points out that the Hebrew canon (unlike the Greek canon and Christian Old Testament canon) closes with 2 Chronicles 36, which tells of the destruction of Jerusalem by the Babylonians. Although the term *herem* is not used, the many parallels between 2 Chronicles 36 and Joshua 6 give the unmistakable impression that the city has fallen because God has instituted a ban on Israel. The classical prophets toyed with the possibility of Yahweh turning against Israel for breaking covenant;[34] now it has happened. Yahweh disowns his people and brings devastation upon the holy city. No mercy is shown to its inhabitants; the chosen people are either killed or carried off into exile. "Yahweh begins the story as the compassionate, patient God of a disobedient people. As the story progresses, Yahweh becomes a wrathful avenger whose actions are confused with and indistinguishable from those of an earthly tyrant."[35]

---

31. Nelson-Pallmeyer, *Against Christianity*, 37; cf. 40.
32. McEntire, *Blood of Abel*, 90.
33. Ps 68:20–23; cf. Hab 3:13–16.
34. Amos 2:4–16; 5:27; Isa 43:28; see Niditch *War*, 78.
35. McEntire, *Blood of Abel*, 114.

To be sure, bringing such episodes of divine violence into the limelight in this way is potentially misleading, for there is quite another side to God's character in the biblical accounts as well. Hosea 11, for example, depicts Yahweh in emotional turmoil, torn apart by conflicting feelings of outrage at his people's sin and tender compassion for their plight, contemplating terrible punishment but recoiling in horror from the prospect of executing fierce anger against them and promising never again to destroy Ephraim. Elsewhere, too, God is revealed as a God of mercy, forgiveness and love, a God who displays a special concern for the most vulnerable members of the covenant community, a God who liberates the poor from oppression and who heals and restores the victims of violence.[36] Indeed this biblical notion of a God who sides with the weak and the downtrodden is radically different than that which prevailed in the ancient Near East, where the gods inaugurated and upheld the hierarchical structures of wealth and power.[37] Even so, God's concrete actions at times belie God's words. Yahweh appears not only as the God of victims but also as the God who devours victims, and the problem of how the head-smashing God of the historical narratives, the psalms and the prophets can be reconciled with the nonviolent God disclosed by Jesus still needs to be answered.

HERMENEUTICAL STRATEGIES

Many different interpretive strategies have been employed to try to resolve this problem. One common tactic is to *refuse to question anything God does*, as a matter of principle, for God's ways are higher than our ways and God's thoughts higher than ours (Isa 55:9). God is sovereign and holy, and it is simply wrong for human beings as mere creatures to subject God's actions to moral scrutiny. But this pious concern to safeguard God from all criticism merely ducks the problem. Even Abraham was prepared to challenge God's projected violence against the inhabitants of Sodom on the ground that the judge of all the earth has a moral obligation to abide by the principle of justice (Gen 18:16–33). If God's deeds are beyond all moral valuation, so that nothing God ever does can be called bad, then it is equally true that nothing God does can ever be called good, and no way finally exists to differentiate between God and

---

36. For a discussion of how biblical tradition often affirms modern human rights convictions, see my book *Crowned with Glory*.

37. McEntire, *Blood of Abel*, 44.

the Devil. There is also no ground for challenging religious zealots today who cast themselves in the role of human agents of divine wrath on the basis that whatever God is said to have done in sacred Scripture must be inherently good.

Another common strategy is to offer *pleas of mitigation on God's behalf*, to find in each episode of bloodletting a justifiable reason for divine judgment. The dispossession and extermination of the Canaanites, for example, is seen as fitting punishment for their idolatry and wickedness. It is also often observed that given Israel's precarious predicament in a hostile world, God simply had to employ lethal violence in order to safeguard the chosen instrument of salvation for the benefit of us all. God's violence is an example of "good violence" rather than "bad violence" because it is a redemptive or salvific violence.[38] But such appeals to mitigating circumstances come perilously close to an ends-justifies-the-means style of moral reasoning. It is true that the conquest of Canaan is sometimes defended in the biblical text as deserved retribution for the idolatry of the inhabitants.[39] But the justice of the penalty is by no means self-evident. As McEntire points out, "The inhabitants of Jericho, and Canaan in general, are never accused of anything other than two dubious transgressions. They happen to live in the land Yahweh promised to Abraham and they do not exclusively worship a god, Yahweh, who has never been revealed to them. As punishment for these transgressions, they become victims of destructive violence." The net result is "people minding their own business becoming dead so that nomads can become farmers."[40]

It is also true that the continued existence of Israel as a holy people is of overriding importance to the story of salvation and that God favored their interests for the ultimate good of all humanity. But it is extremely

---

38. In his book *Violence, Hospitality, and the Cross*, Hans Boersma argues that in a sinful world violence is necessary to defend the boundaries that enable hospitality to function. In such a world, God employs "redemptive" violence, which is a "good violence" because it serves to uphold monotheism, to punish immorality, and to protect the poor and underprivileged. But Boersma makes little attempt to measure this sweeping defence of divine violence against the concrete suffering endured by its victims. See my critical "Review of Hans Boersma" in *Stimulus* 13/3 (2005), 51–52, which includes my own attempt to spell out the semantic parameters of the term "violence."

39. For example, Gen 13:13; 15:16; Deut 9:5; 20:17–18. The general perfidy of the Canaanites is pervasive in the biblical tradition, although the purported wickedness of the Canaanites is never actually substantiated within the conquest accounts.

40. McEntire, *Blood of Abel*, 118.

doubtful that every episode of divinely sanctioned bloodshed was critical to the maintenance of Israel's national and religious integrity. Sometimes relatively minor infractions attract massive retribution while at other times mercy is extended to serious breaches of covenantal boundaries. It also needs saying that the ease with which some interpreters defend the necessity and morality of the "redemptive violence" employed in biblical history attests to an imaginative failure on their part to recognize the hideous suffering endured by its victims. Christian readers recoil in horror at the Christmas story of Herod's slaughter of the infant boys in Bethlehem (Matt 2:16–18), yet often barely flinch when reading of God ordering the massacre of the Amalekite infants—and that some two centuries after the offence for which the people were allegedly being punished.[41] Readers may delight in the sparing of Rahab and her family when Joshua "fit de battle of Jericho," but spare no thought for all the other inhabitants of the city who were "devoted to destruction by the edge of the sword, both men and women, young and old, oxen, sheep, and donkeys" (Josh 6:21).

A third interpretive strategy is to *sanitize the real-life violence of the biblical text by allegorizing or spiritualizing it.* There is a long and venerable approach to biblical interpretation that is so convinced of the text's divine origins that where the literal sense of the words produces impossible results, one must look for a deeper allegorical meaning, a meaning, as Origen put, "worthy of God." By this method stories of war and mayhem are transposed into uplifting moral and spiritual truths. But despite its impressive pedigree, allegorizing is hardly a viable method in the modern world for dealing with offensive texts. Moreover, even if the allegorical meaning may be counted as worthy of God, the literal historical meaning remains deeply problematic.[42] Allegorists and Sunday school teachers may find comforting spiritual messages disclosed by violent texts, but the texts themselves were initially intended to portray and validate actual bodily suffering and death.

Yet another hermeneutical strategy is to *dismiss the violent portrayals of God in the biblical text as historically and theologically false.* They are the product of the biblical authors projecting onto God their own violent fantasies and vengeful impulses, seeking to justify human atrocities by claiming God decreed them. God thus gets the blame for what in reality were acts of human malice. This means that rather than blithely accepting

---

41. 1 Sam 15:2–3; cf. Exod 17:14, 16; Num 24:20; Deut 25:17–19.
42. So Collins, "Zeal of Phinehas," 24–25.

the truthfulness of everything the text says about God as guaranteed by divine revelation, it is important to separate the wheat from the chaff, to distinguish the voice of divine truth from the voice of human self-deception.[43] Nelson-Pallmeyer makes this point with uncompromising clarity:

> The Bible tells us more about human beings than it does about God, and it does so even when it claims to be talking about God. Revelation within the biblical story, in my view, is rare, and often overwhelmed by distorted human projections. The Bible is both sacred and dangerous. It is sacred because God is revealed partially within the experiences of those responsible for its pages. That is why many of us return to it day after day and year after year in search of meaning and guidance. It is also a dangerous book because we often ascribe divine will to the many human distortions it contains. We undermine the sacredness of the Bible and fuel its dangers whenever we fail to discern the difference between distortion and revelation . . . Stated simply, the Bible can inform our religious experience, but it is often wrong about God.[44]

For Nelson-Pallmeyer it is not enough just to recognize the metaphorical character of the violent images used for God. Violent metaphors must be utterly repudiated as false and abusive. They distort the truth of God and should be expunged from the language of theology and worship. Other scholars, however, warn against discarding such morally offensive material, for, as John Collins suggests, violent texts still possess revelatory power insofar as they give "an unvarnished picture of human nature and of the dynamics of history, and also of religion and the things that people do in its name."[45]

This fourth hermeneutical strategy is helpful in alerting us to the complexity of the interface between divine revelation and human reception. Comprehending God's self-disclosure in the biblical narrative is like following a fine silver thread woven into a dense and colorful tapestry, a tapestry embroidered of a wide range of human reflections and actions that are always culturally conditioned and ideologically slanted. Accordingly, every time God's permission is evoked by biblical figures does not necessarily mean that God has spoken. Yet how do we make allowance for this possibility without remaking God in our own image? How do

---

43. So Anderson, "Genocide or Jesus," 51.
44. Nelson-Pallmeyer, *Jesus Against Christianity*, 16.
45. Collins, "Zeal of Phinehas" 25.

we avoid simply favoring those parts of Scripture that suit our own prejudices and biases and discarding the rest as false projections, thus reducing the text to an echo chamber of modern liberal values and preconceptions? And how is the canonical status of the text sustained if we accept only the nice bits? In any case, the violence-of-God material is not easily separable from other more peaceful conceptions of divine activity. In one form or another, divine violence is woven into warp and woof of almost the entire biblical tradition. The self-same texts that extol God's graciousness and mercy and forgiveness and slowness to anger, also warn of God visiting the iniquity of the parents on their children for three or four generations.[46] No wonder Nelson-Pallmyer is forced to conclude that revelation is rare in the Bible.

This brings us to a final, and more promising, hermeneutical strategy, one that allows for a substantial *change in God's relationship to violence in the course of the biblical story*. In this approach, the violent texts are not to be rejected as a simple distortion of divine reality. They are a reliable reflection of how God was experienced at this time. In the midst of the violence that pervaded human life and society, people encountered God as someone directly involved in the messiness of human life and conflict. They knew that God abhorred the squandering of human life, for it was invested with sacred significance. Yet they also wanted a God who would employ coercive power in great measure to punish, protect, and correct. Elijah, for instance, invited God to cast fire down from heaven to consume his opponents, for this was how any self-respecting deity should prove his superiority when challenged by competitors.[47] But with the coming of Jesus a fresh experience of God is afforded. When Jesus's disciples wanted to emulate Elijah by calling down fire on a Samaritan village, Jesus "turned and rebuked them" (Luke 9:54–55). He did so not simply because such an extreme reprisal would be unfair in this particular circumstance, but because he considered violent vengeance to be wrong in principle and because he knew that God should no longer be understood to work in this way.[48] God has disarmed! God's perceived involvement in the infliction of violence is over. God no longer fights fire with fire. God has changed—or, more accurately, the human experience of God's association with violence has changed. God will no longer

---

46. Exod 34:6–7; Num 14:18–19; Deut 5:9–10.
47. 2 Kgs 1:11–12; cf. Gen 19:24; Lev 10:1–2; Job 1:16; Ps 97:3.
48. So rightly Allison, "Violent Judgment," 476.

permit his identity to be defined by violence; God actively repudiates the violent behavior that has hitherto clouded his character so that the duplicity of violence itself may be exposed and defeated.

GOD'S CHANGED RELATIONSHIP TO VIOLENCE

I noted earlier that the creation narratives presuppose a divine ontology of peace. Violence is not part of God's creative activity or of God's internal being. Violence appears only after the human community has fallen into sin. Interestingly the subsequent account depicts an initial reluctance on God's part to employ violence, then a decision to do so, followed by a recoiling from its drastic consequences. This imaginative portrayal of divine ambivalence towards violence in the early scenes of the human story is, I suggest, an important key for understanding what follows. It dramatizes a profound insight into the perversity of violence, namely, that once violence is entrenched in human society, even the sacred is captured by its allure. Once "the earth is filled with violence" (Gen 6:11, 13), humanity's apprehension of the divine is inescapably framed by its desire to have a deity whose power is greater than that of human violence and whose greatness is shown precisely in a heightened capacity for violence. The violence-of-God material that pervades the biblical narratives is thus both symptomatic of this capture and disclosive of it.

God's reply to Adam and Eve's disobedience is not, at first, a violent one. Along with other consequences they are banished from the Garden to prevent their fallen condition from becoming everlasting (Gen 3:22–24). When in the second generation the problem of sibling rivalry arises, God tries to warn Cain off from succumbing to his feelings of jealousy and resentment, without success. Sin is personified as a hungry animal lying at the door ready to spring (4:6–7). It is so powerful that it overcomes the will of God and overtakes the passions of Cain, and he turns to violence.

After Cain murders his brother, God still does not respond violently; instead the Lord acts to protect the life of the killer, though now *threatening* sevenfold vengeance against any who disregards the protective mark on Cain (4:15). God's next response to human sinfulness is to impose a 120-year limit on the human life span (6:3) and to express regret over the decision to create human beings in the first place (6:6). But as violence spins out of control and fills the land, God plans, for the first time, an act of violent retribution in which "everything that is on the earth shall die" (6:17). In due course God carries out the plan, blotting out all but a tiny handful of creatures (7:21–24).

Afterwards, however, God is deeply disturbed by the indiscriminate nature of the punishment employed. Non-human creation has been made to bear the brunt of humanity's sin. At the same time, God recognizes that wiping out sinful people still has not actually removed the problem of sin, "for the inclination of the human heart is evil from youth" (Gen 8:21; cf. 6:5). God therefore promises never again to curse the ground and destroy all living creatures because of human evil (8:21–22; 9:11, 15). As McDonald observes, "God tried violence once and now knows better."[49]

God then makes two telling concessions to the descendants of Noah: humans may now kill animals for food (9:3–4), and those who take human life will face the death sentence (9:5–6), an attempt to use judicially circumscribed violence to break the spirit of vendetta displayed earlier by Lamech (4:23–24). In a sense, God makes a compromise with violence. Lethal violence in the human community is forbidden, but those who resort to it can expect God to respond in like manner.

The patriarchal narratives that follow are remarkably peaceful. There is very little violence described at all, although God is often involved in what does occur, such as the destruction of Sodom and Gomorrah,[50] and God's long-term plan to dispossess the Canaanites of their land is frequently alluded to.[51] Violence becomes more pronounced only during and after the deliverance from Egypt, and especially during the conquest of Canaan where, as we have seen, genocide is commanded. Thereafter in the waxing and waning of Israel's fortunes, God is frequently depicted as the author and instrument of violence, ranging from incidents of individual retribution to episodes of large-scale war making.

God's *actual* responsibility for authorizing this violence is, of course, doubtful, if not impossible. It is a standard feature of biblical idiom to ascribe a causative role to God for almost everything that happens, both good and bad, as well for narrators to assume a God's-eye perspective in interpreting events. It is crucial to recognize this interpretive technique. Raymund Schwager divides the texts that speak of God's violence in the Old Testament into four categories: those where Yahweh strikes out

---

49. McDonald, *God and Violence*, 54; cf. 57.
50. Gen 12:3, 17; 14:20; 15:14–16; 18:20; 19:15–29; 22:1–19; 38:10.
51. Gen 12:7; 13:14–17; 15:16; 17:8; 22:17; 28:3–4, 13–15; 35:12; 48:4; 50:24.

irrationally for no apparent reason (which are extremely rare),[52] those where God personally takes revenge on human wrongdoing,[53] those where God uses other human beings to punish evildoers,[54] and those where the wicked are punished by their deeds rebounding back on them under God's supervision.[55] But the distinction between these categories is more rhetorical than real, for the narrative texts show that even where God's direct retribution is talked of, it is almost always mediated through human instruments.[56] Both direct and indirect divine violence amount to the same thing; "it is always a question of human power interpreted as God's action."[57] Direct heavenly intervention is rare, though it does happen (and presumably here natural calamities are being attributed to God).[58] Much the same applies to those texts that speak of self-punishment. The penalty may be conceptualized as the inherent consequence of a wrongful deed boomeranging back on the doer, but in practice the penalty might still be inflicted by another person or be initiated by God.[59] Taken together then, while violence is explicitly ascribed to God in the biblical text, it is almost always committed by human beings. Texts on Yahweh's violence normally refer to *human* deeds that are thought in some way to be related to God's will, so that we may safely assume that "human violence is meant when there is talk of divine anger and retribution."[60]

But why is it that human violence is so naturally identified with the action of God? Why is God conceived as the author of so much carnage? Why are harmful human experiences viewed as the punishments from God? Part of the answer lies in the desire to affirm God's transcendent immanence in all of historical experience, and part of it lies in the corrupting impact of violence itself. Such is the intrinsic nature of violence that once unleashed it changes everything, including humanity's experience of God. In the Genesis story God is initially portrayed as one who

52. For example, Exod 4:24-26; 2 Sam 6:6-7.
53. See Lev 26:14-39; Exod 12:29; Ezek 21:3-4, 9-15; Jer 25:32-33.
54. For example, Deut 20:16-17; 1 Sam 15:2-3; Isa 19:2; Jer 51:20-24; Ezek 21:31; Ps 44:11-12; Zech 8:10.
55. For example, Isa 50:11; Jer 44:8; Ps 7:13-17; Prov 8:36; 26:27.
56. See, for example, Ezek 21:31; Jer 22:25-26; Isa 19:2; 13:17.
57. Schwager, *Scapegoats*, 63.
58. For example, Gen 19:24; Num 16:29-32.
59. See, for example, Isa 64:6-7; Ps 81:11-12.
60. Schwager, *Scapegoats*, 63.

resists and opposes violence, albeit without success. But as violence grows and spreads God is driven to counter-violence. Once this step is taken, however, God is enmeshed in the very problem that needs addressing.[61] Redemptive violence takes on an irresistible logic of its own, so that even the knowledge of God falls victim to it.

It is almost as though once it is imagined that God compromises with violence, God ends up being compromised. Consistently in the biblical story the experience of violence changes peoples' identity, the way individuals are perceived and known and relate to one another.[62] The same happens to God's identity, as the peaceable God of creation is inexorably defined in militant and aggressive ways. Counter-themes of love and mercy and forgiveness and restraint are always present, but the larger conceptual framework fundamentally remains one of redemptive violence.

Once conceived as violent, God's only option is to tarry with humanity in its misconceptions in order to win redemption by other means. God is forced to accommodate revelation to the limitations of human perception, not least so that the ultimate futility of redemptive violence—already intimated in Genesis 8:21—might become apparent.[63] In the process horrendous acts of violence are attributed, or misattributed, to God. But God's apparent capture by the categories of sacred violence becomes the precondition for exposing violence for what it is—an enslaving and self-perpetuating deception that contaminates all that it touches, including knowledge of God.[64] With the coming of Jesus, however, God finally casts off the illusions surrounding righteous violence to disclose "the plan of the mystery hidden for ages in God who created all things" (Eph 3:9)—to reconcile all things by an act of self-giving, nonviolent, victorious love. Significantly this requires God-in-Christ personally to fall victim to divinely sanctioned lethal violence,[65] making it plain once and

61. Whether some actual primeval act of violence by God is the reason for God's subsequent identification with violence, or whether the flood story itself is the product of prior projection of violence onto heaven is open to discussion.

62. This is one of the major findings in McEntire's study *Blood of Abel*.

63. Cf. Wink, *Engaging the Powers*, 146–47.

64. God's sovereign self-disclosure is the necessary presupposition for all and any knowledge of God. But divine revelation is also necessarily filtered through fallible human language and categories, which can distort as well as report God's truth, and often both at the same time. For a helpful discussion of the relationship between revelation and Scripture, see Placher, *Transcendence*, 181–200.

65. Jesus is condemned to death on the charge of blasphemy (Mark 14:55–64), a

for all that God-authored violence is a falsity, that "whenever sacred violence is mentioned, it is always human beings attacking one another."[66]

It is God's definitive renunciation of redemptive violence in the life, death, and resurrection of Christ that requires us to re-read the earlier biblical narratives of divine violence in such a way that God can no longer be seen as the ultimate author of the cruelty and killing they record. Certainly, these bloody narratives attest to God's providential presence in the midst of human degradation. But insofar as they ascribe to God responsibility for acts of barbarism, they attest only to the veil of violence through which the experience of God has been filtered since the days of Cain. In Christ, however, the veil is taken away and God stands fully revealed.

I am suggesting then that the biblical accounts of divine violence are both true to how God was experienced following the entry of sin, yet ultimately untrue to God's real character. In this respect they are hermeneutically complex. It could be objected that allowing for such misrepresentation of God's initiative in violence by the biblical authors undermines the authority and trustworthiness of the scriptural text.[67] But this is not necessarily so. The text remains trustworthy in that it reliably discloses how God has been apprehended in history and how God perseveres with human fallibility. Those passages that ascribe violence to God should not be censored or sanitized or discarded; instead they should be read with a "critical charity" that embraces them, for all their gruesomeness, as a gift of God to aid in our instruction and formation.[68] But neither should such passages be absolutized as an unassailable revelation of God's true being; that role belongs to Christ alone.

Objections might also be raised to the notion of God being "captured" by the mythology of violence, of God allowing the divine identity to be clouded by images of vengeance and viciousness. But this phenomenon can be seen as testimony to the seriousness of the cognitive and moral distortions created by the entry of sin and the irruption of violence.[69] Also, there are precedents within Scripture itself for ques-

---

capital crime in Mosaic law (Lev 24:15–16).

66. Schwager, *Must There Be Scapegoats?*, 67.

67. Collins is clear that what makes violent religious texts dangerous is not their violent content but the certitude with which they are received by readers as divine revelation, "Phineas," 23–26. So too Nelson-Pallmeyer, *Jesus Against Christianity*, 277.

68. I borrow this term from Ellen Davis, "Critical Traditioning."

69. Cf. Rom 1:18–23.

tioning whether established understandings of God's behavior are truly consonant with the character of God. Jeremiah, for example, despite repeated affirmations in sacred tradition that God employs the practice of collective punishment, extending down through many generations,[70] looks forward to the day when this will no longer be so (Jer 31:29-30), and Ezekiel is rebuked by God for failing to see that the principle no longer applies (Ezek 18:1-4).

An even more instructive analogy is the way in which the apostle Paul rethinks the role of the law in salvation. Paul confronts a similar hermeneutical dilemma to the one explored above. He discovered that when God played his trump card in Jesus Christ, it looked disconcertingly different from what God's hand had hitherto looked like. Up until that point God had insisted that obedience to the Torah was the indispensable source of righteousness for the chosen people and the ultimate ground of hope for Israel's redemption. The law was absolutely central to God's saving purposes. But then something unexpected happened. When God finally intervened to secure salvation for Israel, it took place "apart from the law" (Rom 3:21; 8:1-4), in some respects even contrary to the law. Paul was therefore forced to think his way through how and why God's familiar ways in the past had altered so dramatically. The zealous young Pharisee, who himself had been prepared to use righteous violence to defend and uphold the law,[71] was compelled to read the Scriptures afresh, to interpret them from a new perspective, to discern in a them a new understanding of God hitherto hidden from sight but now revealed through his Son. In doing so Paul suggests a relationship between God, sin, death, and the law that parallels, in broad outline, the relationship between God and violence I have sketched above.

PAUL'S TREATMENT OF THE LAW AS A HERMENEUTICAL PRECEDENT

The meaning and self-consistency of Paul's extensive reflections on the place of the Mosaic Law in the Christian era is a storm center in current Pauline scholarship. Over the last 30 years, the so-called "New

---

70. Exod 34:6-7; Num 14:18-19; Deut 5:9-10.

71. Gal 1:13; Phil 3:6; 1 Cor 15:9; cf. Acts 9:1-2; 22:4; 26:9-11. On the violent implications of "zeal," see Donaldson, "Zealot"; Smiles, "Concept of 'Zeal'"; Fairchild, "Pre-Christian Zealot." For a thematizing of the place of zeal in the biblical tradition and American self-understanding, see Jewett and Lawrence, *Captain America*.

Perspective on Paul" has thrown up a series of objections to the traditional or "Lutheran" understanding that has dominated the interpretation of Paul since the time of the Reformation. Yet the New Perspective is itself coming under sustained criticism, with some scholars claiming that it lacks the theological depth and exegetical precision of the traditional model. No consensus has yet emerged although there is a growing feeling that some mediating position is required that combines the insights of both older and the newer perspectives.

There is no room here to explore this further. Suffice it to say that any satisfactory explanation of Paul's critique of the law must, in my opinion, do justice to three main realities: the diversity of views on the Torah in first-century Judaism, Paul's radical commitment to Gentile inclusion in the messianic community, and the apostle's darkly pessimistic view of the human condition. All three inform and shape his reconsideration of the role of the law in God's purposes, now that Messiah has appeared.

It is noteworthy that Paul approaches the issue within a narrative framework. That is to say, he reads Scripture primarily as a story, with an overarching plot, a set of characters, and a forward-reaching momentum that climaxes in the life, death, and resurrection of Christ. Paul recognizes that there are different ways of interpreting this story. As a Pharisee, he read the biblical story through the lens of the Torah, with Moses being the key actor in the drama and Israel's holiness being its central concern. Now as a Christian, Paul has learned to read the story through the lens of Jesus Christ, with Abraham being the key figure, and the eschatological uniting of Jew and Gentile in a new covenant community being its true message. Of course, for Paul, these two readings of the biblical narrative are not equally valid. The former is the product of viewing Scripture through a "veil" of ignorance, of lacking true enlightenment about the real import of God's saving righteousness. Only in Christ is this veil removed; only in him do the lights come on.[72] Only then does the true meaning of God's activity in preceding history come clearly into view.

From this hermeneutical vantage point, Paul is able to see the Torah in a completely new light. Once he viewed the law as God's answer to Adam's sin, the gracious means by which Israel could recover humanity's true role in the world and secure admission to the world to come. Now however Paul considers the law to be part of the problem, not part of the solution. Paul faults the law on three main counts. First, the law *has*

---

72. See 2 Cor 3:12–18; Rom 10:2–4.

proven powerless to free God's people from the grip of sin. Far from controlling sin, as God intended, the law actually makes the situation worse because it simultaneously highlights Israel's accountability to God's requirements (Rom 2:12; 3:19) and her impotence to achieve genuine righteousness no matter how sincerely she strives for it (9:31; cf. 2:17–29). Consequently, the law cannot deliver the hoped-for vindication; on the contrary it brings "the knowledge of sin" (3:20; 5:13; 7:7), the weight of God's wrath (4:15), and the inevitability of God's curse (Gal 3:10). More than that, it actually exacerbates human sinfulness. The law functions to stir up the very passions it condemns (Rom 7:5), so that the coming of the law resulted in trespasses being multiplied rather than being reduced (5:20).

The reason for this sorry state of affairs is that the law, for all its divine qualities, is unable to overcome the indwelling and all-pervasive power of sin (Rom 3:9–18; 7:14–25; Gal 3:22). The law is fatally "weakened by the flesh" (Rom 8:3; 7:14, 25); it is stymied by that fallen human condition that "does not submit to God's law, indeed it cannot" (8:7). The law has even become a weapon in the hands of sin (7:7–13), so much so that Paul can boldly declare that "the power of sin *is* the law" (1 Cor 15:56; cf. Rom 7:22–23). What God intended for life has become a vehicle of death.[73] The source of the problem is not the law itself, which Paul considers to be "holy, just and good" (Rom 7:12, 14, 16). The problem is the deep-rootedness of sin, which lies beyond the reach of any external legal code, even one given by God.

The second problem Paul finds with the law is that it is *limited to one ethnic community*. Notwithstanding the ironical tone of his comments, Paul accepts the premise that the law was given uniquely to Israel to enable her to be "a guide to the blind, a light to those who are in darkness, a corrector of the foolish, a teacher of children, having in the law the embodiment of knowledge and truth" (Rom 2:19–20). But this mission has been subverted by Israel's failure to practice what she preaches, so much so that Paul can even charge the covenant people with causing God's name to be blasphemed among the Gentiles (2:24). What Israel's track record proves, Paul argues, is that sin is no respecter of ethnic boundaries. Nor, conversely, is the capacity to perceive and obey God's will. Paul believes that it is quite possible for uncircumcised Gentiles, who do not possess the Torah, "instinctively to do what the law requires" since "what the law

---

73. Rom 7:5, 9–10; 10:5; Gal 2:19; cf. 3:12, 21; 1 Cor 15:56; 2 Cor 3:6–7.

requires is written on their hearts, to which their own conscience bears witness" (2:14-15, 27). So, law and righteousness are not co-extensive realities; there is no necessary overlap. If there were, justification could legitimately come through the law and Gentiles would need to become observant Jews in order to appropriate it. But Israel's own servitude to sin proves that this is not the case.

In any event, even if it were the case, an additional problem would arise, for God would then be reduced to the status of a tribal deity rather than universal lord, and God's promise to bless all the nations of the world through Abraham would be null and void (4:9-16; Gal 3:15-22). If the unity, sovereignty and justice of God—to which the law itself bears witness—are to be vouchsafed, justification must come by some means other than the law. It must potentially be open to every member of the human family.

> For we hold that a person is justified by faith apart from works prescribed by the law. Or is God the God of Jews only? Is he not the God of Gentiles also? Yes, of Gentiles also, since God is one; and he will justify the circumcised on the ground of faith and the uncircumcised through that same faith. Do we then overthrow the law by this faith? By no means! On the contrary, we uphold the law (Rom 3:28-31; cf. 10:11-13).

The third problem Paul has with the law is that an overriding emphasis on law keeping *shifts the spotlight from God's empowering grace to autonomous human achievement.* Paul is adamant that justification cannot come from reliance on "the works of the law."[74] Now, it is true that by this phrase Paul most likely has in mind ceremonial practices such as circumcision, food laws, purity regulations and Sabbath observance, which served visibly to demarcate the boundary between the law-keeping covenant community and the Gentile world. He is not thinking of legalism in a moral sense but of proud reliance on badges of ethnic distinction. He is not accusing Judaism of advocating an individualistic works-righteousness whereby people can earn their own salvation by merit. He is more likely targeting some conception of national-righteousness, whereby adoption of certain Jewish distinctives was thought essential to securing final vindication.

Even so, Paul still recognizes the potential for a law-centered spirituality to over-emphasize human capability and to underestimate the insidiousness of sin and the necessity of grace. Viewed from the perspective

74. Rom 3:20, 27-28; Gal 2:16; 3:2, 5, 10, 12; cf. Rom 4:2, 6; 9:12, 32; 11:6; Eph 2:9.

of law-keeping, sin tends to get equated with a set of external behaviors that can be avoided with sufficient vigilance, rather than being recognized for what it really is—a deadly poison that permeates the entire life-system of humanity, a cosmic power that enslaves all humanity by habituating everyone to self-centeredness and idolatry.[75] A certain kind of complacency can therefore emerge that is so assured of its own sincerity that it underrates the unmerited nature of grace (cf. Phil 3:4–16). This is partly why Paul sets law and grace in such stark opposition.[76]

The only solution to this predicament, Paul argues, is the rupturing of sin's lordship and the radical renewal of human nature from the inside out so that God's law is written on the human heart by means of the indwelling of the Spirit. This is exactly what Christ achieves through his death and resurrection on behalf of all humanity, as a kind of second Adam.[77] Those who participate through baptism in Christ's victory (Rom 6:1–14) are empowered by the eschatological Spirit to fulfill the true intention of God's law (8:1–4). That intention is a life of freedom wholly devoted to the love of God and the love of neighbor,[78] including even the love of enemies (12:9–21). Paul saw his own life-experience as proof of the pudding. Once supremely zealous for God's law, he perpetrated violence on God's behalf.[79] Now graciously freed from the grip of sin through faith in Christ, he proclaims the peace of God, even taking up the cause of his former opponents in the interests of universal reconciliation.

In light of this analysis, Paul concludes that God only ever intended the regime of law to be a temporary holding-measure, until Christ should come (Gal 3:19–26). It served negatively to imprison all under sin (Gal 3:22; Rom 10:32) in preparation for the great liberation that Christ would win through his vicarious death and resurrection. Those united with Christ in this way are no longer "under law but under grace" (6:15). They have "died to the law" (7:4; Gal 2:19), they are "discharged from the law" (7:6), they are "freed" and "redeemed" from the law (Gal 3:13; 4:5; 5:1), "no longer subject" to the law's rule (Gal 3:25) or its condemnation (Rom 8:1). "For Christ is the end-goal (*telos*) of the law" (10:5). Things have changed!

75. Rom 1:18–32; 3:9–20; 5:12–21; 6:12–14, 20–21; 7:7–25, etc.
76. Rom 4:16; 5:20–21; 6:1, 14; 11:5; 1 Cor 15:10; Gal 1:6; 2:21; 5:4; cf. Eph 2:5–6.
77. Rom 5:6–21; 1 Cor 15:42–49; Col 1:10; 3:10.
78. Rom 5:5; 13:8–10; 14:15; Gal 5:6, 13–14, 22–23; Phil 1:9; 1 Cor 8:1; 13:1–8; 16:14; Col 3:14; cf. Eph 4:32–35.
79. Gal 1:13; Phil 3:5–6; 1 Cor 15:9; cf. Acts 9:1–2; 22:4; 26:5, 9–11.

In none of this, of course, is Paul wrestling with the problem of divine violence (he is actually struggling to make sense of the prodigiousness of God's mercy!).[80] But there are several features of Paul's approach to the law that constitute a kind of hermeneutical template for the type of approach to divine violence I have advocated above.

To begin with, in both cases, the presenting problem is *a substantial shift in God's modus operandi from what was apparent in previous tradition*. Paul openly acknowledges that God's methods have changed. This is implicit in the ringing adversative declaration, "But now, apart from law . . ." that commences his account of the revelation of saving justice in Christ in Romans 3:21–26. It is also evident in the way he divides Israel's story into sequential phases (Adam to Abraham, Abraham to Moses, Moses to Christ), with the law entering 430 years after the promise to Abraham and serving as a disciplinarian "until Christ came," after which time "we are no longer subject to a disciplinarian" (Gal 3:15–26). Paul thus allows for *real* change in God's ways.

The sheer radicalism of this change ought not to be underestimated. It required for Paul a thoroughgoing revision of understanding of what had hitherto been the most fundamental ingredients of covenantal faithfulness—circumcision, Sabbath observance, food laws and separation from all sources of impurity, including Gentiles. That the apostle can boldly declare that "I know and am persuaded in the Lord Jesus that nothing is unclean in itself" (Rom 14:14) and that "neither circumcision nor uncircumcision is anything but a new creation is everything" (Gal 6:15) is a measure of the extent to which he reckoned on a major revolution having occurred in God's way of working.

Second, in problematizing the law Paul seeks an explanation that both *accords with the plot of the canonical story and explains why God appears to act differently than previously thought*, which is what I have said is needed in order to deal with the issue of divine violence. Paul accepts that radical changes have taken place in God's priorities, but he is equally emphatic that there is a profound consistency between the realities of the present and the revelation of the past. The "new creation" afforded in Christ is not arbitrary or capricious; it accords with the deepest themes of the previous story. It is both "attested by the law and the prophets" (Rom 3:21, 31) and compatible with God's own being (3:29). That authentic righteousness can come "apart from the law," Paul argues, is already

---

80. See Rom 11:28–36.

evident in the story of Abraham as a foreshadowing of what was to come (4:1-25), and it is only by transcending the limitations of Mosaic law that the promise of universal blessing to Abraham can possibly be realized (Gal 3:6-17). The negative role of the law is thus balanced by its positive role in anticipating and illuminating eschatological events.[81] Even Moses can now be heard to speak of "the word of faith that we proclaim" (Rom 10:8)! It is the fulfillment of eschatological hope in Christ and the Spirit that accounts for *why* God's activity now seems so different. It is also what impels Paul to *read the canonical story afresh* to discern in it a meaning and dynamic once hidden from view. A similar strategy is needed, I have suggested, with respect to the narratives of divine violence.

Finally, and most tellingly, Paul does not shrink from depicting God's law as having been *captured by the power of sin and becoming a source of enslavement and death*. The law itself, Paul is clear, is imbued with the very attributes of God; it is "holy, just and good," it is even "spiritual" (Rom 7:12, 14, 16). But irrespective of its divine credentials the law has been bamboozled by sin. Seizing the opportunity created by the revelation of God's will, sin commandeered the law in order to deceive and kill its adherents (7:11). Consequently, despite its intrinsic goodness, and despite its promise of life to those who observe its commandments, the law has in effect functioned to lock in, as it were, Israel's servitude to sin and death.

This is an incredibly daring claim for Paul to make. He asserts that not only has Gentile humanity's knowledge of God been corrupted by the tyranny of sin (1:18-23; cf. 1 Cor 1:20-25), even Israel's apprehension of God's intentions in the law has fallen victim to sin's death-dealing deception. It is only by taking this insight with full seriousness that we can begin to make sense of the attribution of violence to God in the biblical record. Arguably part of sin's deception is the identification of human violence with the will of God. Jesus Christ explodes this deception, and in him a new humanity emerges that is now in the process of "being renewed in knowledge according to the image of its Creator" (Col 3:10).

In these ways, then, Paul's grappling with the ambiguities of the law in salvation history furnishes something of a hermeneutical analogy for the approach to divine violence sketched out in this chapter. To be absolutely clear: I am not suggesting that Paul's ruminations on the law in themselves relate to the issue of God's recorded violence, only that he

---

81. Cf. Rom 4:23-24; 15:4; 1 Cor 10:11; 9:10.

models a style of hermeneutical engagement with Scripture that can be usefully reapplied to this question. Whether the biblical stories of violence caused any discomfort for the apostle is hard to say. Certainly, he never explicitly disavows a violent God. If anything, the real scandal for Paul was not the violent exclusivity of God's past actions but the gratuitous inclusiveness of God's saving activity in the present. When Paul takes refuge in the inscrutableness of God's ways it is not to justify divine violence but to underscore the mystery of God's indefatigable mercy, a mercy displayed equally towards disobedient Israel and towards wider Gentile humanity (Rom 11:28–36).

Paul may never have consciously reflected on how best to reconcile this present experience of God's mercy with past episodes of grotesque violence. But it was his apprehension of the crucified and risen Christ as the "image of the invisible God" (Col 1:15) that transformed Paul from a violent religious terrorist into a peacemaker *extraordinaire*. It was this that led him to speak distinctively of God as "the God of peace,"[82] the God who has reconciled the entire world to God's self not by violent conquest but by self-giving sacrifice. This crucified God is the same God who made the world and everything in it, the same God who called Abraham and chose Israel, the same God that Jesus called Father, and the same God to whom he pointed his followers as the supreme paradigm for the way of nonviolent discipleship.

---

82. The phrase "God of peace" is a favorite of Paul's (Rom 15:33; 16:20; 2 Cor 13:11; Phil 4:9; 1 Thess 5:23; 2 Thess 3:16; cf. Eph 2:14), though he did not invent it (Heb 13:20). In early Jewish literature the phrase occurs only once (*Test. Dan* 5:2).

8

Atonement, Violence, and the Will of God

EXPOSURE TO THE ANABAPTIST-MENNONITE tradition has been one of the most formative influences on my Christian life. My encounter with Anabaptism began with reading key books by Mennonite authors during my student days in New Zealand in the early 1970s. It developed during my four years of doctoral research in Britain in the early 1980s, when my wife and I were members of the London Mennonite Fellowship. It was deepened further by a period of sabbatical leave at a Mennonite seminary in the United States in the early 1990s, and again in the late '90s. And throughout the past 35 years it has been continually enriched by fellowship with Mennonite friends and scholars around the world.[1]

From my contact with the Anabaptist tradition, I have come to believe that a commitment to nonviolence is an essential feature of Christian discipleship. At first I saw a peace commitment largely in connection with questions of war and militarism. It is a commitment to forswear lethal violence as incompatible with the worship of a crucified God. But I have since learned that violence is systemic and institutionalized, not just episodic and personal. Violence is arguably the primary social manifestation of sin;[2] it is all pervasive in human experience. It shapes the way we view the world and influences how we exercise moral and theological discernment.

It is important, therefore, that those who take seriously Jesus's call to nonviolence learn to read the Bible, to do theology, and to think about God in light of this basic commitment. This is by no means easy. The

1. See further C. D. Marshall, "Following Christ."
2. Cf. Gen 4:1–16, 23–25; 6:11.

Bible itself is full of violence, much of it ascribed directly to God. Also, the long history of Christian theological interpretation has been affected by the Church's profound compromise with violence—by its preparedness not only to sanction the violence of the state but even to authorize violence in pursuit of its own interests. This in turn has rested upon, and has strongly reinforced, a view of God as a violent and punitive deity, a God who gets his own way—whether in the short term, through crusade or inquisition, or in the long term, through eschatological judgment and everlasting torment—by use of overwhelming coercion.

Such a God is increasingly hard for people to believe in. Many people today prefer atheism or agnosticism or some vague form of pantheism to the violent deity of traditional religion. And who can blame them, especially in these days when violence fueled by religious fundamentalism is on the upsurge around the world? In such circumstances, atheism may be the morally better choice. "When persons take leave of God," Clark Pinnock reminds us, "we need to ask what sort of God did they take leave of?"[3] Surely it is better *not* to believe in God than to believe in a violent God who bullies, hurts and humiliates people for his own ends. Given, then, that religiously sanctioned violence puts the very existence and character of God in the balance, it is incumbent on Christian believers to think carefully about how our hermeneutics, our theological method, and our vision of God have been conditioned more by Christendom's longstanding accommodation to violence than by conformity to the revelation of God we see embodied in Jesus.

There can be little doubt that Jesus himself lived and taught nonviolence. This is generally, if not universally, accepted by New Testament scholarship, and is well entrenched in the popular mind as well. But three issues arising from this fact are much more disputed. First, *why* did Jesus advocate nonviolence? Was it merely a calculated, pragmatic response to the particular political or social circumstances he faced? Or is it a normative principle of action for all times and in all circumstances? Second, *how* do Christians obey Jesus's word on this matter? Should we confine his call to nonviolence to the sphere of interpersonal relations alone? Or do we extend it to social and political relationships as well? And third, *what* does Jesus's teaching and practice tell us about the nature of ultimate reality? Should Jesus's rejection of the sword determine, not just Christian ethics, but the entire theological endeavor? Is God nonviolent?

---

3. Pinnock, *Most Moved Mover*, 1–2.

Or does Jesus reserve to God alone the right to use violence to achieve his purposes?

This last question is perhaps the most acute one for the Christian witness against violence. It is true that Christian nonviolence does not strictly depend on the supposition of a nonviolent God. Indeed Miroslav Volf argues that nonviolence is only possible in a violent world by the conscious deferment of violence to God: "Vengeance is mine, I will repay, says the Lord."[4] But it makes much better sense theologically to assume that Jesus practiced nonviolence and demanded it of his followers because he believed that nonviolence corresponds to the essential nature of the deity,[5] of whom he himself was the visible image and "exact imprint" of his being.[6] Christian nonviolence, in other words, is ultimately grounded in the Christian apprehension of God as a God who loves his enemies, who sends rain on the just and on the unjust, and who overcomes evil through self-sacrificing love rather than through violent retribution.

It is this conviction that has forced me, in my own work, to seek to go behind the violent imagery so often used in the Bible to portray God's work to find a deeper, nonviolent reality beneath. In my book entitled *Beyond Retribution,* which attempts to furnish biblical and theological foundations for the so-called restorative-justice movement, I argue that the biblical witness to God's justice is better characterized in restorative or redemptive categories than in retributive or punitive ones.[7] Two of the biggest hurdles I faced in arguing for this thesis are New Testament passages about Final Judgment, which anticipate wrath and damnation on God's enemies, and popular theologies of the atonement which attribute the salvific power of the cross to some cosmic act of substitutionary punishment. In both cases, God's justice appears to be definitively vindicated through violent, death-dealing retribution, something that has disturbing implications for peace theology and practice. I am convinced, however, that in both cases the deeper reality of what transpired at the cross and will happen at future judgment is non-retributive and nonviolent in character. Indeed, both events represent God's ultimate conquest of violence and disclose the true nature of divinity.

---

4. Deut 32:35; Rom 12:19; Heb 10:30. See further Volf, *Exclusion and Embrace,* especially 275–306.

5. Cf. Matt 5:9, 43–48.

6. Col 1:15; Heb 1:1–4; John 14:8–13.

7. C. D. Marshall, *Beyond Retribution.*

In what follows I want to revisit the question of the atonement, not this time to examine the link between atonement and justice, as I do in that book,[8] but to explore more specifically the connection between atonement and violence. I also want to engage in some initial dialogue with a book entitled *The Nonviolent Atonement* that appeared shortly after mine.[9] Its author, Mennonite theologian J. Denny Weaver, shares my concern to expose and break the link between atonement theology and retributive violence, though we do so in different ways, and there are features of his position that I would take issue with.

ATONEMENT THEOLOGY AND VIOLENCE

To say that Jesus died on a cross is to make an objective historical statement. To say that "Christ died for our sins" (1 Cor 15:3) or that "he was handed over to death for our trespasses and was raised for our justification" (Rom 4:25), is to offer a theological interpretation of the meaning of that death. It is to assert something unique about the dying of Jesus, to claim it achieved something no other death achieved—it effected the salvation of the world. This is what is meant when we speak of Christ's death and resurrection as the "atonement."

There is no single or definitive way of explaining the atoning power of Jesus's death. In the history of Christian thought, several theories have been elaborated to account for how and why Christ's death secures salvation. These are often grouped into three great families—the "Christus Victor" model, which stresses Jesus's triumph over Satan; the "Moral Influence" theory, which emphasizes the transforming impact on observers of the cross as a demonstration of God's love for humanity; and the "Satisfaction" model, which sees Jesus's death as satisfying the demands of God's honor or God's justice.[10] Each of these theories has enjoyed currency at some time, but none of them, on its own, is fully adequate to comprehend the mystery of the cross.[11]

---

8. See C. D. Marshall, *Beyond Retribution*, 38–69.

9. Weaver, *Nonviolent Atonement*. A second edition of the book was released in 2011, but Weaver's argument remains fundamentally the same. All references in the present discussion are to the first edition.

10. See, for example, Aulén, *Christus Victor*; Finger, *Christian Theology*, 1:303–48.

11. Some scholars seek to address this problem by blending all three approaches. The problem with this approach is that each model rests on differing presuppositions and the resulting synthesis still tends to favor one approach over the others.

It is the satisfaction model that has exercised greatest dominance in Western theology.[12] It was formulated by Anselm in the eleventh century and was refashioned by the Protestant Reformers in the sixteenth century into the more strictly legal doctrine of "penal substitution." Several scholars have argued that substitutionary punishment is basic to how the New Testament, especially Paul, understands the atonement.[13] Furthermore, in popular Christian thought some version of penal substitution remains the dominant way of explaining, and proclaiming, the work of the cross. Tom Smail deems penal substitution to be "one of the main bastions of evangelical orthodoxy, second only in importance to the supreme authority of Scripture . . ."[14] According to the penal theory (which comes in several versions),[15] God passed the verdict of condemnation on humanity that God's law demanded, but carried out the penalty on a substitute. A legal transfer took place. Our guilt and its punishment were imposed on Christ and his righteousness was imputed to us. The genius of the cross lies in the fact that it allowed God to satisfy the demands of retributive justice by inflicting the penalty of sin on Christ, while at the same time satisfying his desire for mercy by conferring forgiveness on sinners.

There have always been dissenters from the satisfaction or penal theory. But criticism of it has grown in intensity in the past generation, especially among feminist, black and other advocacy theologians.[16] Criticism has centered not simply on the logical coherence of the model,[17] but on at least four other, interrelated features as well—its underlying

---

12. "Satisfaction atonement assumes that the sin of humankind against God has earned the penalty of death, but that Jesus satisfied the offended honor of God on their behalf or took the place of sinful humankind and bore their punishment or satisfied the required penalty on their behalf. Sin was atoned for because it was punished vicariously through the death of Jesus, which saved sinful humankind from the punishment of death they deserved. That is, sinful humankind can enjoy salvation because Jesus was killed in their place, satisfying the requirement of divine justice on their behalf." Weaver, *Nonviolent Atonement*, 3; cf. 16–17, 179–224.

13. See, e.g., Packer, *Penal Substitution*; Morris, *Cross in the New Testament*, 382–88.

14. Smail, "Can One Man Die," 75.

15. See Fiddes, *Past Event*, 96–104.

16. For an excellent review of feminist, womanist and black theology, see Weaver, *Nonviolent Atonement*, chapters 4–6. See also Moltmann-Wendel, "Feminist Theology"; Duff, "Atonement." On advocacy theology generally, see Patte, *Ethics*.

17. See, e.g., Talbot, "Punishment"; Fiddes, *Past Event*, 83–111; Gorringe, *Just Vengeance*; Smail, "Can One Man Die," 84–86; Brinsmead, "The Scandal of God's Justice [Part 3]"; Baxter, "Cursed Beloved."

concept of God, its class or gender interest, its ethical abstraction, and its pastoral impact.

To begin with, many feminist critics allege that traditional satisfaction theology evokes the horrifying scenario of "divine child abuse." It portrays God the Father in an abusive relationship with the Son, demanding unquestioning obedience and imposing unmerited suffering upon him in order to defend his own dignity.[18] As Julie Hopkins writes, "It is morally abhorrent to claim that God the Father demanded the self-sacrifice of his only Son to balance the scales of justice. A God who punished through pain, despair and violent death is not a God of love but a sadist and despot."[19]

Critics also assert that although satisfaction theology masquerades as objective, universal truth, it actually represents the interests and perspectives of particular groups. All theology is contextual or "interested" in nature, and satisfaction theology is no different. Anselm's account depends on the logic of the medieval penitential system and the presuppositions of feudalism, where protecting the lord's honor was an all-important consideration.[20] Penal substitution similarly reflects the "law and order" priorities of those thoroughly identified with the prevailing system — ruling-class, white, male clerics.

Not only that, but the abstract or mythical nature of such atonement theology has permitted the ruling elite to participate in systems of oppression without any sense of inconsistency with their Christian commitment. If salvation from sin is a purely spiritual matter that takes place outside of history through some invisible transaction between Father and Son, and if the benefits of this act of salvation are appropriated by individuals solely on the basis of their believing it has happened, then theology becomes divorced from ethical commitment, and this permits oppression to continue unchallenged. Accordingly a pious slave-owner could believe all the "right" theology and feel secure in his salvation without ever questioning his participation in the violence of slavery. A man like John Wesley could accompany condemned criminals to the scaffold,

---

18. The charge of divine child abuse is not leveled solely against satisfaction theology. Insofar as all the traditional models portray God demanding unquestioning obedience from the Son and imposing suffering on him in order to achieve some higher good, all have been accused of depicting abuse in a positive light. But the main target of the accusation has been satisfaction atonement.

19. Hopkins, *Feminist Christology*, 50.

20. On this, see Weaver, *Nonviolent Atonement*, 179-95.

encouraging them to pray for the salvation of their souls, without ever questioning the violent institution of capital punishment.[21] Not only can satisfaction atonement accommodate violence, it may even *encourage* violence. As Timothy Gorringe has documented, the belief that God punished Christ retributively for the sins of the world to uphold his law has frequently been used in Western history to justify excessively harsh treatment of criminals. "Wherever Calvinism spread," Gorringe observes, "punitive sentencing followed."[22]

A fourth major criticism of satisfaction atonement concerns its pastoral impact. Its depiction of Jesus obediently accepting death without protest to meet some divine obligation represents an unhealthy pattern for other victims of oppression to emulate. The model exalts innocent suffering as somehow salvific and discourages active resistance to injustice. In this way it contributes to the victimization of marginalized groups. If those who live in abusive or oppressive situations are encouraged to forge their faith identity by identifying with a Jesus who sacrifices himself utterly for the sake of the One who demands his submission to suffering, their own victim-status is reinforced and sustained. In accepting a worldview of divinely sanctioned redemptive suffering, victims can even become complicit in their own oppression by failing actively to resist and repudiate it.

Such, then, are some of the ill-effects that have been imputed to satisfaction theologies of atonement. In view of them, it is not surprising that several critics jettison atonement theology entirely. All talk of atonement, they urge, is inextricably bound up with the promotion and justification of violence and so must be dispensed with altogether. This usually goes hand-in-hand with an attempt to recover from the Gospel tradition an emphasis on love, justice, peace, inclusiveness or liberation as the true center of Christian faith. But to abandon the doctrine of atonement entirely is surely a counsel of despair, and one that threatens to dissolve the heart of the biblical gospel. The real challenge is to find ways to understand and articulate the salvific character of Christ's death and resurrection that make sense to our generation, that stand in continuity with the rich diversity of ways in which the New Testament writers speak of the cross, and that do not depend on discreditable views of God nor sanction violence of any kind.

---

21. See Gorringe, *Just Vengeance*, 1–7.
22. Ibid., especially 83–219 (quote from 140).

One recent attempt to do this is that of J. Denny Weaver in his book, *The Nonviolent Atonement*. Weaver proposes a new atonement model, which he calls "narrative Christus Victor," which takes the nonviolence of Jesus as normative for atonement theology (and Christology as well). "Narrative Christus Victor," he writes, "is atonement from a nonviolent perspective."[23] It is also, he maintains, "the dominant and preferred reading of atonement in the Bible."[24] Before assessing this claim, a brief summary of Weaver's position is in order.

ATONEMENT THEOLOGY AND THE NONVIOLENT CHRIST

Working from an historic peace church perspective, Weaver's basic methodological assumption is that, "the rejection of violence, whether the direct violence of the sword or the systemic violence of racism or sexism, should be visible in expressions of christology and atonement."[25] Weaver observes a similar conviction at work in many feminist, womanist and black theologies as well, and devotes the central chapters of his book to reviewing, and largely validating, the criticisms each of these streams has leveled at traditional atonement theology (and Christology). He also adds several fresh criticisms of his own and makes some intriguing observations about how the early development of Christian doctrine served the interests of Constantinianism.

Weaver's chief assertion is that satisfaction atonement theology depends on the idea of a God who sanctions violence, indeed a God who *requires* violence in order to satisfy his own honor or justice. The accumulated violence of our evil deeds is balanced by the compensatory violence of God's retributive punishment. There is no escaping this conclusion. "Make no mistake about it," Weaver asserts, "Satisfaction atonement *in any form* depends on divinely sanctioned violence that follows from the assumption that doing justice means to punish."[26] Historically this fact has not much bothered Christian theologians, but it deeply perturbs Weaver, and for similar reasons to those listed earlier.

---

23. Weaver, *Nonviolent Atonement*, 74.
24. Ibid., 69.
25. Ibid., 7, 12.
26. Ibid., 203; also 2, 17, 17, 72.

First, it exhibits a disturbing view of God as a violent and vengeful deity. This is not merely distasteful; it creates significant theological problems. The God of satisfaction theology is said to act in ways that contradict the nonviolent Christ of the Gospel tradition.[27] God uses the violence Jesus rejects. This in turn undermines classic Trinitarian doctrine that holds that all the attributes of God are present in each person of the Trinity, and that what is true for each person of the Trinity must also be true for God as One.[28] Since Jesus's life and teaching are the benchmark for understanding the reign of God,[29] and since Jesus's rejection of lethal violence is fundamental to his vision of God's reign, satisfaction atonement must go.

Second, in common with feminist and womanist critics, Weaver objects to the way satisfaction theology makes passive submission to abusive authority rather than active resistance to it a positive virtue. This is both a destructive model for other victims of injustice and a problematic ethical example for all other Christians. It also overlooks the fact that throughout his ministry Jesus himself engaged in active, though nonviolent, resistance to injustice and evil.[30]

Third, satisfaction atonement not only exalts divine violence, it actively accommodates human violence, both the overt violence of the sword and the systemic violence of racism and sexism. It does so because it conceives of atonement as something that takes place outside of actual history. It depends on some abstract transaction between Father and Son that somehow cancels human guilt and preserves God's honor or sense of justice, but does nothing to confront or change actual historical structures of oppression. Satisfaction atonement also takes place outside the particular history of Jesus's earthly ministry. It reduces the meaning of Jesus's life to some elaborate scheme whose purpose was to produce his death. Like creedal Christology,[31] it moves directly from incarnation to crucifixion, with all that transpired in between having no ultimate significance for salvation or atonement. Consequently salvation becomes separated from ethics, and it is this that has permitted orthodox Christianity to regard violence as compatible with the gospel of Jesus Christ.

27. Ibid., 65–66.
28. Ibid., 202, 209.
29. Ibid., 223.
30. Ibid., 34–46.
31. On the limitations and accommodationist impulse of Nicene-Chalcedonian Christology, see ibid., especially 92–96.

Fourth, in satisfaction theology there is no necessary role for the resurrection. Payment is rendered by Christ's death, with the resurrection serving some other purpose. But the resurrection in the New Testament is the ultimate victory of the reign of God over sin and evil. As Weaver puts it, "the resurrection signifies that the order of the universe has been determined, that the reign of God has been revealed as ultimately established, whether or not rebellious human beings recognize it."[32] If such a victory was the outcome of God's act of retributive violence, then it merely shows that might is right, not that there is a power in the universe greater than violence.

Finally, Weaver's Mennonite perspective becomes most obvious when he links the ethical abstraction and violence-accommodating nature of satisfaction atonement with the legacy of the Constantinian synthesis—that coalition between church, state and culture known as "Christendom." Briefly put, Weaver argues that atonement theology and Christology give expression to an underlying ecclesiology; that is to say, they reflect the place the church occupies in society. In the pre-Constantinian period, the church existed on the periphery of society. It saw itself as the earthly manifestation of God's kingdom that it stood in contrast to, and as a witness to, the prevailing imperial order that did not acknowledge God. The dominant atonement model at this time was Christus Victor, which, in its various forms, emphasized the cosmic victory of God over the forces of Satan and evil. Believers had been set free from these evil powers, but the powers were still seen to exert their baleful influence in the surrounding social and political order of paganism.

After the Constantinian settlement, however, the church moved from the periphery to the center of society. It came to identify with the institutional structures of the empire, which were no longer thought to stand over against God's kingdom but were now under the control of divine providence and could be used to advance the church's own goals. Whereas the pre-Constantinian church looked to Jesus as the norm for its faith and practice, and hence was pacifist, the church of Christendom looked to "Christian" society, and to the interests of the emperor himself, for its norms, and hence it accepted the sword. "In a manner of speaking," Weaver observes, "*not* applying the teaching of Jesus became the 'Christian' thing to do."[33]

32. Ibid., 155, 147.

33. Ibid., 85. For an account of how this became reflected in Christendom's initiation processes, see Kreider, *Change of Conversion*.

At the same time, employing the abstract ontological categories of Greek philosophy, conciliar Christology became preoccupied with defining the two natures of Christ and the oneness of divine substance uniting Father and Son. Nothing was said in the creeds about the social or ethical character of God's reign, as made known in Jesus's life and teaching. "If all we know of Jesus is that he is 'one substance with the Father' and that he is 'fully God and fully man,'" Weaver observes, "there is nothing there that expresses the ethical dimension of being Christ-related, nothing there that would shape the church so that it can witness to the world."[34] In a sense it was no longer necessary, for the church had now made peace with the world, and with war.

> I suggest that it is the church which no longer specifically reflected Jesus' teaching about nonviolence and his rejection of the sword that can proclaim christological formulas devoid of ethics as the foundation of Christian doctrine. The abstract categories of "man" and "God" in these formulas allow the church to accommodate the sword and violence while still maintaining a confession about Christ at the center of its theology.[35]

The same applies to atonement theology. Weaver points out that satisfaction theory, unlike Christus Victor, has no real place for Satan in the mechanics of atonement. It was no longer felt necessary, for there are few, if any, structures left for Satan to rule in Christendom! His activity could be limited to deviant individuals and infidels beyond the boundaries of Christian Europe.[36] And so, banishing Satan on the one hand, and accepting the prevailing hierarchical structures of feudal society on the other, Anselm rethought atonement around the image of God as an offended overlord exacting satisfaction from his human vassals.[37]

But the time has come, Weaver suggests, to put the devil back into the equation, not as a personified being but as a way of speaking about the accumulated sinfulness of institutional structures that refuse

---

34. Weaver, *Nonviolent Atonement*, 93. It should be emphasized that Weaver does not regard the Nicene or Chalcedonian formulas as wrong, invalid or superfluous to Christology, only that they are contextual rather than universal or timeless statements and that they are inadequate in themselves for a Christian peace theology.

35. Ibid., 94.

36. Ibid., 212–14.

37. Although scattered references to satisfaction can be found in earlier writings, Gorringe insists that "to all intents and purposes the theology of satisfaction begins with Anselm" (*Just Vengeance*, 90).

to acknowledge the rule of God and so become the vehicles of evil and oppression. It is over these powers that Christ triumphed in his mission, and thus secured atonement.

NARRATIVE CHRISTUS VICTOR: A NEW MODEL

This leads to Weaver's constructive proposal for a new "narrative Christus Victor" model of atonement, a model that stands in continuity with classical Christus Victor but also differs in important ways. As the name implies, the model emphasizes *Christ's* nonviolent *victory* over the forces of evil, as recorded in the biblical *narrative* of Jesus's life and teaching, and confirmed in his resurrection.

The purpose of Jesus's mission, Weaver suggests, was to make the reign of God visible and overcome the forces of evil that resist God's rule. In his actions, Jesus brought healing, deliverance and restoration to the victims of oppressive situations and systems. In his teaching, he dealt with how people's relationships change when they are governed by the reign of God. In both word and deed, he actively but nonviolently challenged the structures that oppress and dehumanize people. When he encountered evil or violence, he refused to respond in kind, thus exposing and breaking the cycle of hatred and revenge. Jesus was ready and willing to die for the sake of his mission. But death was not the goal or culmination of the venture, even if it was an inevitable consequence of resisting the powers, especially those represented by imperial Rome and the Jewish holiness code. These powers were so threatened by Jesus that they conspired to kill him. Jesus submitted to their violence rather than meeting it on its own terms, thus showing that the rule of God does not depend on violence. He died a violent death. But God raised him from the dead, demonstrating that God's power is greater even than the annihilation of death that comes from the exercise of violence. Jesus's resurrection serves as objective evidence that the fundamental balance of power in the universe has now shifted.

Weaver makes a compelling case, and I concur with a good deal of what he says. I agree that is necessary to think through atonement from a nonviolent perspective; that our understanding of atonement must square with and make sense of the New Testament narratives of Jesus's proclamation and embodiment of God's kingdom; that salvation is more a matter of liberation from the grip to evil than the discharging of a debt owed to God; and that Jesus's refusal of the sword and his call to love of enemy are a crucial clue to understanding *how* he defeated sin and brought deliverance. So I am in general sympathy with the direction of Weaver's thought. But there are two features of Weaver's explanation that I am much less sure of.

First, because he considers it "very important to underscore that violence originates with humans and not with God,"[38] Weaver is adamant that the death of Jesus was not willed or intended or orchestrated by God. Nor was it a demonstration of God's love. "In narrative Christus Victor the death of Jesus is anything but a loving act of God; it is the product of the forces of evil that oppose the reign of God. While God loved sinful humankind enough to send Jesus to witness to the rule of God, Jesus's death is not a loving act of God, but the ultimate statement that distinguishes the rule of God from the reign of evil."[39] Nor did Jesus choose death. "Jesus came not to die but to live, to witness to the reign of God in human history. While he may have known that carrying out that mission would provoke inevitably fatal opposition, his purpose was not to get himself killed."[40] Weaver seems to believe that any suggestion that Jesus's death was intended by God or chosen by Jesus is tantamount to sanctioning violence. To say that God willed Jesus's violent death is the same as saying that God approved of or even perpetrated the violence that killed him. But is this necessarily so?

The second feature of Weaver's explanation that creates difficulties for me is his claim that the cross was not a salvific necessity. Jesus's death, he says,

> accomplishes nothing for the salvation of sinners, nor does it accomplish anything for the divine economy. Since Jesus' mission was not to die but to make visible the reign of God, it is quite explicit that neither God nor the reign of God needs Jesus' death in the way that his death is irreducibly needed in satisfaction atonement.[41]

His death was an unavoidable consequence of him posing an ultimate threat to the powers of evil, but it was not a necessary outcome for the work of salvation. Yet "while Jesus' death was not the will of God, the

---

38. Weaver, *Nonviolent Atonement*, 49.
39. Ibid., 45.
40. Ibid., 211, 132.
41. Ibid., 72.

ultimate power of the reign of God manifests itself in the resurrection of Jesus because he was killed. Then resurrection overcomes death, the last enemy."[42]

In a sense, then, Weaver transfers the work of atonement from the cross to the earthly ministry of Jesus on the one hand, and to the resurrection of Jesus on the other. Narrative Christus Victor proposes "a *how* explanation that focuses on Jesus' life as the reign of God rather than on Jesus' death as an act of God."[43] The cross happened because the evil powers made it happen; but there was no soteriological necessity for it to happen. But when it did happen, God achieved victory over the powers by raising Jesus from the dead. This would seem to imply that, in principle, Jesus could have achieved universal redemption without the cross. His ministry of healing the sick, delivering the oppressed, embracing the outsider and loving the enemy was enough to establish God's rule. His death was an inevitable, but inessential, circumstance, although one turned to greater good by God's response of resurrection.

Now both these claims—that Jesus's death was not willed by God and it was not itself a saving necessity—seem to me to fly in the face of the accumulated weight of New Testament evidence. Nor are they indispensable to a nonviolent account of atonement. What if there was no possibility of defeating violence without enduring violence nonviolently? What if Christ's victory actually required him to absorb the worst that the powers could do, yet without retaliation? What if there was no other way to overcome death but to pass through death? What if God could not will our salvation without willing a final and definitive showdown with the supreme power of sin, its power to inflict violent death on the innocent? Could it be that this is why the New Testament writers do not shrink from presenting Jesus's death as God's will for the salvation of all?

THE AGENCY OF JESUS'S DEATH IN THE NEW TESTAMENT

Weaver, as we have seen, is insistent that the cause of Jesus's death lies solely with the powers of evil. God had nothing to do with it. But when measured against New Testament teaching, it would appear that Weaver is correct in what he affirms but wrong in what he denies.

42. Ibid., 133.
43. Ibid., 226; my emphasis.

It is certainly the case that the prosecution and execution of Jesus are attributed in the New Testament records to the powers of evil, operating through human malice in general and the self-interest of the Jewish and Roman authorities in particular. Mark, for example, frequently comments on how the Pharisees, Herodians and Sadducees plotted to kill Jesus out of fear, resentment and jealousy.[44] Matthew echoes this perspective, accenting even more sharply the combined hostility of the Jewish leaders to Jesus. Luke attributes the betrayal of Jesus to Satan entering Judas,[45] and aligns the Temple authorities who seize Jesus in Gethsemane with "the power of darkness."[46] John also ascribes Jesus's betrayal to Satan entering the heart of Judas (John 13:2, 27). Under the influence of its evil "ruler" (John 14:30), the world in general hated Jesus without cause,[47] for people "loved darkness" and "their deeds were evil."[48] The speeches in Acts frequently accuse the Jewish leaders of having "betrayed," "rejected," "murdered," "condemned" and "crucified" Jesus despite his complete innocence.[49] A conspiracy of Jewish and Gentile powers united to destroy him.

> '... The kings of the earth took their stand, and the rulers have gathered together against the Lord and against his Messiah.' For in this city, in fact, both Herod and Pontius Pilate, with the Gentiles and the peoples of Israel, gathered together against your holy servant Jesus, whom you anointed, to do whatever your hand and your plan had predestined to take place.[50]

Paul also notes the involvement of the Jews (1 Thess 2:14–15) and "the rulers of this age"[51] in the killing of Jesus. The writer to the Hebrews speaks more generally of Jesus enduring "hostility from sinners" (Heb 12:2–3), and 1 Peter speaks of him being "rejected by human beings" (1 Pet 2:4, 7). Finally, John's Apocalypse posits a radical opposition between

44. See, for example, Mark 3:6; 12:12–13; 14:1–3, 10–11; 15:10; cf. 1:22; 2:7; 6:3; 7:1–5; 8:11–23; Luke 23:48; John 19:12.

45. Luke 22:3; cf. 22:31.

46. Luke 22:53; cf. 23:45.

47. John 15:18, 25. The term "world" in John's Gospel, when used negatively, represents the sum of everyone and everything that sets its face against God's revelation in Christ. See Marrow, "Κοσμος."

48. John 3:19; cf. 1:11.

49. Acts 2:23, 36; 3:13–15; 4:10, 26; 7:51–52; 13:27–29; cf. Luke 23:14, 20, 22; 23:47.

50. Acts 4:26–28; cf. 13:27.

51. 1 Cor 2:8; cf. Col 2:14.

the Lamb who was slain and the powers of evil, which continue to "make war on the Lamb" (Rev 17:4).[52]

So when Weaver attributes responsibility for the violent death of Jesus to the powers of evil or "Satan," a term which designates "the accumulation of earthly structures that are not ruled by the reign of God,"[53] he is certainly echoing a notable New Testament motif. But when he goes on to eliminate God's agency entirely from the explanation of Jesus's death, he departs significantly from what is the prevailing emphasis of New Testament teaching. By setting up the responsibility for Jesus's death in simple either-or terms, Weaver flattens out an important New Testament paradox. And to affirm this paradox is not simply "to play a sleight-of-hand language game";[54] it is to do justice to the full witness of the text.

The Synoptic Narratives

In several ways the Synoptic writers indicate the death of Jesus fulfilled the will and purpose of God.[55] To begin with, they all portray Jesus as always being in control of his own destiny. From the moment of his baptism onwards, where the voice from heaven unites his messianic appointment with the mission of the Suffering Servant of Yahweh,[56] Jesus freely embraces a vocation that he knows will end in death. This does not mean Jesus passively accepts *all* suffering and rejection as invariably the will of God. Far from it. On several occasions when he encounters attempts to arrest or assassinate him, he acts to protect himself and his disciples,[57] for his appointed "hour" had not yet come.[58] Nor does he encourage an

---

52. Weaver gives a helpful account of the nonviolent theology of the book of Revelation in *Nonviolent Atonement*, 20–33.

53. Ibid., 210.

54. Ibid., 211.

55. Ideally the perspective of each gospel writer should be considered separately. But there is substantial enough narrative agreement between them in how they present the purpose and outcome of Jesus's mission to permit some broad generalizations about features common to each account.

56. It is often noted that the voice from heaven at Jesus's baptism (Mark 1:11/Matt 3:17/Luke 3:22) unites the messianic designation of Psalm 2:7 with the identification of the Servant of Yahweh in Isaiah 42:1, whose task involves suffering and rejection. There may also be an allusion to Gen 22:2, 12, 16.

57. Mark 4:35–41/Matt 8:23–27/Luke 8:22–25; Mark 6:47–52/Matt 14:22–32/John 6:15–21; Luke 4:29–30; Matt 12:14–15; cf. Matt 2:13–15. See also John 17:11–12, 15.

58. Mark 14:35, 41; Matt 26:55; Luke 22;14, 53; cf. John 2:4; 7:30; 8:20; 12:23, 27; 13:1; 16:32; 17:1.

unhealthy martyr complex among his followers,[59] even though they too must reckon on the certainty of arrest, torture and execution in the future.[60] So Jesus did not court death as such, and he did not sanctify all suffering. Yet he knows the time must come when the "bridegroom" will be forcibly "taken away," and this climactic event he will not seek to evade.[61]

On the contrary, Jesus chooses to walk into the very jaws of death. "When the days drew near for him to be taken up," Luke says, "he set his face to go to Jerusalem" (Luke 9:51-52). He is therefore unfazed by reports of Herod's plans to kill him, "because it is impossible for a prophet to be killed outside of Jerusalem" (Luke 13:31-33). On his journey to the city, Jesus repeatedly and explicitly speaks of the fate that awaits him at his destination; his predictions sometimes employ the impersonal verb *dei* ("it is necessary," "must") to underline the divine necessity of what is to come. "The Son of Man *must* undergo great suffering, and be rejected by the elders, the chief priests, and the scribes, and be killed, and after three days rise again."[62] A sense of divine purpose is also implied in sayings where Jesus speaks of having a "cup" (of suffering) to drink, a "fire" to kindle, and a "baptism" to undergo.[63] It is even clearer in the important saying where Jesus declares that the Son of Man came "not to be served but to serve and to give his life as a ransom for many."[64]

After a carefully choreographed entry to the city, Jesus engages in highly confrontational tactics with the Temple rulers, which finally seals his fate.[65] The authorities are anxious to move against Jesus but are afraid to do so because of his popular support.[66] Knowing this, and that he is about to be betrayed, Jesus effectively delivers himself into the hands of his enemies by going to the one place where his betrayer knows he can be caught alone (Luke 22:6, 53). He is unsurprised when the authorities turn up, and he does not resist arrest. When put on trial, he refuses to

---

59. Matt 10:23; 24:15-20/Mark 13:14-18/Luke 21:2.
60. Matt 10:17-23, 28; 24:9-10/Mark 13:9-13/Luke 21:12-19; John 16:4.
61. Mark 2:19-20/Matt 9:15/Luke 5:35.
62. Mark 8:31-34/Matt 16:21-23/Luke 9:21-22; cf. 13:33; 17:25; Mark 9:9/Matt 17:9; Mark 9:12/Matt 17:12; Mark 9:22-23/Matt 17:22-23/Luke 9:44; Mark 10:32-34/Matt 20:17-19/Luke 18:31-34.
63. Mark 10:38-40/Matt 20:22-23; Luke 12:49-50; cf. John 18:11.
64. Mark 10:45; Matt 20:28; cf. 1 Tim 2:5.
65. Mark 11:1-33; Matt 21:1-27; 23:37-24:2; Luke 19:29—20:8; cf. John 2:13-22.
66. Mark 11:18; 12:13; 14:1-2, 10-11; Luke 22:6.

defend himself against any of the charges brought against him, much to the irritation of his accusers and the amazement of Pilate.[67]

So throughout their respective narratives, the Gospel writers depict Jesus moving steadfastly and knowingly towards his divinely given destiny of suffering, death and resurrection. His death is seen as more than simply the foreseeable or inevitable consequence of his confrontation with injustice, though it is that too. It is portrayed as a unique event, the climactic expression of his vocation of manifesting God's reign and the fulfillment of God's intention for his mission.

This is nowhere more clearly evident than in the Gethsemane episode where Jesus speaks explicitly of his struggle to submit to this dimension of God's will. In the garden he prays, "Abba, Father, for you all things are possible; remove this cup from me; yet, not what I want, but what you."[68] Each Synoptic account has different ways of underscoring the fact that for Jesus to accept death was to accept the will of God. Mark has Jesus pray the same prayer three times before submitting to God's will. Matthew records only two petitions, but the wording of the second ("My Father, if this cannot pass unless I drink it, your will be done" [Matt 26:42]) intentionally echoes the second petition of the Lord's Prayer ("your kingdom come, your will be done on earth as it is in heaven").[69] The implication is plain: it is precisely through Jesus embracing death that God's kingdom comes and God's will is done on earth as in heaven. Luke records an angel appearing from heaven to strengthen Jesus for what lies ahead rather than to deliver him from it (Matthew has Jesus consciously forego the possibility of angelic deliverance).[70]

Another way in which the Gospel writers underscore the divine necessity of Jesus's death is by presenting it as the fulfillment of Scripture. The entire Passion Narrative is constructed as a kind of dramatization of a large group of psalms—particularly Psalm 22—in which the righteous person suffers unjustly and cries out to God for vindication.[71] Sometimes selected details of Jesus's passion experience are expressly said to "fulfill"

---

67. Mark 15:2–5/Matt 27:11–14/Luke 23:8–12; John 19:8–10.

68. Mark 14:32–42/Matt 26:36–42/Luke 22:39–46.

69. Matt 6:10; cf. 11:12.

70. Luke 22:42; cf. Matt 26:53. Even the writer to the Hebrews suggests that Jesus's prayers were heard by "the one who was able to save him from death because of his reverent submission . . . and obedience" (Heb 5:7–10).

71. For a full listing of the texts and how they are reflected in the passion narrative, see Jansen, *Resurrection*, 68–75.

specific Old Testament texts, including an occasional reference to Isaiah 53.[72] Furthermore, in several of Jesus's own sayings he expressly declares that his sufferings are attested in Scripture. "Then he took the twelve aside and said to them, 'See, we are going up to Jerusalem, and everything that is written about the Son of Man by the prophets will be accomplished.'"[73] In refusing Peter's sword in Gethsemane, Jesus says:

> Put your sword back into its place; for all who take the sword will perish by the sword. Do you think that I cannot appeal to my Father, and he will at once send me more than twelve legions of angels? But how then would the scriptures be fulfilled, which say it must happen in this way?[74]

In Luke 24, the risen Jesus explains to his confused disciples, first to the pair on the Emmaus Road, then to the eleven hiding in Jerusalem, that Messiah's sufferings were both necessary and foreshadowed in the scriptures.

> "Oh, how foolish you are, and how slow of heart to believe all that the prophets have declared! Was it not necessary [edei] that the Messiah should suffer these things and then enter into his glory?" Then beginning with Moses and all the prophets, he interpreted to them the things about himself in all the Scriptures.[75]

> Then he said to them, "These are my words that I spoke to you while I was still with you—that everything written about me in the law of Moses, the prophets, and the psalms must [dei] be fulfilled." Then he opened their minds to understand the Scriptures and he said to them, "Thus it is written, that the Messiah is to suffer and to rise from the dead on the third day and that repentance and forgiveness of sins is to be proclaimed in his name to all nations, beginning from Jerusalem.[76]

---

72. See, e.g., Mark 14:27/Matt 26:31; Mark 14:62/Matt 26:64; Luke 22:37; cf. also John 13:18; 18:9; 19:23, 28, 36; Acts 8:32–33. The place of Isaiah 53 in New Testament reflection on the meaning of Jesus's death, and especially its role in the mind of the historical Jesus, has long been debated. For a thorough, helpful, and up-to-date review of this issue, see Bellinger and Farmer, *Suffering Servant*.

73. Luke 18:31; cf. Luke 22:22, 37; Matt 26:24.

74. Matt 26:52–54; cf. 21:42; Acts 4:11; 1 Peter 2:7.

75. Luke 24:26–27; cf. Acts 17:1–3.

76. Luke 24:44–47.

Now in presenting the death of Jesus against the backdrop of biblical testimony, the Evangelists are not necessarily regarding all the specific texts they have in mind as predictive prophecies. They view them more as prefigurements in redemptive history of what God has now definitively accomplished in the death and resurrection of Jesus. And it is the existence of such divinely given anticipations and foreshadowings in Scripture that proves that the death of Jesus accords with, and brings to fullness, the will of God.

John's Gospel

In John's Gospel, Jesus is identified at the outset as "the Lamb of God who takes away the sin of the world" (John 1:29). Throughout the ensuing narrative, Jesus moves steadily towards the appointed "hour" of his death,[77] which is also the hour of his "glory."[78] John's Jesus speaks of God "sending" and "giving" his Son to save the world as an expression of his great love (John 3:16–17) and declares that, "my food is to do the will of him who sent me and to complete his work."[79] In contemplating the hour when the Son of Man will be "lifted up from the earth" on the cross (John 12:32–33), Jesus asks,

> "What should I say—'Father, save me from this hour'? No, it is for this reason that I have come to this hour. Father, glorify your name." Then a voice came from heaven, "I have glorified it, and I will glorify it again" (John 12:27–28).

Several times John suggests that the details of Jesus's prosecution and death fulfill Scripture.[80] Even more striking, however, is John's emphasis on the fact that Jesus's life is not taken from him against his will but is freely laid down by him.

> I am the good shepherd. The good shepherd lays down his life for the sheep . . . I am the good shepherd. I know my own and my own know me, just as the Father knows me and I know the Father. And I lay down my life for the sheep . . . For this reason the Father loves me, because I lay down my life in order to take it up again. No one takes it from me, but I lay it down of my own

---

77. John 2:4; 7:30; 8:20; 12:23, 27; 13:1; 16:32; 17:1.
78. John 12:23, 27–28; 17:1–5; cf. 21:19.
79. John 4:34; cf. 6:37–40; 12:27–28; 17:4–5.
80. John 13:18; 18:9; 19:23, 28, 36.

accord. I have power to lay it down, and I have power to take it up again. I have received this command from my Father" (John 10:11, 14–18).

At his arrest, Jesus identifies himself to the soldiers and forbids Peter to defend him, since he must "drink the cup the Father has given me."[81] Accordingly when Pilate claims authority to crucify him, Jesus retorts: "You would have no power over me unless it had been given you from above" (John 19:11). It is impossible to avoid the conclusion, then, that John understands the death of Jesus to be willed by God and freely chosen by Jesus.

Acts and Epistles

As noted earlier, the author of Acts expressly ascribes the death of Jesus to the malice and ignorance of the prevailing religious and political powers, for which they are culpable. But that is only one side of the story, for Luke also states quite clearly that these evil actions enabled God's will and plan, as attested in Scripture, to be accomplished. The mysterious interface between divine will and human responsibility is captured well in Peter's Pentecost sermon in Acts 2: "This man, handed over to you *according to the definite plan and foreknowledge of God*, you crucified and killed" (Acts 2:23). A similar juxtaposition features in Peter's sermon at Solomon's Portico in Acts 3: "Now, friends, I know that you acted in ignorance, as did also your rulers. *In this way God fulfilled what he had foretold through all the prophets*, that his Messiah would suffer" (Acts 3:17–18). The same idea features again in Paul's sermon at Pisidian Antioch in Acts 13:

> Because the residents of Jerusalem and their leaders did not recognize him or understand the words of the prophets that are read every Sabbath, they fulfilled those words by condemning him. Even though they found no cause for a sentence of death, they asked Pilate to have him killed. When they had carried out everything that was written about him, they took him down from the tree and laid him in a tomb.[82]

In his own writings, the Apostle Paul himself constantly asserts the divine initiative behind the death of Jesus. He discerns in Jesus's death, not just a tragic expression of human evil, but a purposeful act of God,

---

81. John 18:11; cf. 4–8.
82. Acts 13:27–29; cf. 8:32–35; 17:1–3.

foretold in Scripture, to achieve the redemption and reconciliation of the world. "Christ died for our sins in accordance with the Scriptures," Paul affirms, just as "he was raised on the third day in accordance with the Scriptures."[83] Not only his resurrection but also his death and burial manifest the will and eternal purpose of God.[84] Accordingly Paul speaks of God "sending his own Son" into the world to "deal with sin" and to "redeem those under the law" from its curse.[85] God "did not withhold his own Son, but gave him up for all of us" (Rom 8:32). In giving him up to death, "God put [him] forward as a sacrifice of atonement by his blood . . . to show his righteousness" (Rom 3:25). In some mysterious way, God "made him to be sin who knew no sin, so that in him we might become the righteousness of God" (2 Cor 5:21). However we understand this text, God's active involvement in Jesus's death is clearly asserted. For "in Christ," Paul says, "God was reconciling the world to himself."[86] He was also "proving his love for us in that while we still were sinners Christ died for us" (Rom 5:7).

As well as God's initiative, Paul also stresses Christ's willing submission to death. He was not merely killed by others against his will; he graciously "died for us"[87] as an "act of righteousness" and "obedience" (Rom 5:18–19) and as a demonstration of self-abnegation and self-surrender.[88] The crucifixion of Christ is therefore an event to be "proclaimed" as a demonstration of God's power and God's wisdom (1 Cor 1:20–25; 11:26), as well as an event to be shared in and emulated by others.[89]

None of these texts requires a satisfaction theory of atonement. But the cumulative weight of New Testament evidence does strongly suggest that Jesus's death is understood to be, in some significant sense, an act of God that demonstrates God's love and faithfulness, exemplifies Jesus's utter self-giving for the sake of others, and clarifies and fulfills the biblical testimony to God's saving purposes. This feature cannot simply be ascribed to the rhetorical tendency of the biblical writers to see God as

---

83. 1 Cor 15:3–4; cf. Rom 1:1–4.

84. Cf. Eph 2:13; 3:11–12.

85. Rom 8:3; Gal 4:4; cf. 2:21; 3:13; cf. also Titus 3:4.

86. 2 Cor 5:19; cf. Rom 5:10; Col 1:20–21.

87. Rom 5:6, 8; 1 Cor 15:3; 1 Thess 5:10; 2 Cor 1:5; 5:14; Gal 3:13; cf. Eph 5:2; Titus 2:14.

88. Rom 15:3–4; Phil 2:5–8; cf. 1 Tim 2:6.

89. Gal 2:19; 6:14; Rom 6:3–14; 2 Cor 1:5; 4:10; Phil 3:10; Col 1:2; cf. 2 Tim 2:11. See further C. D. Marshall, "'For Me to Live Is Christ,'" 96–116, especially 111–13.

responsible for everything that happens, even while not holding God responsible for sinful actions. God's initiative behind and saving achievement in Jesus's death is positively celebrated. The crucial issue is not *whether* God intended Jesus to die, but *why* he did and whether doing so is tantamount to God underwriting sacred violence.

A BRIEF PROPOSAL

To accept that God *did* will or need the death of Jesus is not to say that God wanted or required it to satisfy his own holiness, as satisfaction atonement maintains. God willed it for a different reason. God willed it because he willed our salvation, and the only way to achieve our redemption was for Jesus to tread the path of suffering and death, for only thus could sin's power be broken.

I began by suggesting that violence is the foremost social manifestation of sin; it is all-pervasive in human experience. Sin has usurped God's loving rule over humanity, and violence is the principal external evidence of sin's deleterious lordship. "Sin came into the world through one man," Paul writes, "and death came through sin" (Rom 5:12). It is through death that "sin exercises its dominion."[90] Death destroys relationships and the fear of death dominates the human psyche and governs human behavior (Heb 2:14–15). Significantly, the first recorded death in the biblical story is a violent death (Gen 4:8), stemming from the envy or covetousness that most reveals sin's interior grip on the human heart.[91] Just before Cain strikes out against his brother, God observes Cain's jealous anger and warns him that "sin is lurking at the door; its desire is for you, but you must master it" (Gen 4:7). But instead sin masters Cain, and he turns to violence. This connection between internal desire and external violence is highlighted in the epistle of James: "You want something and do not have it; so you commit murder. And you covet something and cannot obtain it; so you engage in disputes and conflicts" (Jas 4:2).

Because of sin, we seek to impose our will on others, and violence enables us to do so through engaging the fear of suffering and death. Sin creates rivalry between people, and violence, or threatened violence, is the ultimate power sin employs to bring success. At the same time, however, the imposition of violence evokes in the victim a "pay-back"

---

90. Rom 5:21; 6:23; 7:7, 13.
91. Gen 3:6; cf. Rom 7:7–12; Mark 7:21–22.

response, an intense desire to strike back in kind, to retaliate blow for blow, stripe for stripe, loss for loss. For victims, this seems to be the only way to appease the pain they have suffered and the resentment they feel. But the pay-back instinct actually manifests the most terrifying characteristic of sin's lordship, its pernicious power to turn those who have been sinned against into sinners in their own right, to suck victims into a pattern of imitative behavior that allows violence to spiral on forever.

So there is a real sense in which the power to inflict violent death, and the capacity to evoke counter-violence from victims, is the most potent evidence of sin's grip over humanity. If sin is to be defeated then, violence must be overcome once and for all. This is what Jesus sought to do. But to succeed in doing so, it was not enough simply to avoid inflicting violence on others, or to teach people to love their enemies. He also had to withstand the temptation to hit back; he had to break the cycle of violence and revenge, hatred and counter-hatred. This meant he had to endure violence himself—the supreme violence of torture and an unjust execution—without seeking or desiring retaliation. He had to absorb the very worst that the powers could do, he had to go the very limits of human desolation, and at that point pray, "Father forgive them, for they do not know what they are doing" (Luke 23:34). In so doing Jesus deconstructed the power and logic of evil.

The power of sin was broken, then, not by some violent act of substitutionary punishment but through Jesus's own definitive refusal to perpetuate the cycle of violence and revenge. In his passion, Jesus adopted the position of supreme victim of human evil and depredation. Yet he refused to respond to his victimization by victimizing those who victimized him. Instead he absorbed the sin of human violence in his own bodily experience without retaliation. "When he was abused, he did not return abuse; when he suffered, he did not threaten; but he entrusted himself to the one who judges justly. He himself bore our sins in his body on the cross, so that free from sins we might live for righteousness . . ." (1 Pet 2:23–24). In so doing Jesus broke the mimetic or payback mechanism that lies at the heart of sin's power (something beyond the reach of any display of coercive power, even God's power), and unleashed the liberative power of forgiveness.

God sent his Son into the world for this purpose. It was God's will to make "the one who knew no sin to be sin for our sake, so that we might become the righteousness of God in him" (2 Cor 5:21). This highly compressed, shorthand summary of what happened at the cross does not mean that God made Christ into a sinner, in order to punish him retributively for our sins. It means that God made the Sinless One to bear the full consequences of sin's dominion over humanity, displayed most graphically in the inescapable logic of violence. In Christ sin did its very worst, and Christ died. But God raised him from the dead and in so doing triumphed over the power of sin and death. "The death he died he died to sin, once for all," with the result that "death no longer has dominion over him" (Rom 6:9–10). And those who by faith are united with Christ in his death share also in his liberation, "so that as Christ was raised from the dead by the glory of the Father, we too might walk in newness of life" (Rom 6:4). Supremely characteristic of this newness of life is freedom from the fear of death, on which violence feeds,[92] and participation in a new humanity in which hostility is put to death and "the things that make for peace" are pursued.[93]

---

92. Cf. Rom 8:35–39.
93. Luke 19:42; cf. Rom 14:1–15:13; Gal 3:25–29; 2 Cor 5:18–21; Eph 2:1–22.

9

For God's Sake!
Terrorism, Religious Violence, and Restorative Justice

OVER THE PAST THIRTY years there has been a dramatic upsurge in terrorist violence in many parts of the world. There is nothing new about terrorism of course; it has been around for a very long time. In the past, terrorist activity was largely local in its impact and intention; it was aimed at a defined audience and witnessed only by those physically present. But modern terrorism is performed on a global stage for a global audience. It is global in three senses: its targets are spread throughout the world; its instigators are increasingly linked together in elaborate international networks, facilitated by the digital revolution; and its audience includes the world-wide television viewing public, which at times watches events as they unfold.

  It is not surprising, then, that terrorism today is often deemed to be the gravest threat to world peace and security. Its gravity far exceeds the small number of people involved in terror organizations or the limited strategic gains they make. Modern terrorism is considered such a serious risk because it scorns international borders and treaties, exposes the impotence of conventional military might to control it, and has the potential to unleash weapons of enormous destructive power on civilian populations anywhere on earth. It may be only a matter of time before we experience nuclear or biological terrorism. As terrorism expert Michael McKinley observes: "The rule of thumb used to be that terrorists did not want millions of people dead, they wanted millions watching. That's changed. They are now quite happy for both to take place."[1]

As well as its epic proportions, another striking feature of much modern terrorism is its *religious* character. Only a generation ago, many Western academics were confidently predicting that secularization would soon see an end of religion and the final death of God—or at least God's belated retirement from public life. With religion banished to the benign fringes of privatized devotion, no need would remain to slaughter opponents on God's behalf. How wrong such predictions have been![2] The proportion of known terrorist organizations claiming a religious identity has increased sharply in the last two decades, and the use of religious language to describe their deeds is commonplace. After the destruction of the Twin Towers, Osama bin Laden declared, "Here is America, struck by God in one of its vital organs, so that its greatest buildings are destroyed."[3] Following the attack on the Australian embassy in Jakarta in September 2004, Jemaah Islamiyah posted an internet statement saying: "We decided to call Australia to account, which we consider one of the worst enemies of God and of God's religion Islam."[4] Not to be out-theologized, George W. Bush once told a Christian gathering in the U.S: "God told me to strike at al-Qaeda and I struck them, and then he instructed me to strike at Saddam, which I did."[5] Religion has re-surfaced in the public square of international affairs with, literally, a bang!

This does not mean, of course, that all terrorism is religiously motivated, nor that all religious violence takes the form of terrorism. But so much terror today is inflicted in the name of God that it revives for

1. Cited in Masters, "Terror on Our Minds."

2. So rightly, Boulton, "Who Needs Religion?" See also Ward, "Churchless Future"; Berger, *Desecularization*.

3. Cited in Juergensmeyer, *Terror in the Mind*, 149.

4. Cited in *New Zealand Herald*, September 11, 2004, B12.

5. Cited in Austin, Kranock, and Oommen, *God and War*, 9. See also the claims made at http://www.buzzflash.com/interviews/04/05/int04024.html. Accessed 12 May, 2004. Bruce Bartlett, a past Republican presidential policy advisor, says of George Bush, "This instinct he's always talking about is this sort of weird, messianic idea of what he thinks God has told him to do . . . This is why George W. Bush is so clear-eyed about Al Qaeda and the Islamic fundamentalist enemy. He believes you have to kill them all. They can't be persuaded, that they're extremists driven by a dark vision. He understands them, because he's just like them. He truly believes he's on a mission from God. Absolute faith like that overwhelms a need for analysis." Cited by Ron Suskind, who tracks the evolution of what he calls Bush's "faith-based presidency" in Suskind, "Without a Doubt." See also Goldhammer, "Fundamentalist Shadow."

our generation the centuries-old debate about the connection between religion and violence. Why do religious devotees engage in so much conflict and war? Does religion inescapably generate violence? Or is religion itself a casualty of violence, a violence that originates elsewhere and co-opts religious conviction for its own ends? Could religion even be a *cure* for human violence, and if so, how? These are profound and complex questions that cannot be considered here. But when passenger planes are flown into skyscrapers, ritual decapitations are displayed on the internet, night clubs and restaurants become slaughter houses and school children are blown to pieces by suicide bombers, all ostensibly at God's behest, the question about religion and violence is far from academic. It demands serious reflection by all people of good will, not least by those who are practicing religious believers.

In this chapter, however, I want to focus more specifically on whether restorative justice has anything to contribute in the search for solutions to the scourge of religious violence and terrorism. This, we will see, is a very difficult question to answer. Before venturing to do so, we need to be clear on what we mean by "religious terrorism" and on why it is such a difficult phenomenon to combat.

WHAT IS RELIGIOUS TERRORISM?

The term "terrorism" comes from the Latin *terrere*, meaning "to cause to tremble." At its most general level, terrorism designates "the intentional effort to generate fear through violence or the threat of violence and the further effort to harness these fears in pursuit of some goal."[6] This definition captures the three key components of terrorism: its reliance on violence, its strategy of fostering fear, and its teleological intent. Yet there is a real sense in which *all* violence generates fear and serves some ancillary purpose, not least the violence associated with conventional warfare. Recall the name given to the American invasion of Iraq—Operation Shock and Awe—a clear indication that premeditated violence was being employed to heighten fear and demoralize the opposition. So the question of what distinguishes terrorism from other forms of violence is politically and ideologically highly loaded. Often it is only a matter of political expediency that deems some episodes of violence as terrorism and others as foreign policy.

---

6. Griffith, *War on Terrorism*, 6.

Within this broad category, *religious* terrorism designates those "public acts of violence . . . for which religion has provided the motivation, the justification, the organization, and the world view."[7] It shares many common features with political terrorism, such as its use of "performative" violence, that is, violence that serves a theatrical as well as a practical purpose.[8] But insofar as it depends upon a religious worldview, faith-based terrorism is marked out by four things in particular: the absolutism of its categories, its tendency to spread contagiously, its heightened symbolism, and its relative unconcern for measurable success. It is precisely these features that make religious violence such a formidable challenge to restorative-justice theory and practice, so each deserves a brief comment.

Absolutism

Religious militancy is characterized, first, by strong claims to moral justification and by a thoroughgoing dualism that divides the world into "us" and "them," truth and falsehood, innocent and guilty, good and bad, with the fault line dividing the categories being absolute. After interviewing many violent activists, Jessica Stern of the Kennedy School of Government at Harvard University writes: "I've noticed that one thing that distinguishes religious terrorists from other people is that they know with absolute certainty that they're doing good. They seem more confident and less susceptible to self-doubt than most other people."[9]

Such people see themselves as caught up in a transcendent battle between good and evil, and consider it their religious duty to purify the world of corruption by force. This results in an unwillingness to make concessions, for how can one compromise with the devil or tolerate impiety? Accordingly, religious zealots are willing to do virtually anything necessary to overcome the enemy, for evil cannot be transformed or accommodated, it must be utterly destroyed. "Religious terrorist groups are more violent than their secular counterparts," Stern observes, "and probably are more likely to use weapons of mass destruction."[10] Holy wars

---

7. Jeurgensmeyer, *Terror in the Mind*, 7; also Griffith, *War on Terrorism*, 179.

8. This is Juergensmeyer's term, which he borrows from linguistics (*Terror in the Mind*, 126).

9. Stern, *Terror in the Name of God*, 26.

10. Ibid., xxii. McTernan, *In God's Name*, 42, 127.

historically have been notable for their savagery, and religious terrorism is really a contemporary form of unauthorized holy war.[11] And one of the most troubling features of holy war is its contagiousness.

Contagiousness

There is an important sense in which all violence is contagious, but arguably religious violence is more infectious than any other kind, and more addictive. Faith-inspired terrorism is contagious in two ways. First, its use of religious language expands the pool of potential sympathizers and recruits beyond the immediate battle zone to co-religionists all around the world. Once a holy war has been declared, religious hardliners from far and wide flock to join the contest, creating a multinational armed struggle, or what has been famously called a "Jihadi International Incorporated."[12]

Second, once holy war organizations are formed and achieve initial success, they seek additional missions elsewhere. This is something the United States did not reckon on sufficiently when it sponsored pan-Islamic terrorist organizations in Afghanistan to oppose the Soviet occupation.[13] After the Soviet withdrawal, the *mujahideen* turned their sights on new targets, including America itself. Returning jihadis in Pakistan posed such a law and order problem that the government there sent them to fight in Kashmir, deliberately stirring up religious passions to intensify the conflict.[14] Once unleashed, holy wars acquire a momentum of their own. They have no masters. Holy war excites more holy war.[15] Fighting for God becomes addictive.

Any consistent recourse to violence can become physiologically addictive for some individuals. But religious violence is addictive in a psychic and spiritual sense as well. Participation in holy war ranks among the most intense of all religious experiences.[16] Jessica Stern found that only a few of the terrorists she interviewed claimed to be in personal

---

11. On the phenomenology of holy war, see Selengut, *Sacred Fury*, 17–48. See also Bainton, *Christian Attitudes*, 44–52, 56f, 109–16, 143–51, 204–10.

12. Stern, *Terror in the Name of God*, 83–84, 117, 233 (the label "Jihadi International Inc." was coined by Eqbal Ahmad).

13. Cf. Eakin, "Insurgents."

14. Stern, *Terror in the Name of God*, 233–36.

15. Griffith, *War on Terrorism*, 107, 110.

16. Selengut, *Sacred Fury*, 21.

communication with God, but they all described themselves as responding to a spiritual calling, and many reported themselves as being addicted to its fulfillment.[17] They were "spiritually intoxicated" by their cause,[18] Stern observes, and experienced "a kind of bliss."[19] "[T]he bottom line, I now understood, is that purifying the world through holy war is addictive. Holy war intensifies the boundaries between Us and Them, satisfying the inherently human longing for a clear identity and a definite purpose in life, creating a seductive state of bliss."[20] Such bliss is its own reward, which leads to the third distinctive feature of religious combat.

Heightened Symbolism

All terrorist acts are symbolic events to some degree, in that they are staged events calculated to attract public attention to some cause, but religious violence is almost exclusively symbolic.[21] That is to say, its creations of terror are done not primarily to achieve a strategic goal but to make a symbolic statement. It is a statement about the real condition of the world and about who possesses true power in the universe. The presupposition of religious terrorism is that the world is already at war, an apocalyptic war between good and evil. This war is being played out on the worldly stage of power politics, though few are aware of it. Terrorist acts dramatize or materialize the spiritual struggle that is invisibly underway behind the scenes. Victims are chosen not because they are a threat to the perpetrators but because they serve as symbols of this larger spiritual confrontation.

The symbolic character of current Islamist terrorism is highlighted well in an article by Jason Burke on Abu Musab al-Zarqawi, believed to have been personally responsible for the beheading of three Western hostages in Iraq in September and October 2004. These videotaped executions, Burke explains, were carefully scripted dramas intended for the world's 1.3 billion Muslims. They were laden with symbolic meanings missed almost entirely by Westerners. Zarqawi justifies his actions by

17. One terrorist operative told Stern, "I am spiritually addicted to jihad" (*Terror in the Name of God*, 200); cf. 217, 221.
18. Ibid., 281–82.
19. Ibid., xxvii.
20. Ibid., 137.
21. Juergensmeyer, *Terror in the Mind*, 125.

appealing to "one of the single most emotive issues in the Islamic world: the supposed imprisonment, and abuse, of Muslim women by non-Muslim men," even though, in reality, very few such prisoners existed. After evoking other sources of Muslim resentment, the videotape climaxes with an act of ritualized slaughter, re-enacting myths about how the first warriors of Islam killed the enemies of God. "Islamic militant terrorism," Burke explains, "is primarily propaganda and not usually tied to a specific political objective. Though frightening vital Western contractors out of Iraq... is useful, Zarqawi's primary goal is to communicate."[22] Zarqawi was killed in 2006 by an American airstrike.

Assessment of Success

Secular terrorists assess the utility of their acts to ensure that their violence will advance their political or nationalist goals. Sacred terrorists, by contrast, do not measure success in such worldly or human terms. Their aim is to not to gain strategic advantage in a tactical campaign but to champion God's will, oppose God's enemies, and galvanize God's people.[23] In fact, Mark Juergensmeyer finds that its perpetrators have often turned to holy war precisely because there was no hope of human success. Their violent acts, he suggests, are "devices for symbolic empowerment in wars that cannot be won and for goals that cannot be achieved."[24] For their campaign is not ultimately about politics or economics or even territory, though such concerns may also be involved. It is about the vindication of their theological vision of the world and the fulfillment of their eschatological hopes. Their sense of achievement comes simply from being involved in the struggle, confident that God is on their side and buoyed by contemplation of spiritual or heavenly rewards.

Such, then, is the distinctive shape of sacred terrorism. Why such a style of terrorism has exploded in recent decades is still debated by the experts. Is it the result of *need*, or of *greed*, or of *creed*, or of the *speed* of global change?

My own proposal is that religious terrorism emerges where four elements come together: an external situation of real or perceived human

22. Burke, "Zarqawi."

23. Selengut, *Sacred Fury*, 224–26; cf. *New Zealand Herald*, "Terror," October 19, 2004, B1.

24. Juergensmeyer, *Terror in the Mind*, 218.

suffering; a set of psychological and emotional responses to this situation on the part of certain individuals within larger cultures of resentment; the availability of religious resources to explain present experience and justify violent remedies; and the influence of charismatic religious leaders who exploit feelings of alienation to issue a call to holy war. No single ingredient is sufficient to spawn holy terror; it is the combination that is critical. Yet any attempt to combat religious terrorism must take all four elements individually into account, as well as the circumstances of their combination.

RESPONDING TO HOLY TERROR

Enough has been said already to indicate that religious terrorism is a particularly complex and dangerous reality to deal with. It is vital that internationally coordinated efforts are made to counteract it. A coherent strategy is required that balances short-term and long-term remedies. The short-term need is to shut down or contain terror groups and networks and bring known perpetrators of murder to justice. The long-term need is to ensure that terrorist ideology loses its appeal among populations made vulnerable to it by perceived humiliation, human rights abuses, economic deprivation, indebtedness, unemployment, military occupation, and other forms of collective distress. The challenge is to achieve the goal of containment without making the goal of prevention more difficult. There is also need for a third kind of response, a *therapeutic* response that addresses the pain of those who have been personally caught up in terrorist atrocities and that promotes reconciliation between estranged communities. It is here that restorative justice could have a role to play. Each of these responses needs teasing out in more detail.

The Task of Containment

Since 9/11, the international response to terrorism has focused primarily on the job of containment. Huge efforts have been made to hunt down known terrorist leaders, to destroy the material and financial bases of their operations, and to enhance domestic security. The predominant means of containment has been by the use of raw military power. Billions of dollars have been spent and tens of thousands of lives sacrificed in the so-called global war on terrorism.

War is always a blunt and bloody instrument for resolving conflict. But the strategy of warring against holy war is a particularly unsophisticated and fruitless way to respond to religious violence.[25] The problem is not only that large-scale military assaults compound the suffering and the humiliation felt by the constituency from which terrorists emerge in the first place, making future recruitment much easier. The main pitfall of waging war on religious terrorism is that the religious zealots' underlying ideology of holy war is actually strengthened every time military power is directed against them.

Military reprisals prove that their diagnosis of the world is correct: a great battle for religious truth truly is underway, the enemy really is a satanic monster, and believers must now rally to defend true religion. Displays of massive counter-violence may even be welcomed by terrorist leaders, for it helps to spread the seeds of burning rage and religious zeal that guarantee "the enlistment of a whole new generation of faith-based terrorists, ready and willing to wage a life and death struggle for the global soul."[26]

Making war on terrorism also validates something even more fundamental—the terrorist conviction that violence is ultimately a *redemptive* medium. Religious warriors believe in the saving efficacy of righteous violence. But so too, apparently, does their main opponent.[27] When President Bush initially referred to the attack on Afghanistan as a "crusade," he was saying more than he realized.[28] The term was quickly abandoned because of its sensitivity to Muslims. But changing the label does not change the product. The war on terrorism retains many of the

---

25. See Utley, "Thirty-Six Ways."

26. McTernan, *In God's Name*, 155. As Lederach observes, "Military action to destroy terror ... will be like hitting a fully mature dandelion with a golf club. We will participate in making sure the myth of why we are evil is sustained and we will assure yet another generation of recruits" ("Challenge of Terror").

27. On the universal appeal of the myth of redemptive violence, see Wink, *Powers That Be*, especially 42–62. Wink calls the myth "the simplest, laziest, most exciting, uncomplicated, irrational, and primitive depiction of evil the world has ever known" (55), and deems it to be "the dominant religion in our society today" (42). See also the telling analysis by Jewett and Lawrence, *Captain America*, 245–72 and passim.

28. In a speech given on September 16, 2001, Bush said, "This is a new kind of thing—a new kind of evil—and we understand. And the American people are beginning to understand. This crusade, this war on terrorism, is going to take a while." Bush used the term again in a speech given in Alaska in mid-February 2002. See the insightful discussion by Suskind, "Without a Doubt."

hallmarks of a crusade—which is the Christian word for "jihad" or holy war.

The campaign is strongly dualistic, with an overt demonizing of the opponent;[29] it sees total annihilation of the enemy as the only way to lasting peace;[30] it refuses any thought of compromise or negotiation with evildoers;[31] it expresses suspicion towards those who inquire into the causes of terrorism or who call for moderation;[32] it claims to be fulfilling a sacred duty;[33] it is bolstered by claims of moral purity and certainty;[34] and, most revealing of all, it favors pre-emption over preven-

29. See C. D. Marshall, "But Deliver Us," 6–7. Bush has frequently called Osama bin Laden "the evil one," which a conservative Christian constituency clearly identifies with Satan. See Achcar, "Clash," available online from http://www.monthlyreview.org/0902achcar.htm.

30. In an insightful discussion, Jewett and Lawrence suggest that the crusading ideal of redemptive violence, which has imparted a unique mystique to American wars, leads to a tendency to use unrestrained violence to obliterate the evil foe. If violence is universally redemptive, then why not use it universally against the enemy, including women and children, *Captain America*, 250–51.

31. For a helpful discussion of evil from a conflict-resolution perspective, see Cloke, "Mediating Evil," www.mediate.com/articles/cloke4.cfm.

32. Richard Perle, a Bush advisor, has argued that we must "decontextualize terror," which means refusing to ask about the context in which it emerges. "Any attempt to discuss the roots of terrorism is an attempt to justify it . . . It simply needs to be fought and destroyed." Johann Hari rightly dismisses this as absurd, something that "invites us all to participate in a strange, wilful ignorance of cause and effect. How can this be a serious response to our problems?" Hari, "Jihadism," argues that "Islamo-fascism" or "jihadism" is a better term for the current problem than "terrorism."

33. An analogy can be drawn between the way terrorists co-opt religion to justify violence and the way that state does. Wink observes that in the myth of redemptive violence, the welfare of the nation becomes the supreme good. People are expendable; the state is not. "Not only does this myth establish a patriotic religion at the heart of the state, it gives divine sanction to that nation's imperialism. The myth of redemptive violence thus serves as the spirituality of militarism. By divine right the state has the power to demand that its citizens sacrifice their lives to maintain the privileges enjoyed by the few. By divine decree it utilizes violence to cleanse the world of enemies of the state. Wealth and prosperity are the right of those who rule in such a state. And the name of God—any god, the Christian God included—can be invoked as having specially blessed and favored the supremacy of the chosen nation and its ruling caste." Wink, *Powers That Be*, 56–57.

34. In his perceptive account of George Bush's evangelical faith, Joe Klein suggests that the real problem with it is not dogmatism but its easy certitude. His faith "does not discomfort him enough; it does not impel him to have second thoughts, to explore other intellectual possibilities or question the consequences of his actions." Accordingly, his faith "offers no speed bumps on the road to Baghdad; it does not give

tion or deterrence. In the judgment of ethicist Edward Leroy Long, the Bush Administration's adoption of the doctrine of pre-emptive strike "clearly illustrates how deeply the model of crusade has taken over as the controlling paradigm since the attacks on the World Trade Center and the Pentagon."[35] Holy war, it appears, has elicited holy war, a holy war fought on behalf of American civil religion.[36]

Yet imitation is the greatest compliment that can be paid to terrorism. Not only do both parties compete to instill the greater fear and exact the higher price, but both insist that purity of motive justifies immense cruelty of action. Both conceive of the problem as a battle to be won rather than an injustice to be resolved. But if terror is to be reduced, rather than ratcheted up ever higher, the issue must be conceptualized in different terms. How we speak of a problem is surprisingly important, for it determines how we conceive of solutions. Lee Griffith bemoans,

> the growing American incapacity to address any problem without resorting to war. This is more than a matter of semantics. Behind the linguistic style that speaks of a war on crime, a war on poverty, a war on drugs, and a war on terrorism lies a style of being and acting. The enemies must be identified, not merely as abstract social problems to be solved, but as real flesh-and-blood enemies to be vilified (which is why the "war on poverty"

---

him pause or force him to reflect. It is a source of comfort and strength but not of wisdom." See "Glare," 14. A similar conclusion is reached by Suskind, who describes Bush as "one of history's great confidence men . . . in the sense that he's a believer in the power of confidence," "Without a Doubt." On the influence of the Christian right on United States' unilateralism, see Oldfield, "Evangelical Roots." For an evangelical critique of Bush's theology of war, see "Evangelicals Slam Bush," http://www.ekklesia.co.uk/content/news_syndication/article_041012bsh.shtml.

35. Long, *Facing Terrorism*, 90 (see further 44-50, 85-86). In point of fact, the American tendency to turn wars into holy crusades has been present since the beginning of the nation, while crusading idealism has been dominant in American civil religion over the past 60 years, as Jewett and Lawrence document, *Captain America*. In an interview, Tony Blair defended the pre-emptive strike on Iraq, saying: "What changed for me is, post September 11, you no longer wait for the thing to happen. You go out actively and try to stop it. That's the thing that has changed now." Rawnsley and Hinsliff, "Blair."

36. The contagiousness of the war on terrorism is also worth noting. Stassen points out that "as the United States declared its military war against terrorism, Indonesia canceled peace talks with the rebels in Aceh and instead made war against them; Israel increased its military attacks against Palestinian leaders; and Russia pursued its destructive war against Chechnya free of US government criticism" (Stassen, "Just Peacemaking").

so quickly turned into a war on the poor). The enemies must be defeated rather than being transformed, much less loved (which is why there is profligate spending for prisons and executions but scant resources for drug treatment). When there is a problem, America goes to war because the world is viewed as ripe for conquest rather than ripe for redemption.[37]

Instead of conceptualizing the issue in terms of fighting a war, it is more helpful to think of it in criminal justice terms, or within a law enforcement framework.[38] Global terrorism, notwithstanding its ideological agenda, may be classified as a type of organized criminal activity in which the whole global community has a stake. Attempts to track down its perpetrators should therefore take the form of international police action, with intelligence gathering serving as the equivalent of sound detective work.

This is not merely tinkering with words. Police action differs from military action in terms of its normative character. Police work is subject to judicial restraint; it is guided by the requirements of procedural fairness; it has strictly limited aims (visually, to control wrongdoing, not to kill all wrongdoers; it does not exercise judgment or administer punishment; its coercive power is applied to the offending party alone; and it is expected to employ minimal force in performing its duties. It is also usually successful in achieving its purpose, and is compatible with longer term restorative objectives. In all these ways, policing differs from soldiering. Police action against terror cells could still employ military personnel. But their methods and goals need to conform to the normative character of police work, rather than the normal practices of war making.[39]

---

37. Griffith, *War on Terrorism*, 76; Stern, *Terror in the Name of God*, 238.

38. Writing only a week after September 11, Cuzzo offers an excellent commentary on what should be done from a restorative perspective in her "Code of the Peaceful Warrior."

39. Gerald Schlabach rightly observes that "the just war theory has gained much of its credibility by imagining war to be like police action without facing up to how different the dynamics of warfare can be from policing. But if war is justified through an appeal to the virtually irrefutable need for policing, it consistently becomes something quite different from policing, and just war reasoning itself all too often devolves into propaganda. It becomes permissive rather than stringent—and it sometimes becomes permissive precisely through the reassuring guise of having been stringent" ("Just Policing," 6).

Even so, as the analogy of domestic justice shows, police action by itself is never sufficient to significantly reduce crime. Efforts at prosecution must be matched by efforts at prevention. The same is true of terrorism. The long-term task of prevention is ultimately more important than the immediate goal of containment.

The Task of Prevention

Religious terrorism is often likened to a deadly virus that spreads contagiously in deprived, oppressed, and traumatized communities where traditional forms of religious adherence are high. This being the case, the most promising remedy is one that boosts the collective immune system so that it does not succumb to the infection.[40] This requires treating the environmental risk factors that predispose communities to violence, such as poverty, joblessness, human rights abuses, indebtedness, ready access to weapons, state failure, political or military repression, and other perceived injustices and humiliations, many of which stem from United States foreign and economic policy.[41]

In this connection, advocates of the new paradigm of "just peacemaking"[42] have several specific proposals to make for helping to prevent or reduce terrorism, such as working to advance human rights, democracy and religious liberty; developing the institutions of civil society; promoting co-operative methods of conflict resolution; strength-

---

40. I am indebted to Lederach, "Challenge," for this analogy.

41. See, for example, Achcar, "The Clash of Barbarisms." Achcar notes, for example, that the "sanctions of mass destruction" used against Iraq caused more deaths than have all the casualties from use of weapons of mass destruction combined (estimated at four hundred thousand). The US has bombed more than two dozen countries since the end of World War II and has been involved in direct or indirect support for revolts, coups, and invasions in more than seventy different nations (so Griffith, *War on Terrorism*, 90–91).

42. Just peacemaking is a new, third, paradigm for considering the ethics of war and peace, alongside pacifism and just war theory. It addresses not the "permission" question ("Is it morally permissible to make war in this situation?") but the "prevention" question ("What strategies should be used to prevent war?"). It identifies 10 principles that are normative for adherents of both just war and pacifist streams. It is not a narrowly Christian paradigm, although one of its architects, Glen Stassen, in "Peacemaking Theory," shows how it coheres with the teaching of Jesus in the Sermon on the Mount. For a large-scale treatment of Jesus's teaching from this perspective, see Stassen and Gushee, *Kingdom Ethics*. More fully on just peacemaking, see Stassen, *Just Peacemaking*.

ening the rule of law; identifying common security interests between adversaries; and, perhaps most crucially of all, making concerted efforts to resolve the Palestinian-Israeli conflict.[43]

Yet religious terrorism is more than a simple response to poverty and oppression; it is also a way of acting out a violent theological worldview that claims absolute divine sanction. This means that prevention must also involve conscious attempts to counter theologies of sacred violence and to forge theologies of peacemaking and toleration in their place.[44] Such theological work must be undertaken within (and between) every religious tradition. Fresh thought must also be given to how religion can inform and shape public life in a non-coercive, life-affirming way. Western modernity has sought to banish religion from the public square and to ground civil society on secularist assumptions. Religious terrorism is a violent protest at this model of marginalization, and especially at its global export. While terrorist ideologues strive for a totalitarian theocracy, what the majority of their co-religionists want is a religious civil society, one in which religion continues to provide a moral and spiritual beacon for collective life but which does not impose its will by force and which respects basic human rights.[45] Nurturing such a form of civil society is a critical factor in combating religious militancy.[46]

---

43. On the critical importance of this issue in terrorism, see New, *Holy War*.

44. One powerful example of this process working is the case of Hamoud al-Hitar and four other Islamic scholars in Yemen who challenged five al Qaeda members in prison to a theological contest over whether terrorist violence could be justified by the Koran. The agreement was that if the prisoners could convince the scholars of their case, they would join their campaign. Conversely if the scholars won the debate, the prisoners would agree to renounce violence. The results of this unconventional counter-terrorism methodology have been spectacular, with a dramatic decline in terror attacks in the country over recent years. See further Brandon, "Koranic Duels."

45. Etzioni, "Religious Civil Society." See also the important piece by Michael Hirsch, "Misreading Islam." Hirsch cites a poll in Iraq in May 2004 that showed that 58 percent of Iraqis want their religious communities to have a "great deal of influence" in selecting members of a new election commission. Hirsch contests the current Washington orthodoxy that secular-style democracy in the Arab world is the answer to terrorism, a view that he traces to the work of historian Bernard Lewis (who first coined the phrase "clash of civilizations"). Hirsch points out that the US invasion of Iraq effectively toppled a secular state and heightened the appeal and influence of Islamic radicalism. Progress in the Arab world will come, Hirsch insists, not by secularizing it from above but by rediscovering a more tolerant form of Islam, which actually predates modern radicalism. This may be a long, long time in coming, and the West may need to allow Arab states to experience the failures of fundamentalism first.

46. On this see Juergensmeyer, *Terror in the Mind*, 242–49. Selengut, *Sacred Fury*,

Prevention and prosecution, therefore, belong inseparably together in the campaign to reduce terrorist violence. But a third kind of response is also needed, one that seeks to meet the therapeutic needs of individuals and communities whose lives have been blighted by deeds of terror and counter-terror. Every bomb that explodes leaves victims battered and bereaved in its wake, and every perpetrator of violence who callously extinguishes human life is left morally and spiritually diminished by such actions, and more able to do it again. The wall of hostility between embittered communities also grows higher as mutual recriminations go unanswered and stereotypes get blacker. These human realities need attention if strategies of prevention and containment are to be successful.

The Therapeutic Task: Can Restorative Justice Help?

There is a temptation for those who believe in the power of restorative justice to view it as a panacea for the world's ills and constantly seek new frontiers where its magic can be applied. But caution is advisable. Experience teaches that even in the most promising of circumstances, restorative methods do not always achieve restorative outcomes. Practice does not always validate theory. If this is true in relatively straightforward cases of interpersonal offending, how much will it be true in situations of such enormous complexity as religious terrorism? Indeed, at first sight, the characteristic features of religious terrorism seem so antithetical to restorative-justice values, processes, and principles that it is hard to imagine any convergence between the two whatsoever.

Take *values* to begin with. According to restorative-justice philosophy, "justice processes may be considered restorative only inasmuch as they give expression to key restorative values, such as respect, honesty, humility, mutual care, accountability, and trust."[47] But many of these values are alien to the psychology of religious killers. They do not respect their victims. On the contrary, they explicitly repudiate the equal dignity of their opponents, whom they view as ontologically and spiritually inferior beings. They do not accept any duty of care towards them, or the existence of any communal bonds that unite them. To admit to

---

236, 135. For a very different solution that depends on global acceptance of a non-realist God and an earth-centered spirituality, see Geering, *World to Come*, especially 109–21, 135–49.

47. Bowen, Boyack, and Marshall, "Restorative Justice," 265–76.

social kinship with their foes would be to repudiate their entire dualistic worldview.

Again, restorative justice values restoration over retribution. Religious killers however extol vengeance as a moral duty. "Islam says an eye for an eye," claims Abu Shanab, a Hamas leader. "We believe in retaliation."[48] Yitzhak Ginzburg, a militant Jewish rabbi, describes revenge as a purifying experience, something that accords with the essence of one's being. "It is like a law of nature," he says. "He who takes revenge joins the 'ecological currents of reality' . . . Revenge is the return of the individual and the nation to believe in themselves, in their power and in the fact that they have a place under the sun and are no longer stepped on by everybody."[49] A former Mossad official expresses the same sentiment even more memorably: "An eye for an eye gives you nothing. You have to go after the head!"[50]

Yet again, restorative justice values the opponent's right to life and rejects the death penalty. But dealing out death is the stock in trade of terrorism. A document captured in Afghanistan in 2002 included a written oath by an al Qaeda operative that states: "I Abdul Maawia Siddiqi, son of Abdul Rahmen Siddiqi, state in the presence of God that I will slaughter infidels all the days of my life."[51] Clearly, then, a vast gulf separates the values of restorative justice and the values of religious terrorism.

A similar incongruity exists with respect to *process*. Restorative justice is a dialogical process where people come together to share their thoughts and feelings. Genuine dialogue can only happen when there is a willingness to shift ground and to compromise. But religious violence represents a radical rejection of dialogue and compromise. The tactic of suicide bombing in particular is proof that establishing dialogue is not the aim of religious terrorists. Yet without a preparedness to dialogue—without give and take, without a willingness to accept differences, without some degree of humility—restorative-justice processes simply cannot work.

Similar problems exist over *practice*. The primary participants in restorative-justice conferences occupy the roles of victim and offender, and the main goal is to identify the needs of the victim and hold the

---

48. Cited in Stern, *Terror in the Name of God*, 40.
49. Cited in ibid., 91.
50. This is the comment of Rafi Eitan, quoted in Laura Blumenfeld, *Revenge*, 219.
51. Cited in Selengut, *Sacred Fury*, 43.

offender accountable for taking steps to meet them. If an offender denies responsibility for the harm inflicted, or refuses to see it as morally wrong, restorative-justice conferences cannot proceed. But a distinctive attribute of religious killers is a refusal to see themselves as culpable offenders. They are not murderers; they are soldiers fighting in a just cause, defending the rights of their own victimized communities against the assaults of an inhuman enemy. As one former Irish paramilitary puts it: "Within every terrorist is the conviction that he is a victim."[52] One of the Chechen fighters at Beslan reportedly told one of the hostages: "Russian soldiers are killing our children in Chechnya, so we are here to kill yours."[53] It is difficult to see how roles could be assigned at a meeting between the perpetrators and recipients of terror when only "victims" are available!

So initial indications are not encouraging. The attitudes and beliefs that induce people to take up terror are precisely the attitudes and beliefs that make restorative encounters difficult to achieve, such as self-righteousness, disavowal of guilt, refusal of dialogue, unwillingness to compromise, and lack of respect for the dignity of the other. The victims of terror, as well, frequently exhibit a parallel set of attitudes and emotions. They view the perpetrators of terror as unnatural monsters bereft of all human feeling and value, incapable of remorse and deserving only of extermination. Political pronouncements constantly reinforce this judgment, stereotyping terrorists as irremediably evil and ruling out any kind of dialogue with them or their supporters as a form of appeasement.[54] Just prior to an American assault on Fallujah in late 2004, US Colonel Gareth Brandl told his troops, "The enemy has got a face. He's called Satan. He's in Fallujah and we're going to destroy him."[55]

For all these reasons, then, religious terrorism is an extraordinarily difficult environment for collaborative, dialogical mechanisms to operate

---

52. Cited in Juergensmeyer, *Terror in the Mind*, 170; cf. McTernan, *In God's Name*, 84.

53. Alibhai-Brown, "Sons of Islam."

54. Dr. Garret Fitzgerald, former Irish Prime Minister, reflecting on the experience of dealing with the IRA, insists that negotiations with terrorists should only occur when they want a final settlement of the conflict. But they should not be treated in any way that further alienates people who share their grievances. British negotiation with the IRA in 1970s made matters worse because it made the IRA believe that by murdering more people they would get more concessions. A better approach is to negotiate with moderates, and thus try to separate extremists from their wider base of support. See McCurdy, "Lessons from Violence."

55. Fisk, "Showdown at Fallujah."

in. Is the situation therefore hopeless? Is restorative justice dead in the water as a viable response to terrorism? Not necessarily. With due modesty, with stubborn faith in the capacity of the human spirit, and with flexibility of practice, restorative justice *does* have something special to offer.

Modesty

This is needed because restorative justice cannot do it all by itself. It is not a cure-all. It is not some miraculous formula that will cause people long indoctrinated in hatred to fall into each other's arms like long lost relatives. It can ever be only one small, fallible tool among many needed to redress terrorism. Yet one of the great virtues of restorative justice is that it is a community-centered process. Most discussions of counter-terrorism focus almost exclusively on what governments, armies, and political institutions must do. But non-governmental organizations and informal community groups also have a vital role to play.

Terror groups themselves are kinds of community association gone bad, whose members are bound together by extremely strong relational bonds. These groups are so attractive to young men because they offer a sense of identity, power and self-respect to those who feel disempowered by their circumstances and disconnected from others. Restorative justice offers an alternative, nonviolent form of community empowerment that can help promote reconciliation between mutually hostile communities.

Peter Shirlow of the University of Ulster has said that "one of the main problems facing Northern Ireland is that everyone sees him or herself as a victim of the other side and is unable to recognize that self as a perpetrator of violence and intimidation."[56] The challenge, he believes, is to help people on both sides to see that they are *both* victims *and* perpetrators in the current conflict. Restorative justice as a community-based mechanism is perfectly placed to assist this to happen. Typically, in restorative-justice meetings, the roles of victim and offender are discrete. One party has suffered unjustly at the hands of the other, and the duty of repair runs only one way. But sometimes the roles are not so neatly distinguished. Sometimes both parties have injured each other; both are victims and both are offenders. In these cases, it is helpful for both parties to have the chance to speak as victims, and for both to accept their

---

56. Cited in McTernan, *In God's Name*, 84.

role as offenders. This allows for the victimized status of each side to be validated and for the duty of repair to run both ways.

Such an approach has real potential in settings where rival communities are victims of mutual terror attacks. Even if individual perpetrators and their victims cannot or will not meet, the communities to which both belong, and which usually harbor bitter antagonism towards each other, can do so in their stead. If members of mutually hostile communities can meet to express the bitterness of victimization they have personally experienced, and to accept some measure of collective responsibility for deeds of violence done on their behalf, the groundwork for peace has been laid. And peaceful co-existence is *always* possible between human beings.

Faith in Shared Humanity

Among other things, religious terrorism is a sign that we live in a world where people's controlling belief systems differ radically from one another. Some commentators have sourced modern terrorism in a putative "clash of civilizations" that has ensued in the trail of globalization, and expressed pessimism about the capacity for peaceful co-existence, especially between fundamentalist Islam and the West.[57]

Without denying there are civilizational factors involved,[58] a restorative-justice response to terror rests on a fundamental faith in our common humanity. It makes the bold assumption that, whatever divides us, people are always capable of living together peacefully, that there is no difference that cannot be resolved peacefully with dialogue. It rejects the view widespread today that there are some people so evil that annihilation is the only option for dealing with them.

Ultimately this confidence in shared humanity is a matter of faith or belief (just as trust in the saving power of violence is also a matter of belief). But it is not blind faith. There *are* examples of terrorists changing. One Christian extremist in America abandoned his plans to blow up an abortion clinic when he was unexpectedly overcome with an awareness of the humanity of his potential victims, one of whom reminded him of his grandmother. A Kashmiri militant gave up his violent path after becoming aware of how crippling hatred is. "To hate is venom," he explains.

---

57. For a discussion and critique of Huntington's well known thesis, see McTernan, *In God's Name*, 1–10. See also the valuable observations by Hirsch, "Misreading Islam."

58. See Selengut, *Sacred Fury*, 141–81.

"When you hate, you poison yourself . . . Hate begets hate. You cannot create freedom out of hatred."[59]

Even more telling is the example of Patrick Magee, the so-called "Brighton bomber," who killed five people and injured thirty in a failed attempt in 1984 to annihilate the British cabinet staying at the Grand Hotel in Brighton. In sentencing Magee, the judge described him as "a man of exceptional cruelty and inhumanity," and to this day Magee stands by his actions as a justifiable act of war. But, now out of prison, Magee has become a strong supporter of the peace process.

What precipitated this change was a series of meetings he had with Jo Tuffnell, the daughter of one of his murder victims. The meetings began after Tuffnell was overcome by "an incredible feeling" as she prayed in a church one day "for the strength to understand those who had done this and not to stay a victim." She arranged to meet Magee, who says of their first meeting:

> "I had an overwhelming urge to talk to Jo alone. It felt like the presence of anyone else was intrusive and would stop me opening up and being as frank as I needed." He added however, "I wasn't prepared, and I felt totally inadequate with someone sitting there with all that pain, telling it to me, while at the same time trying to understand me. There was certainly guilt there, that I'd caused this woman's father's death. But that feeling only came to the forefront when we were coming out of the [IRA] struggle, because during the struggle there wasn't time and you couldn't have engaged in it if you'd had that mind."

Jo Tuffnell said of that meeting:

> "Only Pat could understand how I felt—he was the only person who actually wanted to hear how I felt. When we first met, he said, 'I want to hear your anger and feel your pain.' No one else had ever said that to me." She added: "I'm no longer scared of my darkest feelings, because I know however negative and awful they are, I can transform them into a passion for change."

This remarkable story is not unique. Similar initiatives have been taken by other republican and loyalist ex-prisoners, and dozens of victims' groups have been formed, some of which have sought meetings with former terrorist perpetrators.[60]

---

59. Syed, quoted in Stern, *Terror in the Name of God*, 137.
60. McKittrick, "Brighton Bomber."

Flexibility of Practice

The moving story of Patrick Magee and Jo Tufnell is also significant from a practice perspective. The meetings between the two appear to have been unfacilitated, were spread over several years, and entailed "long and searching conversations dissecting their roles as victim and perpetrator." Most standard restorative-justice conferences, by comparison, are facilitated by a neutral party, take a couple of hours at most to complete, and do not permit disputes about roles.

In the Magee case, a preparedness to hear the victim's pain was evidently more important to the victim than the offender's full acceptance of culpability. Magee concedes that his unwillingness to call his actions wrong was hard for Tufnell to hear, and it has been "an impediment" in their relationship. But that did not preclude them continuing to meet for dialogue. This underscores how pliable and open-ended practice needs to be to accommodate the exigencies of particular situations. No one model of practice is sacrosanct, as long as restorative values and principles remain operative.

Of course, given the complexities surrounding religious violence and the degree of trauma involved, it stands to reason that any restorative intervention needs to be skillfully managed and thoroughly prepared. Victims in particular would need careful preparation. They must be at an appropriate stage in their recovery process before venturing to meet those responsible for their suffering. As conflict specialist Vernon Redekop explains, "It is difficult, if not impossible, to start a process of reconciliation when the pain of violence is visceral, recent and overwhelming. When people are traumatized through the loss of loved ones, through having observed many deaths, or having been terrified to the core of their beings, they are not ready to start a discourse or any process that involves their relationship with an enemy."[61] Professional counselling and other forms of therapy may be required before any restorative-justice meeting occurs, and peer support throughout the process would be critical.

Perpetrators also need preparation. The minimal requirement is a willingness to listen and an agreement to speak truthfully about their own motivations and actions. Skillful management of their encounter is imperative. Because both sides will be hyper-sensitive to threatening signals from the other and will amplify the smallest hint of antagonism into a full blown physiological "fight or flight" reaction, extraordinary effort

---

61. Redekop, *From Violence to Blessing*, 290.

must be taken to provide a safe place and safe process. This could include, as in the Magee case, a readiness to meet many times over an extended period. Given that terrorists commonly view themselves as victims rather than victimizers, it would be important that some of these meetings focus the perpetrator's own prior experience of suffering and betrayal. This is not to excuse their later crimes. On the contrary, it is only when an offender's pain is acknowledged that their last refuge from responsibility is removed. If it is flatly denied, they will continue to feel justified in their actions.

In October 2004, an Australian journalist, John Martinkus, was kidnapped by Sunni militants in Iraq. He was interrogated throughout the night, while a large-screen TV tuned into al-Jazeera television played in the background. The mood of his interrogators darkened every time stories of fighting in Iraq appeared. Martinkus spent much of the night contemplating the possibility of execution in the morning. He had seen the videotaped beheadings of other hostages, which he describes as "sickening." He knew the "old trick of humanizing yourself to your captors" and showed some of them a photograph of his girlfriend that he carried in his wallet. One of his captors reciprocated, pulling out a picture of his three-year-old daughter in Fallujah. "I held it and said 'she looks beautiful.' He replied, 'she is dead now in an American air strike' and his face became hard. My effort had backfired."[62] Such is the kind of anguish hidden driving much terrorist brutality. It does not justify their brutality, but it cannot be ignored in any attempt to bring change.

One further lesson from the Magee story is that while violent terrorists may initially lack the values and attitudes essential for involvement in restorative processes, the very act of meeting with their victims has the potential, over time, to evoke them. It is easy to vilify and dehumanize enemies in the abstract; it is much harder to do it to those whose individual identity one has now come face-to-face with. It is easy to rationalize one's violence at a distance; it is much harder to do so when one hears of its impact on actual human bodies and beings.[63] Perhaps the most powerful contribution restorative justice can make is in the re-humanization of the parties. Demons are expelled when human beings meet together in a

---

62. Martinkus, "Hostage."

63. This is one of the lessons of the various truth-and-reconciliation commissions that have been formed. See the excellent analysis by Spencer Zifcak, "Restorative Justice." See also C. D. Marshall, *Beyond Retribution*, 280–84; Wilson, *Politics of Truth*; Kerber, "Overcoming Violence," 151–57; Steinmann, "Spiritual Elements."

state of common weakness to confront the truth about one another and about themselves.

Face-to-face encounters are, of course, the ideal way for this to happen. But given the extraordinary security concerns surrounding detained terrorists, such meetings may be difficult, sometimes impossible, to arrange. Here again flexibility of practice is important; other ways may exist to promote restorative outcomes. In her gripping book, *Revenge: A Story of Hope*, Laura Blumenfeld tells of how she tracked down the individual responsible for the attempted assassination of her father David, a Jewish American tourist, in Jerusalem in 1986, who was the target of a random political shooting by a Palestinian terror group. Her father survived the attack and had no particular desire for retribution. But Laura was consumed with feelings of revenge, and developed an overwhelming desire to understand this most primal and universal of emotions. She set about to "master revenge," to break it down and to study it.[64] She also developed an urge to meet the man responsible for the shooting. "Confronting him was inevitable," she writes. "Not with an act of violence—the revenge I wanted was of a different kind, one that responded to the heart of the crime . . . I wanted him to realize he was wrong."[65]

When she eventually located the assassin, a young man called Omar al Khatib, he was halfway through serving a twenty-five-year prison term for the crime. Posing as a journalist researching a book, Laura contacted the gunman's family, visiting them in their home frequently over the space of a year without ever disclosing her relationship to Omar's victim. Strong bonds of friendship developed between them, despite the fact that the family often expressed admiration for Omar's heroic and honorable deed. Using his brother to smuggle letters in and out of prison, Laura also began corresponding with Omar himself, again without ever letting on that she was his target's daughter. She probed him about how he felt about his actions, both at the time of the shooting and subsequently, what he would want to say to his victim if he ever had the opportunity to meet him, and whether he regretted what he had done.

Through the course of their correspondence both parties were changed. Laura came to recognize how important it was for her that Omar acknowledged his sorrow for shooting an innocent man, and that he came to understand that "this conflict is between human beings, and

---

64. Blumenfeld, *Revenge*, 17.
65. Ibid., 18.

not disembodied Arabs and Jews. And we're people, not 'military targets.' We're people with families. And you can't just kill us."[66] More profoundly, she came to understand that the revenge she craved was not for retaliation—an eye for an eye—but for transformation. "Revenge does not have to be about destroying your enemy; it can mean transforming him, or yourself."[67] Omar was also affected by the correspondence. He later wrote to his victim, David Blumenfeld, that through her letters and actions Laura had been "the mirror that made me see your face as a human person to be admired and respected."[68]

After a year of writing, Laura and Omar did eventually meet in person, not in a restorative justice conference but at a court hearing where Omar was applying for early parole on health grounds. Laura seized the opportunity to address the bench of judges, declaring for the first time that she was the daughter of the man who had been shot, a confession that stunned Omar and his family. Laura argued passionately, though unsuccessfully, for Omar's early release on the grounds that he was truly sorry for his crime and that he had promised never again to harm anyone in pursuit of his political beliefs. Laura's mother even leapt to her feet saying that the Blumenfeld family had forgiven Omar, and so now should the state of Israel!

Throughout the period of his written exchanges with Laura, Omar repeatedly insisted that his shooting of the innocent American tourist was "not personal"; it was a justifiable act in the struggle for freedom for his people. It was clear that Omar, like most violent activists, saw the world in terms of collective rather than individual identities. But at one point in his correspondence, he indicated to Laura that he was coming to respect what he called the "holiness" of other people's lives and the need for people to live in peace. "People are so different when you get to know them from near," he once observed.[69] This, of course, is precisely what restorative justice seeks to achieve by bringing hostile parties into face-to-face contact. But Omar's experience shows that even where such direct encounters are not possible, sustained personal contact by letter or through intermediaries can sometimes have the same effect, or at very

66. Ibid., 344.
67. Ibid., 348.
68. Ibid.
69. Ibid., 280.

least can play a powerful role in preparing the ground for direct interaction at some future point.

CONCLUSION

Again it needs to be emphasized that restorative-justice meetings between the victims and perpetrators of terror cannot, on their own, redress all the harmful effects of terrorism. Without ongoing work at structural transformation and peacebuilding, restorative encounters, however powerful in themselves, are inadequate to bring lasting peace. But even if it is only one tool in the box, restorative justice still has a contribution to make. It can help those caught up in terrorist atrocities to address the inner realities bequeathed by the outer reality of violent acts—the profound emotional pain, the ongoing effects of traumatization, and the deep-seated feelings of hatred, anger and revenge.[70] It may also help those who have inflicted terror to begin to rethink their own identities, to break free from the structures of violence that hitherto have dictated their worldview, and to learn to see reality differently, a world that is populated by the human children of God, not stalked by demons in disguise.

It is important not to shrink back from the challenge at this point in history. In a world racked with anxiety over security, in a world where we are daily commanded to "be afraid, be very afraid," in a world where inflicting terror is commended as the only way to end terror, in a world of demonization and counter-demonization, restorative justice is a still, small voice of protest. As trivial as it may seem, terror is renounced not just in the refusal to endorse war, but in every act of human kindness and decency. Promoting peaceful modes of human engagement is the greatest antidote there is to religiously inspired violence, and restorative justice is all about peaceful forms of human engagement. "Blessed are the peacemakers," Jesus said, "for they shall be called the children of God."

---

70. On the trauma associated with suffering terror attacks, see Office for Victims, *Handbook for Coping after Terrorism*, and Nath, "Consider the Lilies."

Afterword

Thomas Noakes-Duncan

THIS BOOK HAS BEEN published for two reasons. First, to bring together a collection of essays that have previously appeared in various other publications to make them more generally available to readers. If Chris were asked, this is the reason he would give for the volume. There is, however, a second reason, which better explains my interest in the project. The selection of essays included here covers the teaching career of someone who has done more than most people to promote what I will call a "restorative theology." I will explain what this description means shortly. For now, tribute must be given to my teacher and friend, Chris Marshall.

My first memory of Chris was at a gathering of intentional Christian communities exploring what it means to live in light of God's peaceable kingdom. Having just recently moved to the Wellington area, Chris probably felt the need to say a little about what motivated his life work. He told a story about one of his two sons who at a young age had been physically assaulted in the street in a random attack. The incident had had a significant impact on his son, affecting both his sense of meaning and security, and his relationships to those around him. As Chris shared this story, I remember sensing some of the anguish that as a father he had over his young son. It was no surprise to me that some years later Chris would begin to work closely on the text of the Parable of the Prodigal Son.

I mention this early memory because it highlights something important about Chris's character and vision, but also something crucial that he has brought to the task of biblical interpretation. Chris is a deeply attentive person, with a capacity to listen and empathize in a way that shows a genuine concern for the plight of others. While this kind of attunement to others might be expected of a father towards his own son, Chris has not limited himself in this way. For him, the posture of empathetic listening is a way of being in the world, undergirding all relationships. It is also a source of understanding.

Having spent his life working in the fields of New Testament ethics, biblical interpretation, and restorative justice, Chris has learned there is a profound moral logic to our emotions. From his biblical exposition on the themes of love, compassion, lament, shame, and many more besides, he has furnished a language that helps make sense of our fragmented lives. I have personally been upheld by Chris's often perceptive judgments, such as when he counseled me over the meaning of love as I was finding out what it meant to be a father of two sons on the autistic spectrum.

Fundamental to Chris's vision is the understanding that humans are not autonomous beings who merely brush up against each other in life; instead they are beings in relationship. The attention Chris pays to relationships, both in his own life and in his scholarly work, flows from his understanding of our created existence as relational beings. He has dedicated his life to fostering the habits that make space for friendship, mutual learning, and solidarity in suffering and joy. From my first encounter with Chris, he has always been generous in extending hospitality through conversation and in welcoming people into his life. If the Christian life is one of bearing each other's burdens, then I am grateful that God has given us people like Chris as an example of what this looks like.

My gratitude for Chris stems also from sharing many convictions in common, which is often the ground on which friendships are based. Theologically, we both feel at home in the Anabaptist tradition, despite living in a country that lacks any ecclesial descendants of this tradition. Academically, we live betwixt and between. We are both theologians by training and vocation, yet appointed to teach restorative justice within a secular environment not accustomed to reasoning by faith. But it is perhaps our shared commitment to Jesus as the embodiment of God's peace and justice that has set us on such a similar path, a path that led us both to restorative justice.

It may not be immediately obvious how a concern to see God's peace and justice realized on earth as it is in heaven leads to restorative justice. Some explanation is in order. As mentioned in the Foreword, Chris's first encounter with restorative justice came about through doing peace studies at the Anabaptist Mennonite Biblical Seminary in America. It was around this time that he discovered Howard Zehr's book *Changing Lenses*.[1] While initially interested only in the chapter on covenantal justice, it

---

1. Zehr, *Changing Lenses*.

was not long before Chris caught sight of the broader resonance between the restorative vision and the biblical injunction to seek the justice of God's kingdom. It is worth recalling the opening lines of Zehr's seminal book:

> This book is about principles and ideals. It seeks—perhaps presumptuously—to identify and evaluate some of the basic assumptions we make about crime, about justice, about how we live together. It attempts to outline briefly how we came to have these assumptions and to suggest some alternatives.[2]

From this starting point, Zehr goes on to describe the reality of crime from the perspective of those directly affected by it. He does not shy away from the visceral experience of those who have been harmed, nor does he resort to caricatures when speaking about offenders. An understanding of crime and society's response to it begins with deep personal engagement. It arises from attending personally to the plight of others, extending solidarity and empathy to both victims *and* offenders, and working to heal the relationship between them. This not only demystifies some of our assumptions about crime, including the way victims and offenders are often objectified, it also invites others to participate in the work of healing and recovery from crime.

What is equally fascinating in Zehr's book is the way that he seamlessly interweaves theological reflection with the story of victims and offenders. In his account, one cannot speak about the journeys of having done harm or being harmed without recourse to the biblical story. Whether this is a victim's tortured anger expressed towards God, or an offender's deep sense of shame as he pleads for mercy and hope, God is never far removed from the cries of sinners and sufferers, often coalescing in the same person.

As well as recognizing the reality of God in situations of crime, Zehr's broader interest lay in outlining an alternative paradigm for resolving crime. As a criminal-justice historian, he recounted the history of more community-level approaches to dealing with wrongdoing before their colonization by state-centered notions of justice and law. He showed that wherever the influence of Roman law and retributive justice spread, there was a corresponding diminution of more mediated, reparative, and communal approaches to wrongdoing. Zehr was not primarily calling for a whole-scale return to a community model of criminal justice. Rather,

2. Ibid., 15.

he was seeking to facilitate a conceptual shift in the way we think about and practice justice in the modern context.

The chapter titled "Covenant Justice: The Biblical Alternative" has confused many readers as to what kind of book *Changing Lenses* is.[3] For while it continually references Christian claims about forgiveness, reconciliation, and peace, it does not read like a work of theology. It is likely that readers who profess no religious faith simply skip over this chapter to get back to the argument at hand. Yet to do so is to miss a critical juncture in the trajectory towards the restorative paradigm of justice. The contrast Zehr outlines between the retributive ethos of the current justice system and a restorative understanding of justice draws most fully on his reflection on the nature of *shalom* (peace) and covenant-justice in the Old and New Testaments. The entire thrust of the biblical theme of righteousness or justice, he argues, points not towards the punishment of sinners but rather their restoration through the extension of mercy and compassion. It was this more holistic conception of a "peace-making justice,"[4] oriented toward the restoration of right relationships, that Zehr sought to recover as a resource for the development of an alternative response to crime in the contemporary era.

Writing at the dawn of penal populism, Zehr was aware that selective appeals to the Bible were partly responsible for the concerted move towards a more retributive stance in criminal-justice policy. Yet such a move, he argued, owed much more to Greco-Roman antecedents than to the biblical story of God's justice. The image of a blindfolded goddess waging war on crime in order to re-balance the scales of justice belongs to pagan lore, not the Bible. God's justice is satisfied in the biblical story through Jesus's death and resurrection, whereby sinful humanity is brought into the arena of God's saving justice in order that they might share in the peace of his kingdom.

As this brief foray shows, *Changing Lenses* contains a treasure trove of material for seeing restorative justice as giving expression to God's concern for the healing or righting of relationships. It was this same concern that first led a group of Mennonites in Kitchener, Ontario, to imagine a different way of responding to crime and its effects, resulting in the Victim-Offender-Reconciliation-Project, an early forerunner to the

---

3. Ibid., 126–57.

4. For an explanation of restorative justice as a "peace-making justice," see Cayley, *Expanding Prison*, 11.

restorative-justice movement.⁵ It was also this concern that drives all of Chris's reflections in this book, whether they are concerned with crime in contemporary society or with wrestling with the presence of troubling texts in Scripture.

As mentioned earlier, Chris has done more than most people to further the interplay between restorative themes and the biblical text. What Zehr introduced in one chapter has become for Chris a whole way of doing theology. In some respects, Chris has taken Zehr's general insight that the biblical story provides a fresh way of thinking about crime and justice, and tested it on particular texts of Scripture, thereby offering a more fine-grained exposition of what this fresh perspective means. In so doing, he leaves his readers in no doubt as to the demand that God's Word places on Christians.

To take one example, I mentioned earlier Chris's work on the parable of the Prodigal Son. He shows how the characters in this story throw into sharp relief the difference between a restorative understanding of justice, fulfilled in the reintegration of offenders through the practices of repentance and forgiveness, and a justice that prioritizes the law of just deserts through practices of punishment and exclusion. Yet what is most remarkable about Chris's reading of this story is the role he sees for honor and shame in determining the future of the prodigal. Having covered himself in shame through rupturing his bedrock relationships to family and kin, there is little hope for the son's recovery, especially if he is treated according to his deserts. But the father in the story operates, not according to the logic of just deserts, but according to that "divine form of justice" that is committed to "reinstating penitent offenders to full participation in the life of the community they have spurned and even bestows honor on them for choosing again the path of freedom and life in place of alienation and death."⁶ Chris examines the multiple steps that such bestowal of honor entails and how each act restores dignity, citizenship and belonging to the young man. His exposition leaves no doubt about what is expected of Christians today in response to the challenges faced by offenders reintegrating to civil society, and why such work ultimately depends on the divine workings of a compassionate justice.

By means of his exegetical work, Chris has argued that "the first Christians experience[d] in Christ and lived out in their faith communities an understanding of justice as a power that heals, restores, and

---

5. Peachey, "Kitchener Experiment."
6. C. D. Marshall, *Compassionate Justice*, 217.

reconciles rather than hurts, punishes, and kills, and that reality ought to shape and direct a Christian contribution to the criminal justice debate today."[7] The early Christian communities embodied a restorative understanding of justice—and so should Christian communities today as they seek to participate in the outworking of divine justice in the world, as it is revealed in and enacted by Jesus Christ. Chris has sought to do this by bringing a "restorative justice lens to the task of New Testament interpretation," the fruits of which are evident in this book.[8] Yet this is not the only way he has furthered the restorative vision of justice.

In 2013, Chris was appointed as the inaugural holder of the Diana Unwin Chair in Restorative Justice at Victoria University of Wellington, New Zealand. Stepping from the role of Professor of Religious Studies to Professor of Restorative Justice involved more than a change of job title. In his new role, he has assumed responsibility for stewarding the research, teaching, and professional development of the wider restorative-justice community in New Zealand. This has required him to work across the spectrum of civil society, engaging a variety of political actors and ordinary citizens, all in the hope, as he puts it, of "moving the vision of restorative justice, and all that it promises, from the margins of our consciousness to the mainstream of how we live together in society, in faith, hope and charity."[9]

Chris has brought to this work a level of acuity and approachability that few academics master in equal measure. Whether it is over coffee, in front of public servants, or before a gathering of practitioners or professionals, Chris has tirelessly proclaimed the virtues of the restorative way, coaxing others into sharing his enthusiasm for a more restorative society. Through many joint efforts, the restorative-justice community in New Zealand is now experiencing something of a second wind, as restorative interventions migrate into areas outside of the traditional justice domains of police, courts and prisons.

It is important to recall here the hope expressed in *Changing Lenses* of the broader implications of restorative justice for a new way of living together in society. Restorative justice is not just another program for intervening in situations of crime. At its best, it is meant to inspire the imagination as to what human relationships ought to look like in society and how harms can be addressed in a peacemaking way. This helps to

7. C. D. Marshall, *Beyond Retribution*, 33.
8. C. D. Marshall, *Compassionate Justice*, 3.
9. C. D. Marshall, "Restoring What?," 10.

explain the spread of restorative justice into such diverse areas of practice as workplace mediation, human-rights commissions, educational environments, health care, business regulation and even military disciplinary processes. We are now witnessing the emergence of restorative prisons, restorative schools, and even restorative cities. Fresh winds are blowing through the restorative movement, with efforts to develop restorative processes for dealing with cyber-aggression or elder abuse or campus conflict or medical complaints, being just a few examples of work currently underway in New Zealand.

The rising profile of restorative justice in public consciousness is a reason to rejoice, so long as restorative justice doesn't go the way of other reform efforts in propping up the very systems they were originally intended to subvert. Zehr is particularly wary of the dangers associated with early success and rapid growth. He argues that to resist the pressures of diversion and subversion, restorative justice must be grounded in alternative communities of practice, which incarnate the values of a peacemaking justice in ways that safeguard the restorative vision. For Zehr, the most obvious candidate for this role is the church, the very community that gave birth to the restorative vision of justice.

But Zehr's call to the church has gone largely unheeded. The baton of the restorative-justice movement has been passed on by its founders, but the church has been noticeably absent in the hand-off. While practices like Victim-Offender Conferencing or Circles of Accountability and Support have their origins in Christian experimentation, they are no longer seen to be central to the mission of church. Few contemporary practitioners in the restorative movement would even recognize how much their practice owes to the pioneering efforts of Christians responding to their world from the perspective of faith.

While the church may be a missing partner in the contemporary dance of the restorative-justice movement, it is not without its guides. Through books like this one, churches have a resource for understanding God's call upon them to embody relationships that reflect the healing, peace-making, and restoring form of justice they see modeled in Jesus Christ. It is my hope that more and more members of the Christian community will recognize the contribution of people like Chris Marshall in helping it to imagine what it might mean to be a *restorative church* proclaiming a *restorative gospel* in a world of desperate need.[10]

---

10. My own contributions towards this vision can be found in Noakes-Duncan, *Communities of Restoration*.

Bibliography

Achcar, Gilbert. "The Clash of Barbarisms." *Monthly Review* 54.4 (September 2002). http://dx.doi.org/10.14452/MR-054-04-2002-08_3.
Adler, Warren. "Community of Interpreters: Why Christians Should Pursue Truth Communally in the Local Church." Unpublished research paper, Bible College of New Zealand, 2000.
Alibhai-Brown, Yasmin. "Sons of Islam Bring Shame on Religion." *Independent*, reprinted *New Zealand Herald*, September 8, 2004, A19.
Allison, Dale C., Jr. "Rejecting Violent Judgment: Luke 9:52-56 and Its Relatives." *Journal of Biblical Literature* 121 (2002) 459-78.
Anderson, Paul N. "Genocide or Jesus: A God of Conquest or Pacifism?" In *The Destructive Power of Religion: Violence in Judaism, Christianity, and Islam*, edited by J. Harold Ellens, 4:31-52. Westport, CT: Praeger, 2004.
Armstrong, Karen. "Unholy Strictures." *Guardian Weekly*, August 19-25, 2005, 13.
Augsburger, Myron S. *Principles of Biblical Interpretation in Mennonite Theology*. Scottdale, PA: Herald, 1967.
Aulén, Gustaf. *Christus Victor: An Historical Study of the Three Main Types of the Idea of the Atonement*. Translated by A. G. Hebert. London: SPCK, 1931.
Austin, Greg, Todd Kranock, and Thom Oommen. *God and War: An Audit and an Exploration*. Bradford, UK: Department of Peace Studies, University of Bradford, 2004.
Bainton, Roland H. *Christian Attitudes Toward War and Peace: A Historical Survey and Critical Re-evaluation*. Nashville: Abingdon, 1960.
Barclay, Oliver. "The Theology of Social Ethics: A Survey of Current Positions." *Interchange* 36 (1985) 6-23.
Barclay, Oliver, and Chris Sugden. "Biblical Social Ethics in a Mixed Society." *Evangelical Quarterly* 62 (1990) 5-18.
Barrow, Simon, et al. "Evangelicals Slam Bush for His 'Theology of War.'" October 12, 2004. http://www.ekklesia.co.uk/content/news_syndication/article_041012bsh.shtml.
Baxter, Christina A. "The Cursed Beloved: A Reconsideration of Penal Substitution." In *Atonement Today*, edited by John Goldingay, 54-72. London: SPCK, 1995.
Bellinger, William H., Jr., and William R. Farmer, eds. *Jesus and the Suffering Servant: Isaiah 53 and Christian Origins*. Harrisburg, PA: Trinity Press International, 1998.

Belousek, Darrin W. S. *Atonement, Justice, and Peace: The Message of the Cross and the Mission of the Church*. Grand Rapids: Eerdmans, 2012.

Berger, Peter L., ed. *The Desecularization of the World: Resurgent Religion and World Politics*. Grand Rapids: Eerdmans, 1999.

Birch, Bruce C. "Moral Agency, Community, and the Character of God in the Hebrew Bible." *Semeia* 66 (1995) 23-41.

Birch, Bruce C., and Larry L. Rasmussen. *Bible and Ethics in the Christian Life*. Rev. and expanded ed. Minneapolis: Augsburg, 1989.

Bloesch, Donald G. *Freedom for Obedience: Evangelical Ethics in Contemporary Times*. San Francisco: Harper & Row, 1987.

Blumenfeld, Laura. *Revenge: A Story of Hope*. New York: Washington Square, 2002.

Boersma, Hans. *Violence, Hospitality, and the Cross: Reappropriating the Atonement Tradition*. Grand Rapids: Baker Academic, 2004.

Boston, Jonathan. "Moral Dilemmas and the Problems of Compromise: Two Christian Perspectives." *Stimulus* 1 (1993) 2-12.

———. "Sinning Boldly: Helmut Thielicke's Approach to Ethical Compromise and Borderline Situations." *Crux* 29 (1993) 7-17.

Boulton, David. "Who Needs Religion?" *New Internationalist*, August 2004, 14-15.

Bowen, Helen, Jim Boyack, and Chris Marshall. "How Does Restorative Justice Ensure Good Practice?" In *Critical Issues in Restorative Justice*, edited by Howard Zehr and Barb Toews, 265-76. Monsey, NY: Criminal Justice Press, 2004.

Braithwaite, John. *Crime, Shame, and Reintegration*. Cambridge: Cambridge University Press, 1989.

Brandon, James. "Koranic Duels Ease Terror." *Christian Science Monitor*, February 4, 2005. http://www.csmonitor.com/2005/0204/p01s04-wome.html.

Brinsmead, R. D. "The Scandal of God's Justice [Part 3]." *Christian Verdict* 8 (1983) 3-11.

Broughton, Geoff. *Restorative Christ: Jesus, Justice, and Discipleship*. Eugene, OR: Pickwick, 2014.

Brown, Raymond. *The Death of the Messiah: From Gethsemane to the Grave*. New York: Doubleday, 1994.

Burke, Jason. "Zarqawi: Man Behind the Mask." *New Zealand Herald*, September 17, 2004, B3.

Cahill, Lisa Sowle. *Between the Sexes: Foundations for a Christian Ethics of Sexuality*. Philadelphia: Fortress, 1985.

———. "Christian Character, Biblical Community and Human Values." In *Character and Scripture: Moral Formation, Community, and Biblical Interpretation*, edited by William P. Brown, 3-17. Grand Rapids: Eerdmans, 2002.

———. "The New Testament and Ethics: Communities of Social Change." *Interpretation* 44 (1990) 383-95.

Carroll, John T., and Joel B. Green, eds. *The Death of Jesus in Early Christianity*. Peabody, MA: Hendrickson, 1995.

Cavanaugh, William T. "'A Fire Strong Enough to Consume the House': The Wars of Religion and the Rise of the State." *Modern Theology* 11 (1995) 397-420.

Cayley, David. *The Expanding Prison: The Crisis in Crime and Punishment and the Search for Alternatives*. Toronto: Anansi, 1998.

Charry, Ellen T. "Walking in the Truth: On Knowing God." In *But Is It All True? The Bible and the Question of Truth*, edited by Alan G. Padgett and Patrick R. Keifert, 144–69. Grand Rapids: Eerdmans, 2006.

Chase, Kenneth R. "Christian Discourse and the Humility of Peace." In *Must Christianity Be Violent? Reflections on History, Practice and Theology*, edited by Kenneth R. Chase and Alan Jacobs, 119–34. Grand Rapids: Brazos, 2003.

Childress, James F. "Scripture and Christian Ethics: Some Reflections on the Role of Scripture in Moral Deliberation and Justification." *Interpretation* 34 (1980) 371–80.

Childs, Brevard S. "On Reclaiming the Bible for Christian Theology." In *Reclaiming the Bible for the Church*, edited by Carl E. Braaten and Robert W. Jenson, 1–17. Edinburgh: T. & T. Clark.

The Church Council on Justice and Corrections. *Satisfying Justice: A Compendium on Initiatives, Programs and Legislative Measures*. Ottawa: CCJC, 1996. http://www.csc-scc.gc.ca/publications/092/005007-5500-eng.pdf.

Cloke, Ken. "Mediating Evil, War, and Terrorism: The Politics of Conflict." November 2004. www.mediate.com/articles/cloke4.cfm.

Collins, John J. "The Zeal of Phinehas, the Bible, and the Legitimation of Violence." In *The Destructive Power of Religion: Violence in Judaism, Christianity, and Islam*, edited by J. Harold Ellens, 1:12–33. Westport, CT: Praeger, 2004.

Consedine, J. *Restorative Justice: Healing the Effects of Crime*. Lyttelton, NZ: Ploughshares Publications, 1995.

Cook, David. *The Moral Maze: A Way of Exploring Christian Ethics*. London: SPCK, 1983.

Cosden, Darrell. "Christian Morality in a Pluralistic Society: Perspectives for Post-Soviet Cultures." *Evangelical Review of Theology* 22 (1998) 337–45.

Culbertson, R. G. "Perspectives on Punishment and Sentencing." In *Christian Social Ethics: Perspectives and Problems*, edited by Perry C. Cotham, 217–45. Grand Rapids: Baker, 1979.

Cuzzo, Maria Stalzer Wyant. "Code of the Peaceful Warrior: A Restorative Justice Response to Recent Events." September 17, 2001. http://restorativejustice.org/10fulltext/cuzzo-maria-stalzer-wyant.-the-code-of-the-peaceful-warrior-a-restorative-justice-response-to-recent-events.html.

Davies, W. D. "Paul and the Law: Pitfalls in Interpretation." In *Paul and Paulinism: Essays in Honour of C. K. Barrett*, edited by M. D. Hooker and S. G. Wilson, 4–16. London: SPCK, 1982.

———. "The Relevance of the Moral Teaching of the Early Church." In *Neotestamentica et Semitica: Studies in Honour of Matthew Black*, edited by E. Earle Ellis and Max Wilcox, 35–38. Edinburgh: T. & T. Clark, 1969.

Davies, W. D., and Dale. C. Allison. "Reflections on the Sermon on the Mount." *Scottish Journal of Theology* 44 (1991) 283–310.

Davis, Ellen F. "Critical Traditioning: Seeking an Inner Biblical Hermeneutic." *Anglican Theological Review* 82 (2000) 733–51.

Deckert, Marion G. "One Ethic, Two Kingdoms." *Mennonite Life* 59.4 (December 2004). https://ml.bethelks.edu/issue/vol-59-no-4/article/one-ethic-two-kingdoms/.

De Vries, Simon John. "Human Sacrifice in the Old Testament: In Ritual and Warfare." In *The Destructive Power of Religion: Violence in Judaism, Christianity, and Islam*, edited by J. Harold Ellens, 1:99–121. Westport, CT: Praeger, 2004.

Donaldson, Terence L. "Zealot and Convert: The Origins of Paul's Christ-Torah Antithesis." *Catholic Biblical Quarterly* 51 (1989) 655-82.
Donfried, Karl P. "Alien Hermeneutics and the Misappropriation of Scripture." In *Reclaiming the Bible for the Church*, edited by Carl E. Braaten and Robert W. Jenson, 19-45. Grand Rapids: Eerdmans, 1995.
Douma, Jochem. "The Use of Scripture in Ethics." *European Journal of Theology* 1 (1992) 105-22.
Duff, Nancy J. "Atonement and the Christian Life: Reformed Doctrine from a Feminist Perspective." *Interpretation* 53 (1999) 21-33.
———. "The Significance of Pauline Apocalyptic for Theological Ethics." In *Apocalyptic and the New Testament: Essays in Honor of J. Louis Martyn*, edited by Joel Marcus and Marion L. Soards, 279-96. Sheffield: JSOT, 1989.
Dunn, J. D. G. *The Living Word*. London: SCM, 1987.
Eakin, Hugh. "When U.S. Aided Insurgents, Did It Breed Future Terrorists?" *New York Times*, April 10, 2004. http://www.nytimes.com/2004/04/10/arts/10MAMD.html?ex=1082612982&ei=1&en=10f192e8a9d399ac.
Ellens, J. Harold. "Revenge, Justice and Hope: Laura Blumenfeld's Journey." In *The Destructive Power of Religion: Violence in Judaism, Christianity, and Islam*, edited by J. Harold Ellens, 4:227-35. Westport, CT: Praeger, 2004.
Etzioni, Amitai. "Religious Civil Society Is Antidote to Anarchy in Iraq and Afghanistan." *Christian Science Monitor*, April 1, 2004. http://www.csmonitor.com/2004/0401/p09s01-coop.html.
Fairchild, Mark R. "Paul's Pre-Christian Zealot Associations: A Re-examination of Gal 1:14 and Acts 22:3." *New Testament Studies* 45 (1999) 514-32.
Fiddes, Paul S. *Past Event and Present Salvation: The Christian Idea of Atonement*. London: Darton, Longman & Todd, 1989.
Finger, Thomas N. *Christian Theology: An Eschatological Approach*. Vol. 1. Scottdale, PA: Herald, 1985.
Fisk, Robert. "Showdown at Fallujah." *Independent*, April 1, 2004; reprinted *New Zealand Herald*, November 8, 2004, A1.
Flett, John. "Gospel Is Public Truth: Toward a Trinitarian Account of Mission to Modern Western Culture." Unpublished paper presented to Bible College of New Zealand Postgraduate Seminar, July 21, 2003.
———. "Vision of Theology's Responsibility for Societal Transformation in New Zealand: The Moot as a Case Study in Societal and Cultural Construction via Competent Lay Participation." Unpublished paper presented to the Consultation on Social Transformation in NZ, Bible College of New Zealand, September 2, 2000.
Flood, Derek. *Healing the Gospel: A Radical Vision for Grace, Justice, and the Cross*. Eugene, OR: Cascade, 2012.
Forrester, Duncan B. *Christian Justice and Public Policy*. Cambridge: Cambridge University Press, 1997.
———. "Political Justice and Christian Theology." *Studies in Christian Ethics* 3 (1990) 1-13.
———. "The Scope of Public Theology." *Studies in Christian Ethics* 17 (2004) 5-19.
———. "Welfare and Human Nature: Public Theology in Welfare Policy Debates." *Studies in Christian Ethics* 13 (2000) 1-14.

Foucault, Michel. *Discipline and Punish: The Birth of the Prison*. Translated by Alan Sheridan. New York: Vintage, 1979.
Fowl, Stephen E., and L. Gregory Jones. *Reading in Communion: Scripture and Ethics in Christian Life*. London: SPCK, 1991; rev. ed., 1997.
Fuller, Daniel P. "Paul and Galatians 3:28." *TSF Bulletin* 9 (1985) 9-13.
Fuller, Reginald H. "The Decalogue in the New Testament." *Interpretation* 43 (1989) 243-55.
Furnish, Victor P. "Belonging to Christ: A Paradigm for Ethics in First Corinthians." *Interpretation* 44 (1990) 145-57.
———. *The Moral Teaching of Paul: Selected Issues*. 2nd ed. Nashville: Abingdon, 1985.
———. *Theology and Ethics in Paul*. Nashville: Abingdon, 1968.
Gascoigne, Robert. *The Public Forum and Christian Ethics*. Cambridge: Cambridge University Press, 2001.
Geering, Lloyd. *The World to Come: From Christian Past to Global Future*. Wellington, NZ: B. Williams, 1999.
Goldhammer, John D. "Dr. Bush and Mr. Hyde: The Fundamentalist Shadow of George W. Bush." September 19, 2005. http://www.scoop.co.nz/stories/HL0509/S00292.htm.
Goldingay, John. "Models for Scripture." *Scottish Journal of Theology* 44 (1991) 19-37.
———. "Modes of Theological Reflection in the Bible." *Theology* 94 (1991) 181-88.
Gorringe, Timothy J. *God's Just Vengeance: Crime, Violence and the Rhetoric of Salvation*. Cambridge: Cambridge University Press, 1996.
Griffith, Lee. *The Fall of the Prison: Biblical Perspectives on Prison Abolition*. Grand Rapids: Eerdmans, 1993.
———. *The War on Terrorism and the Terror of God*. Grand Rapids: Eerdmans, 2002.
Gunton, Colin. "Using and Being Used: Scripture and Systematic Theology." *Theology Today* 47 (1992) 248-59.
Gustafson, James M. "The Place of Scripture in Christian Ethics: A Methodological Study." *Interpretation* 24 (1970) 430-55.
———. "The Relation of the Gospels to the Moral Life." In *Jesus and Man's Hope*, edited by Donald G. Miller and Dikran Y. Hadidian, 2:111-16. Pittsburgh: Pittsburgh Theological Seminary, 1971.
Hari, Johann. "Jihadism: The Real Terror of Our Age." *Independent*, reprinted *New Zealand Herald*, September 27, 2004, A17.
Harvey, A. E. *Strenuous Commands: The Ethic of Jesus*. London: SCM, 1990.
Harvey, Nicholas. "Christian Morality." *Scottish Journal of Theology* 52 (1999) 106-15.
Hauerwas, Stanley. "The Moral Authority of Scripture: The Politics and Ethics of Remembering." *Interpretation* 34 (1980) 356-70.
———. "The Sermon on the Mount, Just War and the Quest for Peace." *Concilium* 195 (1988) 36-43.
Haughey, John C. "Jesus as the Justice of God." In *The Faith That Does Justice: Examining the Christian Sources for Social Change*, edited by John C. Haughey, 264-88. 1977. Reprint, Eugene, OR: Wipf & Stock, 2006.
Hays, Richard B. *Echoes of Scripture in the Letters of Paul*. New Haven: Yale University Press, 1989.
———. *The Moral Vision of the New Testament: A Contemporary Introduction to New Testament Ethics*. Edinburgh: T. & T. Clark, 1996.

———. "Scripture-Shaped Community: The Problem of Method in New Testament Ethics." *Interpretation* 54 (1990) 42-55.
Henley, John A. "Eschatology and Community in the Ethics of Paul." *Australian Biblical Review* 27 (1979) 24-44.
Hicks, David. "The Christian Dimensions of Morality." *Studies in Christian Ethics* 9 (1996) 22-35.
Hirsch, Michael. "Misreading Islam." *Washington Monthly*, November 12, 2004. http://www.alternet.org/story/20488/.
Holder, Rodney. "Karl Barth and the Legitimacy of Natural Theology." *Themelios* 26 (2000) 22-37.
Holloway, Jeph. "Will Christian Ethics Be Christian?" *Southwestern Journal of Theology* 42 (2000) 4-29.
Hopkins, Julie M. *Towards a Feminist Christology: Jesus of Nazareth, European Women, and the Christological Crisis*. Grand Rapids: Eerdmans, 1995.
Hoyle, Carolyn, ed. "General Introduction." In *Restorative Justice*, vol. 1, *The Rise of Restorative Justice*, edited by Carolyn Hoyle. London: Routledge, 2010.
Horsely, Richard A. "Ethics and Exegesis: 'Love Your Enemies' and the Doctrine of Non-violence." *Journal of the American Academy of Religion* 54 (1986) 3-32.
Hudson, Barbara A. *Understanding Justice: An Introduction to Ideas, Perspectives, and Controversies in Modern Penal Theory*. Buckingham: Open University Press, 1996.
Jansen, John Frederick. *The Resurrection of Jesus Christ in New Testament Theology*. Philadelphia: Westminster, 1980.
Jenson, Robert W. "Hermeneutics and the Life of the Church." In *Reclaiming the Bible for the Church*, edited by Carl E. Braaten and Robert W. Jenson, 89-105. Grand Rapids: Eerdmans, 1995.
Jewett, Robert, and John S. Lawrence. *Captain America and the Crusade against Evil: The Dilemma of Zealous Nationalism*. Grand Rapids: Eerdmans, 2003.
Johnson, Abigail. "Theological Reflection in a Small Group." *Alban Weekly*, August 14, 2006. http://www.alban.org/weekly/PF/2006/06_0814_SmallGroup.html.
Jones, L. Gregory. "Formed and Transformed by Scripture: Character, Community, and Authority in Biblical Interpretation." In *Character and Scripture: Moral Formation, Community and Biblical Interpretation*, edited by William P. Brown, 18-33. Grand Rapids: Eerdmans, 2002.
Juergensmeyer, Mark. *Terror in the Mind of God: The Global Rise of Religious Violence*. Berkeley: University of California Press, 2003.
Kaye, Bruce. *Using the Bible in Ethics*. Bramcote, UK: Grove, 1976.
Kerber, Guillermo. "Overcoming Violence and Pursuing Justice: An Introduction to Restorative Justice Procedures." *Ecumenical Review* 55 (2003) 151-57.
Kille, D. Andrew. "'The Bible Made Me Do It': Text, Interpretation, and Violence." In *The Destructive Power of Religion: Violence in Judaism, Christianity, and Islam*, edited by J. Harold Ellens, 1:55-73. Westport, CT: Praeger, 2004.
Kilner, John F. "A Pauline Approach to Ethical Decision-Making." *Interpretation* 43 (1989) 366-79.
Klein, Joe. "The Blinding Glare of His Certainty." *Time*, February 24, 2003, 14.
Knapp, G. L. "Prison." In *The International Standard Bible Encyclopedia*, edited by Geoffrey W. Bromiley, 3:973-75. Grand Rapids: Eerdmans, 1979.

Koontz, Ted. "Grace to You and Peace: Towards a Gospel of Peace for the 21st Century." Unpublished paper at Mennonite Central Committee Conference, "Seeking the Peace of the City," Akron, PA, August 2004, 1-9.

———. "Thinking Theologically about the War against Iraq." *Mennonite Quarterly Review* 77 (2003) 93-108.

Kreider, Alan. "Beyond Bosch: The Early Church and the Christendom Shift." *International Bulletin* 29 (2005) 59–68.

———. *The Change of Conversion and the Origin of Christendom*. Harrisburg, PA: Trinity Press International, 1999.

Lampman, Lisa Barnes, and Michelle D. Shattuck, eds. *God and the Victim: Theological Reflections on Evil, Victimization, Justice, and Forgiveness*. Grand Rapids: Eerdmans, 1999.

Lampman, Lisa Barnes, and Michelle D. Shattuck. "Finding God in the Wake of Crime: Answers to Hard Questions." In *God and the Victim: Theological Reflections on Evil, Victimization, Justice, and Forgiveness*, edited by Lisa Barnes Lampman and Michelle D. Shattuck, 1-16. Grand Rapids: Eerdmans, 1999.

Lederach, John Paul. "The Challenge of Terror: A Traveling Essay." www.mediate.com/articles/terror911.cfm.

Lindars, Barnabas. "The Bible and Christian Ethics." *Theology* 76 (1973) 180–89.

Lindbeck, George. "Scripture, Consensus, and Community." In *Biblical Interpretation in Crisis*, edited by Richard J. Neuhaus, 74-101. Grand Rapids: Eerdmans, 1989.

Lischer, Richard. "The Sermon on the Mount as Radical Pastoral Care." *Interpretation* 41 (1987) 157-69.

Long, Edward LeRoy, Jr. *Facing Terrorism: Responding as Christians*. Louisville: Westminster John Knox, 2004.

———. "The Use of the Bible in Christian Ethics." *Interpretation* 19 (1965) 149-62.

Longenecker, Richard N. *New Testament Social Ethics for Today*. Grand Rapids: Eerdmans, 1984.

Mabee, Charles. "Reflections on Monotheism and Violence." In *The Destructive Power of Religion: Violence in Judaism, Christianity, and Islam*, edited by J. Harold Ellens, 4:111-18. Westport, CT: Praeger, 2004.

Malina, Bruce J. "The Bible: Witness or Warrant; Reflections on Daniel Patte's *Ethics of Biblical Interpretation*: A Review Essay." *Biblical Theology Bulletin* 26 (1996) 82-87.

Marcus, Joel. "The Old Testament and the Death of Jesus: The Role of Scripture in the Gospel Passion Narratives." In *The Death of Jesus in Early Christianity*, edited by John T. Carroll and Joel B. Green, 205-33. Peabody, MA: Hendrickson, 1995.

Marrow, Stanley B. "Κοσμοξ in John." *Catholic Biblical Quarterly* 64 (2002) 90-102.

Marshall, Christopher D. "Atonement, Violence and the Will of God." *Mennonite Quarterly Review* 76 (2003) 67-90.

———. *Beyond Retribution: A New Testament Vision for Justice, Crime, and Punishment*. Grand Rapids: Eerdmans, 2001.

———. "'But Deliver Us from Evil': George Bush and the Rhetoric of Evil." *Urban Seed* 5 (2003) 6-7.

———. *Compassionate Justice: An Interdisciplinary Dialogue with Two Gospel Parables on Law, Crime, and Restorative Justice*. Eugene, OR: Cascade, 2012.

———. "Crime, Crucifixion and the Forgotten Art of Lament." *Reality* 9 (2002) 16-22.

———. *Crowned with Glory and Honor: Human Rights in the Biblical Tradition*. Telford, PA: Pandora, 2001.

———. "Following Christ Down Under: A New Zealand Perspective on Anabaptism." In *Engaging Anabaptism: Conversations with a Radical Tradition*, edited by J. D. Roth, 41–52. Scottdale, PA: Herald, 2001.

———. "'For Me to Live Is Christ': Pauline Spirituality as a Basis for Ministry." In *The Call to Serve*, edited by D. A. Campbell, 96–116. Sheffield: Sheffield Academic, 1996.

———. *Faith as a Theme in Mark's Narrative*. Cambridge: Cambridge University Press, 1989.

———. "A Gracious Legacy: Changing Lenses in New Zealand." *Restorative Justice* 3 (2015) 439–44.

———. *Kingdom Come: The Kingdom of God in the Teaching of Jesus*. Auckland: Impetus, 1993.

———. *The Little Book on Biblical Justice*. Intercourse, PA: Good Books, 2005.

———. "Parables as Paradigms for Public Theology." In *The Bible, Justice and Public Theology*, edited by David J. Neville, 23–44. Sheffield: Sheffield Phoenix, 2014.

———. "Restoring What? The Practice, Promise, and Perils of Restorative Justice in New Zealand." *Policy Quarterly* 10 (2014) 3–11.

———. "Review of Hans Boersma, *Violence, Hospitality and the Cross: Reappropriating the Atonement Tradition*." *Stimulus* (2005) 51–52.

———. "The Use of the Bible in Ethics: Scripture, Ethics and the Social Justice Statement." In *Voices for Justice: Church, Law, and State in New Zealand*, edited by Jonathan Boston and Alan Cameron, 107–46. Palmerston North, NZ: Dunmore, 1994.

Marshall, I. Howard. "How Do We Interpret the Bible Today?" *Themelios* 5 (1980) 4–10.

———. "The Use of the New Testament in Christian Ethics." *Expository Times* 105 (1994) 131–36.

———. "Using the Bible in Ethics." In *Essays in Evangelical Social Ethics*, edited by David F. Wright, 45–49. Exeter: Paternoster, 1979.

Martinkus, John. "Hostage in Death's Shadow." *New Zealand Herald*, October 30, 2004, A1, B14–15.

Masters, Catherine. "Terror on Our Minds." *New Zealand Herald*, September 11–12, 2004, B3–B4.

Mathieson, Don. "Principles and Rules in Christian Ethics." *Latimer Journal* 107 (1991) 8–16.

Mauser, Ulrich. *The Gospel of Peace: A Scriptural Message for Today's World*. Louisville: Westminster John Knox, 1992.

McCurdy, Diana. "Lessons from Violence." *New Zealand Herald*, September 11–12, 2004, B5.

McDonald, Patricia M. *God and Violence: Biblical Resources for Living in a Small World*. Scottdale, PA: Herald, 2004.

McEntire, Mark. *The Blood of Abel: The Violent Plot in the Hebrew Bible*. Macon, GA: Mercer University Press, 1999.

McGrath, Alister E. "Doctrine and Ethics." *Journal of the Evangelical Theological Society* 34 (1991) 145–56.

———. "Reclaiming Our Roots and Vision: Scripture and the Stability of the Christian Church." In *Reclaiming the Bible for the Church*, edited by Carl E. Braaten and Robert W. Jenson, 63–88. Grand Rapids: Eerdmans, 1995.

McKanan, Dan. "Is God Violent? Theological Options in the Antislavery Movement." In *Must Christianity Be Violent?*, edited by Kenneth R. Chase and Alan Jacobs, 50-68. Grand Rapids: Brazos, 2003.
McKim, Donald K. *The Bible in Theology and Preaching*. Rev. ed. Nashville: Abingdon, 1994.
McKittrick, David. "'Brighton Bomber' Revisits His Paramilitary Past with Some Sorrow." *Independent*, reprinted in *New Zealand Herald* October 7, 2004, B3.
McTernan, Oliver. *Violence in God's Name: Religion in an Age of Conflict*. Maryknoll, NY: Orbis, 2003.
Meeks, Wayne A. "A Hermeneutics of Social Embodiment." *Harvard Theological Review* 79 (1986) 176-86.
———. "Understanding Early Christian Ethics." *Journal of Biblical Literature* 105 (1986) 3-11.
Mika, Harry, et al. *Taking Victims and Their Advocates Seriously: A Listening Project*. Akron, PA: Mennonite Central Committee Office on Crime and Justice, 2002.
Miles, Jack. "The Disarmament of God." In *The Destructive Power of Religion: Violence in Judaism, Christianity, and Islam*, edited by J. Harold Ellens, 1:123-67. Westport, CT: Praeger, 2004.
Miles, Margaret R. "Imitation of Christ: Is It Possible in the Twentieth Century?" *Princeton Seminary Bulletin* 10 (1989) 7-22.
Moltmann, Jürgen. *Jesus Christ for Today's World*. Translated by Margaret Kohl. London: SCM, 1994.
Moltmann, Jürgen, Nicholas Wolterstorff, and Ellen T. Charry. *A Passion for God's Reign: Theology, Christian Learning, and the Christian Self*. Edited by Miroslav Volf. Grand Rapids: Eerdmans, 1998.
Moltmann-Wendel, Elisabeth. "Is There a Feminist Theology of the Cross?" In *The Scandal of a Crucified World: Perspectives on the Cross and Suffering*, edited by Yacob Tesfai, 87-98. Maryknoll, NY: Orbis, 1994.
Morris, Leon. *The Cross in the New Testament*. Exeter: Paternoster, 1966.
Mott, Stephen Charles. "The Use of the Bible in Social Ethics II: The Use of the New Testament." Part I, *Transformation* 1.2 (1984) 11-20; Part II, *Transformation* 1.3 (1984) 19-26.
Myers, Ched, and Elaine Enns. *Ambassadors of Reconciliation*. 2 vols. Maryknoll, NY: Orbis, 2009.
Nath, Pamela S. "Consider the Lilies: Teaching the Value of Vulnerability." http://www.mcc.org/peacetheology/papers.htm.
Nelson-Pallmeyer, Jack. *Jesus Against Christianity: Reclaiming the Missing Jesus*. Harrisburg, PA: Trinity Press International, 2001.
New Zealand Herald. "Terror Mastermind Pledges His Loyalty to Osama Bin Laden." October 19, 2004, B1.
New, David S. *Holy War: The Rise of Militant Christian, Jewish and Islamic Fundamentalism*. Jefferson, NC: McFarland, 2002.
Newbigin, Lesslie. *The Welfare State: A Christian Perspective*. Oxford: Oxford Institute for Church and Society, 1985.
Niditch, Susan. *War in the Hebrew Bible: A Study in the Ethics of Violence*. New York: Oxford University Press, 1993.
Noakes-Duncan, Thomas. *Communities of Restoration: Ecclesial Ethics and Restorative Justice*. London: Bloomsbury T. & T. Clark, 2017.

Office for Victims of Crime. *OVC Handbook for Coping after Terrorism: A Guide for Healing and Recovery*. Washington, DC: US Department of Justice, Office of Justice Programs, 2001.

Oldfield, Duane. "Evangelical Roots of American Unilateralism: The Christian Right's Influence and How to Counter It." *Foreign Policy in Focus*, March 2004.

Ollenburger, Ben. C. "The Hermeneutics of Obedience: Reflections on Anabaptist Hermeneutics." In *Essays on Biblical Interpretation: Anabaptist-Mennonite Perspectives*, edited by Willard M. Swartley, 45-61. Elkhart, IN: Institute of Mennonite Studies, 1984.

———. "Pursuing the Truth of Scripture: Reflections on Wolterstorff's *Divine Discourse*." In *But Is It All True?*, edited by Alan G. Padgett and Patrick R. Keifert, 44-65. Grand Rapids: Eerdmans, 2006.

Olson, Mark. "The God Who Dared." *The Other Side* 26 (1990) 11-15.

———. "No More Prisons, No Not One." *The Other Side* 25 (1989) 24-25.

Olson, Dennis T. "Truth and the Torah: Reflections on Rationality and the Pentateuch." In *But Is It All True?*, edited by Alan G. Padgett and Patrick R. Keifert, 16-33. Grand Rapids: Eerdmans, 2006.

Packer, J. I. "Infallible Scripture and the Role of Hermeneutics." In *Scripture and Truth*, edited by D. A. Carson and J. D. Woodbridge, 325-56. Leicester, UK: InterVarsity, 1983.

———. *What Did the Cross Achieve? The Logic of Penal Substitution*. Leicester, UK: TSF Monograph, 1974.

Padgett, Alan G. "'I Am the Truth': An Understanding of Truth from Christology for Scripture." In *But Is It All True?*, edited by Alan G. Padgett and Patrick R. Keifert, 104-14. Grand Rapids: Eerdmans, 2006.

Patrick, M. W. "Understanding the 'Understanding Distance' Today: The Love Command of Jesus." In *Interpreting Disciples: Practical Theology in the Disciples of Christ*, edited by L. Dale Richesin and Larry D. Bouchard, 101-29. Fort Worth: Texas University Press, 1987.

Patte, Daniel. *Ethics of Biblical Interpretation: A Reevaluation*. Louisville: Westminster John Knox, 1995.

Peachey, Dean E. "The Kitchener Experiment." In *Restorative Justice*, edited by Carolyn Hoyle, 1:125-35. London: Routledge, 2010.

Perkins, Pheme. "New Testament Ethics: Questions and Contexts." *Religious Studies Review* 10 (1984) 321-27.

Pinnock, Clark H. *Most Moved Mover: A Theology of God's Openness*. Grand Rapids: Baker Academic, 2001.

Placher, William C. *Domestication of Transcendence*. Louisville: Westminster John Knox, 1996.

Ramm, Bernard. *Protestant Biblical Interpretation: A Textbook of Hermeneutics*. 3rd rev. ed. Grand Rapids: Baker Academic, 1970.

Ramsey, Michael. *God, Christ and the World: A Study in Contemporary Theology*. London: SCM, 1969.

Rawnsley, Andrew, and Gaby Hinsliff. "Blair Battling with Shadow of War." *Observer*, reprinted in *New Zealand Herald*, September 28, 2004, B3.

Redekop, Vern Neufeld. *From Violence to Blessing: How an Understanding of Deep-Rooted Conflict Can Open Paths to Reconciliation*. Ottawa: Novalis, 2002.

Richesin, L. Dale, and Larry D. Bouchard, eds. *Interpreting Disciples. Practical Theology in the Disciples of Christ*. Fort Worth: Texas Christian University Press, 1987.

Ricoeur, Paul. "The Golden Rule: Exegetical and Theological Perplexities." *New Testament Studies* 36 (1990) 392-97.
Rodd, C. S. "The Use of the Old Testament in Christian Ethics." *Expository Times* 105 (1994) 100-106.
Schlabach, Gerald. "Just Policing and the Christian Call to Nonviolence." http://www.academia.edu/15491839/Just_Policing_and_the_Christian_Call_to_Nonviolence.
Schluter, Michael, and Roy Clements. "Jubilee Institutional Norms: A Middle Way between Creation Ethics and Kingdom Ethics as the Basis for Christian Political Action." *Evangelical Quarterly* 62 (1990) 48-50.
Schrey, H., et al. *The Biblical Doctrine of Justice and Law.* London: SCM, 1955. Cited in Van Ness, Daniel and Karen Heetderks Strong, *Restoring Justice: An Introduction to Restorative Justice,* Fourth Edition. New Providence, NJ: LexisNexis Anderson Publications, 2010.
Schüssler Fiorenza, Elisabeth. *In Memory of Her.* London: SCM, 1983.
Schüssler Fiorenza, Francis. "The Crisis of Scriptural Authority." *Interpretation* 44 (1990) 353-68.
Schwager, Raymund. *Must There Be Scapegoats? Violence and Redemption in the Bible.* Translated by Maria L. Assad. New York: Harper & Row, 1987.
Scroggs, Robin. "New Testament and Ethics: How Do We Get from There to Here?" *Perspectives in Religious Studies.* 11 (1984) 77-93.
———. *Text and the Times: New Testament Essays for Today.* Minneapolis: Fortress, 1993.
Selengut, Charles. *Sacred Fury: Understanding Religious Violence.* Lanham, MD: Rowman & Littlefield, 2003, 2008.
Shupack, Martin. "Biblical Basis of Public Witness." *MCC Peace Office Newsletter* 33.3 (2003) 4-7.
Sleeper, C. Freeman. "Ethics as a Context for Biblical Interpretation." *Interpretation* 22 (1968) 443-60.
Smail, Tom. "Can One Man Die for the People?" In *Atonement Today,* edited by John Goldingay, 73–92. London: SPCK, 1995.
Smiles, Vincent M. "The Concept of 'Zeal' in Second-Temple Judaism and Paul's Critique of It in Romans 10:2." *Catholic Biblical Quarterly* 64 (2002) 282-99.
Smithies, R., and H. Wilson, eds. *Making Choices: Social Justice for Our Times.* Wellington: Church Leaders' Social Justice Initiative, 1993.
Snyder, T. Richard. *The Protestant Ethic and the Spirit of Punishment.* Grand Rapids: Eerdmans, 2001.
Spohn, William C. *What Are They Saying about Scripture and Ethics?* New York: Paulist, 1984.
Stacey, David. *Interpreting the Bible.* New York: Seabury, 1977.
Stackhouse, Max L. "Public Theology and Political Economy in a Globalizing Era." *Studies in Christian Ethics* 14 (2001) 63-86.
Stassen, Glen H. "Jesus and Just Peacemaking Theory." In *Must Christianity Be Violent? Reflections on History, Practice and Theology,* edited by Kenneth R. Chase and Alan Jacobs, 135–55. Grand Rapids: Brazos, 2003.
———. *Just Peacemaking: Transforming Initiatives for Justice and Peace.* Louisville: Westminster John Knox, 1992.
Stassen, Glen H., and David P. Gushee. *Kingdom Ethics: Following Jesus in Contemporary Context.* Downers Grove, IL: InterVarsity, 2003.

Steinmann, Rebecca. "Spiritual Elements in the Political Processes of South Africa's Truth and Reconciliation Commission." http://www.mcc.org/peacetheology/papers.htm.

Stern, Jessica. *Terror in the Name of God: Why Religious Militants Kill.* New York: HarperCollins, 2003.

Strang, Heather. "The Crime Victim Movement as a Force in Civil Society." In *Restorative Justice and Civil Society*, edited by Heather Strang and John Braithwaite, 69-82. Cambridge: Cambridge University Press, 2001.

Strang, Heather, and John Braithwaite, eds. *Restorative Justice and Civil Society*. Cambridge: Cambridge University Press, 2001.

Suskind, Ron. "Without a Doubt." *New York Times*, October 17, 2004. http://www.truthout.org/docs_04/printer_101704A.shtml.

Swartley, Willard M. *Covenant of Peace: The Missing Peace in New Testament Theology and Ethics*. Grand Rapids: Eerdmans 2006.

———, ed. *Essays on Biblical Interpretation.* Elkhart, IN: Institute of Mennonite Studies, 1984.

———. *Slavery, Sabbath, War, and Women: Case Issues in Biblical Interpretation.* Scottdale, PA: Herald, 1983.

Talbot, T. "Punishment, Forgiveness and Divine Justice." *Religious Studies* 29 (1993) 151-68.

Tate, W. Randolph. *Biblical Interpretation: An Integrated Approach.* Peabody, MA: Hendrickson, 1991.

Thompson, James W. "Ethics of Jesus and the Early Church." In *Christian Social Ethics*, edited by Perry C. Cotham, 45-59. Grand Rapids: Baker, 1979.

Tiessen, Terrance. "Toward a Hermeneutic for Discerning Universal Moral Absolutes." *Journal of the Evangelical Theological Society* 36 (1993) 189-207.

Trulear, H. D. "Go and Do Likewise: The Church's Role in Caring for Crime Victims," In *God and the Victim,* edited by Lisa Barnes Lampman and Michelle D. Shattuck, 70-88. Grand Rapids: Eerdmans, 1999.

Utley, Jon Basil. "Thirty-Six Ways the U.S. Is Losing the War on Terror." August 3, 2004. http://www.antiwar.com/utley/?articleid=3234.

Vanhoozer, Kevin J. "Introduction." In *Dictionary for Theological Interpretation of the Bible,* 20-21. Grand Rapids: Baker Academic, 2005.

Verhey, Allen. "The Bible in Christian Ethics." In *A New Dictionary of Christian Ethics*, edited by James F. Childress and John Macquarrie, 57-61. London: SCM, 1986.

Volf, Miroslav. *Exclusion and Embrace: A Theological Exploration of Identity, Otherness, and Reconciliation.* Nashville: Abingdon, 1996.

Wachtel, T., and P. McCold. "Restorative Justice in Everyday Life." In *Restorative Justice and Civil Society*, edited by Heather Strang and John Braithwaite, 114-29. Cambridge: Cambridge University Press, 2001.

Wansink, C. S. *Chained in Christ: The Experience and Rhetoric of Paul's Imprisonments.* Sheffield: Sheffield Academic, 1996.

Ward, Kevin. "A Churchless Future?" *Stimulus* 12 (2004) 2-12.

Weaver, J. Denny. *Nonviolent Atonement.* Grand Rapids: Eerdmans, 2001.

Welch, D. "Fear and Loathing," *New Zealand Listener,* May 11, 2002, 16-19.

Westerholm, Stephen. *Israel's Law and the Church's Faith.* Grand Rapids: Eerdmans, 1988.

Wilder, Amos N. "Kerygma, Eschatology and Social Ethics." In *The Background of the New Testament and Its Eschatology*, edited by W. D. Davies and D. Daube, 509-36. Cambridge: Cambridge University Press, 1964.
Wilson, Richard A. *The Politics of Truth and Reconciliation in South Africa: Legitimizing the Post-Apartheid State*. Cambridge: Cambridge University Press, 2001.
Wink, Walter. *Engaging the Powers: Discernment and Resistance in a World of Domination*. Minneapolis: Fortress, 1992.
———. *Powers That Be: Theology for a New Millennium*. New York: Doubleday, 1998.
Wolterstorff, Nicholas. *Divine Discourse: Philosophical Reflections on the Claim That God Speaks*. Cambridge: Cambridge University Press, 1995.
———. "Public Theology or Christian Learning?" In *A Passion for God's Reign: Theology, Christian Learning and the Christian Self*, by Jürgen Moltmann, Nicholas Wolterstorff, and Ellen Charry, 65-87. Grand Rapids: Eerdmans, 1998.
———. "True Words." In *But Is It All True?*, edited by Alan G. Padgett and Patrick R. Keifert, 34-43. Grand Rapids: Eerdmans, 2006.
Woolford, Andrew. *The Politics of Restorative Justice: A Critical Introduction*. Halifax, NS: Fernwood, 2009.
Wright, Christopher J. H. *The Use of the Bible in Social Ethics*. Bramcote, UK: Grove, 1983.
Wright, N. T. "How Can the Bible Be Authoritative?" *Vox Evangelica* 21 (1991) 7-32.
———. *Jesus and the Victory of God*. London: SPCK, 1996.
———. *The Last Word: Beyond the Bible Wars to a New Understanding of the Authority of Scripture*. San Francisco: HarperSanFrancisco, 2005.
Yoder, John Howard. "The Authority of the Canon." In *Essays on Biblical Interpretation*, edited by Willard M. Swartley, 265-72. Elkhart, IN: Institute of Mennonite Studies, 1984.
———. "The Hermeneutics of Peoplehood: A Protestant Perspective on Practical Moral Reasoning." *Journal of Religious Ethics* 10 (1982) 40-67.
———. *The Politics of Jesus: Behold the Man! Our Victorious Lamb*. 2nd ed. Grand Rapids: Eerdmans, 1994.
———. "Withdrawal and Diaspora: The Two Faces of Liberation." In *Freedom and Discipleship*, edited by Daniel S. Schipani, 76-84. Maryknoll, NY: Orbis, 1989.
Zehr, Howard. *Changing Lenses: A New Focus for Crime and Justice*. Scottdale, PA: Herald, 1990.
———. *Changing Lenses: A New Focus for Crime and Justice*. 4th ed. Scottdale, PA: Herald, 2015.
———. *The Little Book of Restorative Justice*. Intercourse PA: Good Books, 2002.
———. "Restoring Justice." In *God and the Victim*, edited by Lisa Barnes Lampman and Michelle D. Shattuck, 131-59. Grand Rapids: Eerdmans, 1999.
Zehr, Howard, and Barb Toews, eds. *Critical Issues in Restorative Justice*. Monsey, NY: Criminal Justice Press, 2004.
Zifcak, Spencer. "Restorative Justice in East Timor: A Case Study of the Nation's Truth and Reconciliation Commission." Unpublished paper. Australian National University, 2003.
Zimbelman, Joel. "The Contribution of John Howard Yoder to Recent Discussions in Christian Social Ethics." *Scottish Journal of Theology* 45 (1992) 367-99.

Scripture Index

Genesis

1-2	135
1:28	132
3:6	181n91
3:22-24	146
4:1-16	136, 159n2
4:6-7	146
4:7	181
4:8	135n15, 181
4:15	146
4:23-24	136n17, 147
4:23-25	159n2
6:3	146
6:5-7	136n17
6:5	147
6:6	146
6:11-13	136n17
6:11	146, 159n2
6:13	146
6:17	147
7:1-24	136n18
7:21-24	147
8:21-22	136n18, 147
8:21	147, 149
9:11-17	136n18
9:11	147
9:15	147
9:3-4	147
9:5-6	147
12:3	147n50
12:7	147n51
12:17	147n50
13:13	142n39
13:14-17	147n51
14:20	147n50
15:12	90n23
15:14-16	147n50
15:16	142n39, 147n51
17:8	147n51
18:16-33	141
18:20	147n50
19:15-29	147n50
19:24	145n47, 148n58
22:1-19	147n50
22:2	174n56
22:12	174n56
22:16	174n56
22:17	147n51
28:3-4	147n51
28:13-15	147n51
35:12	147n51
37:24	100n34
37:28	100n34
38:10	147n50
39	97
39:20	100n33
40:1-22	100n33
48:4	147n51
50:24	147n51

Exodus

4:24-26	148n52
10:21-22	90n23
11:4-5	138n24
12	138

Exodus (continued)

12:12	138n24
12:13	138n24
12:23	138n24
12:27	138n24
12:29	148n53
14–15	138
15:1-3	138
17:8-13	139n26
17:14	143n41
17:16	143n41
20:1-17	3n4
20:21	90n23
22:1-3	100n28
22:25	18n49
34:6-7	145n46, 151n70

Leviticus

10:1-2	145n47
11:45	3
19:18	37, 110
19:33	110n3
25:36	18n49
24:15-16	149n65
26:14-39	148n53

Numbers

11:1-6	138n23
12:1-16	138n24
14:10-12	138n23, 138n24
14:18-19	145n46, 151n70
16	129, 139
16:29-32	148n56
16:41-50	138n24
21:1-3	139n26
21:4-9	25n67
21:23-24	139n26
24:20	143n41
25	139
25:6-9	138n24
31	139

Deuteronomy

1:34-40	138n23
2:30-35	139n26
5:9-10	145n46, 151n70
5:22	90n23
6:4-5	37, 110
7:2-6	139n26
7:2	139n27
7:8	104n44
9:5	142n39
10:18-19	110n3
20:16-17	148n54
20:17-18	142n39
23:19	18n49
24:18	104n44
25:17-19	143n41
28:9	90n23
32:35	161n4

Joshua

1	139
6	140
6:1-16	139n26
6:21	143
7:1	139n26
7:24-26a	139n26
11:20	139n27
24:7	90n23

Judges

3:16-25	139n26
4:6-7	139n26
4:9-10	139n26
4:13-15	139n26
4:17	139n26
4:21-22	139n26
15:4-8	139n26
16:21	100n32
16:25	100n32

1 Samuel

2:9	84n12
15:2-3	143n41, 148n54
17:12—18:2	139n26
31:1-13	139n26

2 Samuel

6:6-7	148n52
18:6-9	139n26

18:14-15	139n26	16:16	84n12
22:10	90n23	17:12	84n12
22:12	90n23	18:18	84n12
22:29	84n12	19:8	90n23
		20:26	84n12
		22:11	84n12
		22:13	84n12

1 Kings

3:14	25n67	22:17	84n12
15:3	25n67	24:17	84n12
15:11	98n17	30:26	84n12
22:27	100n31	34:22	84n12
22:31-38	139n26	37:19	84n12
		38:17	84n12

2 Kings

1:11-12	145n47
9:30-35	139n26

Psalms

2:7	174n56
7:13-17	148n55

17:4	100n32, 100n33
18:4	25n67
24:15	95n5, 100n32
25:2-7	95n5, 100n32
25:27-30	100n32

18:9	90n23
18:11	90n23
18:28	84n12
22	82, 85n13, 176
22:1	85n13
44:11-12	148n54

2 Chronicles

6:1	90n23	44:19	90n23
14:9-15	139n26	66	25n67
16:1-10	100n31	68:6	104n44
16:10	98n20	68:20-23	140n33
18:26	98n17, 100n31	77	25n67
36	140	79:11	98n16, 98n18, 104n44, 104n45

Ezra

		81:11-12	148n59
		88:12	84n12
7:26	99n24	88:18	84n12
		91:6	84n12

Nehemiah

		95:8-11	25n67
1:8	90n23	97:2	90n23
		97:3	145n47
		97:8	25n67

Job

		102:19-20	104n44
1:16	145n47	102:19	104n45
3:4	84n12	102:20	98n18
3:18	98	105:28	90n23
5:14	84n12	107:10-16	104n44
10:21	84n12	107:10	84n12, 98n18
11:17	84n12	107:14	84n12
12:22	84n12	118:5	104n44
15:2	84n12	119:105	xxi

Psalms (continued)

135	25n67
136	25n67
139:11	84n12
143:3	84n12
146:6-7	104
146:7	104n44

Proverbs

2:13	84n12
4:19	84n12
8:36	138n55
20:20	84n12
26:27	138n55

Ecclesiastes

5:17	84n12
6:4	84n12
11:8	84n12

Isaiah

2:4	139n26
5:20	84n12
5:30	90n23
8:22	90n23
9:2	84n12
10:6	90
10:12-27	91
11:6-7	20
13:17	148n56
19:2	148n54, 148n56
28:16	25n67
29:18	84n12
42:1	174n56
42:6-7	104n47
42:7	84n12, 104n44
42:16	84n12
42:22	104n46
43:28	140n34
44—66	25n67
45:5	84n12
45:13	104n44
49:8-9	104n44
49:9	84n12
50:10	84n12
50:11	148n55

53	177, 177n72
55:9	84n12, 141
60:14	25n67
61	105n48
61:1	104n44, 104n47
63:11-14	25n67
64:6-7	148n59

Jeremiah

2:6	84n12
2:31	84n12
13:16	90n23
22:25-26	148n56
23:16	90n23
25:32-33	148n53
31:29-30	100n31, 151
32:2-5	100n31
37:16	98
37:20	98n16
39:1-7	95n5, 100n32
44:8	148n55
51:20-24	148n54
52:3-11	95n5, 100n32
52:11	98n20
52:31-34	95n5, 100n32

Lamentations

3:2	90n23
3:6	90n23
3:34-36	101

Ezekiel

18:1-4	151
21:3-4	148n53
21:9-15	148n53
21:31	148n54, 148n56
33	128
34:12	90n23
34:24	25n67
38:14-23	139n26

Hosea

11	25n67, 141

Joel

2:2	90n23
2:31	90n23
3:9-10	139n26

Amos

2:4-16	140n34
5:18	90n23
5:27	140n34

Micah

3:6	90n23
4:1-2	25n67
4:3	139n26
6:3-5	3n4
6:4	104n44
6:8	3n4

Nahum

1:8	90n23

Habakkuk

3:13-16	140n33

Zephaniah

1:15	90n23

Zechariah

8:10	148n54
9:9	104
9:11	104n44
9:12	104
12:8	25n67

Test. Dan

5:2	158n82

Matthew

2:13	90n23
2:13-15	174n57
2:16-18	143
3:17	174n56
4:16	84n12
5:9	161n5
5:13	75
5:21-48	37
5:23-26	100n35
5:43-48	37, 161n5
5:43-44	110n3
5:44-48	133
5:45-47	4n6
5:48	3n5
6:10	176n69
6:23	84n12
6:27	84n12
7:12	110n2
7:24-27	60n42
8:23-27	174n57
9:9-11	111n4
9:15	175n61
10:17-23	175n60
10:23	175n59
10:28	175n60
11:2	100n31
11:12	176n69
11:19	111n4
11:29	60n42
12:3-4	25n67
12:14-15	174n57
13:52	30
14:22-32	174n57
15:32	82n3
16:21-23	175n62
17:9	175n62
17:12	175n62
17:22-23	175n62
18:30	100n35
18:34	98n20
19:21	3n5
20:17-19	175n62
20:22-23	175n63
20:28	175n64
20:34	82n3
21:1-27	175n65
21:42	177n74
22:34-40	37
22:38-40	110n2
23:37—24:2	175n65

Matthew (*continued*)

24:9-10	175n60
24:15-20	175n59
25:30	90n23
25:31-46	111
25:34-40	107

Mark

1:11	174n56
1:22	173n44
1:27	89n21
1:41	82n3
2:7	173n44
2:15-17	111n4
2:18-22	82n6
2:19-20	175n61
3:5	82n4
3:6	173n44
4:35-41	174n57
5:7	89n21
6:3	173n44
6:5	82n4
6:14-29	98n21
6:47-52	174n57
7:1-5	173n44
7:21-22	181n91
8:11-23	173n44
8:12	82n4
8:17-21	82n5
8:31-34	175n62
9:9	175n62
9:12	175n62
9:19	82n5
9:22-23	175n62
10:6	37
10:17-22	37
10:32-34	175n62
10:38-40	175n63
10:45	175n64
11:1-33	175n65
11:18	175n66
12:12-13	173n44
12:13	175n66
12:28-34	110n2
12:28-31	37
13:9-13	175n60
13:14-18	175n59
14:1-3	173n44
14:1-2	175n66
14:10-11	173n44, 175n66
14:27	177n72
14:32-42	176n68
14:35	174n58
14:40	82n5
14:41	174n58
14:55-64	149n65
14:55-59	83
14:62	177n72
15:2-5	176n67
15:6-15	83n8
15:10	173n44
15:15	105
15:25-27	82
15:33-39	82
15:33	90
15:34	89n21
15:37	89n21
15:38	91
15:39	91

Luke

1:79	84n12
3:22	174n56
4:16-20	104
4:29-30	174n57
5:27-32	111n4
5:35	175n61
6:30	19
6:31	110n2
6:35-36	133
6:35	110n3
7:13	82n3
7:32	82n4
8:22-25	174n57
9:21-22	175n62
9:44	175n62
9:51-52	175
9:54-55	145
10:25-28	37, 110n2
10:29-37	110n3
10:37	111
11:34	84n12
12:49-50	175n63
13:31-33	175

13:33	175n62	**John**	
15:1-2	111n4	1:3-4	120, 133
17:25	175n62	1:5	84n12
17:26-37	37	1:11	173n48
18:31	177n73	1:14	55
18:31-34	175n62	1:17	58
19:1-10	111n4	1:29	178
19:29—20:8	175n65	2:4	174n58, 178n77
19:39	86n16	2:13-22	175n65
19:41-44	81	3:14-16	25n67
19:42	183n93	3:16-17	178
20:20-31	82	3:19	84n12, 173n48
21:2	175n59	4:34	178n79
21:12-19	175n60	5:39-40	56
22:3	173n45	6:15-21	174n57
22:6	175, 175n66	6:37-40	178n79
22:14	174n58	7:17	60n42
22:22	177n73	7:30	174n58, 178n77
22:31	173n45	8:20	174n58, 178n77
22:37	83, 177n72, 177n73	8:21	86n15
		8:24	86n15
22:39-46	176n68	8:46	86n15
22:42	176n70	10:11	179
22:52-53	84	10:14-18	179
22:53	173n46, 174n58, 175	11:35-37	81
		11:49-50	83
23:8-12	176n67	12:23	174n58, 178n77, 178n78
23:14-15	83n9	12:27-28	178, 178n78, 178n79
23:14	86n14, 173n49		
23:18-19	83n8	12:27	174n58, 178n77
23:19	100n32	12:32-33	178
23:20	173n49	12:35	84n12
23:22-23	86n14	12:46	84n12
23:22	173n49	13:1	174n58, 178n77
23:32	83	13:2	173
23:34	88, 182	13:18	177n72, 178n80
23:40-41	83n10	13:27	173
23:41	86n14	14:6	51
23:45	173n46	14:8-13	161n6
23:47-48	86n14	14:15	18
23:47	83, 173n49	14:25-31	5n9
23:48	173n44	14:26	60
24	177	14:30	173
24:26-27	177n75	15:18	173n47
24:27	56	15:21—16:15	5n9
24:44-47	177n76	15:25	173n47

John (continued)

16:4	175n60
16:13	60
16:20–22	82n6
16:32	174n58, 178n77
17:1–5	178n78
17:1	174n58, 178n77
17:4–5	178n79
17:11–12	174n57
17:15	119n14, 174n57
18:4–8	179n81
18:9	177n72, 178n80
18:11	175n63, 179n81
18:14	86n16
18:30	83
18:39–40	83n8
19:4	86n14
19:8–10	176n67
19:11	54n29, 179
19:12	173n44
19:17–22	83
19:23	177n72, 178n80
19:28	177n72, 178n80
19:36	177n72, 178n80
21:19	178n78

Acts

2:20	90n23
2:23	173n49, 179
2:36	173n49
3:13–15	173n49
3:17–18	179
4:10	173n49
4:11	177n74
4:23–26	86n16
4:26–28	173n50
4:26	173n49
5:18	100n36
5:19	98n15, 104n44
5:21	100n36
5:22–23	98n15
5:23	100n36
7:2–53	38
7:51–52	173n49
8:3	97n10
8:32–35	179n81
8:32–33	177n72
9:1–2	97n10, 151n71, 155n79
12:6–11	98n15
13:11	90n23
13:27–29	173n49, 179n81
13:27	173n50
14:14–43	38
15:1–35	60
15:13	31
15:28	5n9, 31
16:19–40	97n13, 100n36
16:25–26	98n15, 104n44, 105
16:27–34	107
17:1–3	177n75, 179n81
17:11	1
17:16–34	4n6
22:4–5	97n10
22:4	151n71, 155n79
23:10–21	97n13, 100n36
24:27	97n13, 100n36
26:5	155n79
26:9–11	151n71, 155n79
26:10	97n10
28:16	97n13, 100n36
26:18	84n12
28:20	97n13, 100n36
28:30	97n13, 100n36

Romans

1:1–4	180n83
1:16–17	121, 134
1:18–23	150n69, 157
1:18–32	38, 87n19, 90n24, 155n75
1:28	4n6
2:12	153
2:14–16	4n6
2:14–15	154
2:17–29	153
2:19–20	153
2:19	84n12
2:24	153
2:27	154
3:9–20	87n19, 155n75
3:9–18	153
3:19	153

3:20	121, 134, 153, 154n74	7:7–12	181n91
		7:9–10	153n73
3:21–26	156	7:11	157
3:21	151, 156	7:12	153, 157
3:25	180	7:13	181n90
3:27–28	154n74	7:14–25	153
3:28–31	154, 154	7:14	153, 157
3:29	156	7:16	153, 157
3:31	156	7:22–23	153
4:1–25	157	7:25	153
4:2	154n74	8:1–4	151, 155
4:6	154n74	8:1	155
4:9–16	154	8:3	87n18, 153, 180n85
4:15	153		
4:16	155n76	8:4–6	5n9
4:23–24	157n81	8:7	153
4:25	162	8:13	4n8, 5n9
5:1	121, 134	8:28	4n8
5:5	155n78	8:32	180
5:6	180n87	8:35–39	183n92
5:6–21	155n77	9:1	4n8
5:6–11	91	9:12	154n74
5:7	180	9:31	153
5:8	180n87	9:32	154n74
5:10	180n86	10:2–4	152n72
5:12–21	87n19, 155n75	10:5	153n73, 155
5:12	181	10:8	157
5:13	153	10:11–13	154
5:18–19	180	11:5	155n76
5:20–21	155n76	11:6	154n74
5:20	153	11:28–36	156n80, 158
5:21	181n90	10:32	155
6:1–14	155	12:1–12	43
6:1	155n76	12:1–2	4n6, 29
6:3–14	180n89	12:2	29
6:4	183	12:9–21	155
6:9–10	183	12:15	88
6:12–14	155n75	12:19	161n4
6:14	155n76	13:1	54
6:15	155	13:6	19
6:20–21	155n75	13:8–10	155n78
6:23	181n90	13:9–10	110n2
7:4	155	13:12	84n12
7:5	153, 153n73	14:1–15:13	183n93
7:6	155	14:13–21	17n48
7:7	37, 153, 181n90	14:14	156
7:7–25	155n75	14:15	155n78
7:7–13	153	14:17	4n8

Romans (continued)

15:3-4	180n88
15:4	157n81
15:13	4n8
15:30	4n8
15:33	158n82
16:20	158n82

1 Corinthians

1:16	121
1:18-25	43
1:20-25	157, 180
2:8	84n11, 173n51
2:12	5n9
3:16	5n10
4:5	84n12
6:19	5n10
8:1	155n78
8:13	17n48
9:10	157n81
10:1-11	25n67
10:11	157n81
11:13-15	4n6
11:26	180
12:13	5n10
13:1-8	155n78
14:3	30
14:20-25	76
14:26	30
14:29	5n10, 30
14:35	17n48
14:38	5n10
15:3	162, 180n87
15:3-4	180n82
15:9	151n71, 155n79
15:10	155n76
15:42-49	155n77
15:56	153, 153n73
16:14	155n78

2 Corinthians

1:5	180n87, 180n89
3:6-7	153n73
3:12-18	152n72
3:14	57
3:18	4n8, 52
4:4	120n16, 133n10
4:10	180n89
5:14	180n87
5:17-21	91
5:18-21	183n93
5:19	180n86
5:21	86n15, 87n18, 180, 182
6:5	97n12, 100n36
6:6	4n8
6:14	18n48, 84n12
11:23-28	97n12, 100n36
13:11	158n82

Galatians

1:6	155n76
1:13	151n71, 155n79
2:5	45, 73
2:14	45
2:15	73
2:16	154n74
2:19	153n73, 155, 180n88, 180n89
2:21	155n76, 180n85
3:2	154n74
3:5	154n74
3:6-17	157
3:10	153, 154n74
3:12	153n73, 154n74
3:13	155, 180n85, 180n87
3:15-26	156
3:15-22	154
3:19-26	155
3:21	153n73
3:22	153, 155
3:25-29	183n93
3:25	155
3:28	19
4:4	180n85
4:5	155
5:1	155
5:4	155n76
5:6	155n78
5:13-14	155n78
5:16-26	4n8
5:16	5n9

5:18	5n9
5:22–23	155n78
5:25	5n9
6:1	4n8
6:8	5n9
6:14	180n89
6:15	156

Ephesians

1:10	122, 135
2:1–22	183n93
2:5–6	155n76
2:9	154n74
2:13	180n84
2:14–17	109
2:14	158n82
3:1	97n11, 100n36
3:9	149
3:11–12	180n84
4:1–6	xii
4:8	105n48
4:32	155n78
5:2	180n87
5:8	84n12
5:11	84n12
6:2	37
6:12	84n12
6:21	xi

Philippians

1:9	155n78
1:19–24	98n22
2:5–8	180n88
2:9–11	54n29
3:4–16	155
3:5–6	155n79
3:6	97n10, 151n71
3:10	180n89
4:9	158n82

Colossians

1:2	180n89
1:8	4n8
1:10	155n77
1:13	84n12
1:15	120n16, 121, 133n10, 134, 158, 161n6
1:16	121, 133
1:16–17	121, 135
1:19	120n16, 133n10
1:20–21	180n86
1:20	xxii, 121, 134
2:14	173n51
2:15	84n11, 105n48
3:5–17	52
3:10	155n77, 157
3:14	155n78
4:3	100n36

1 Thessalonians

2:14–15	173
5:4	84n12
5:10	180n87
5:19–22	5n10
5:23	158n82

2 Thessalonians

2:2	5n10
3:16	158n82

1 Timothy

2:5	175n64
2:6	180n88

2 Timothy

1:8	97n11, 100n36
1:13	31
2:15	57
1:16–17	106
2:16	31
2:11	180n89

Titus

2:14	180n87
3:4	180n85

Philemon

1	97n11, 100n36
9	97n11, 100n36

Hebrews

1:1-4	161n6
1:2-3	120, 133
2:14-15	181
3:7—4:11	25n67
4:15	86n15
5:7-10	176n70
7:26-27	86n15
10:30	161n4
10:31	131
11:32	25n67
12:2-3	173
12:2	88n20
12:22	25n67
13:3	98n20, 106
13:5	17n48
13:20	158n82

James

2:11	37
3:18	v, 30
4:2	181

1 Peter

2:4	84n12, 173
2:5-6	25n67
2:7	173, 177n74
2:21	3
2:23-24	182
2:23	88n20
2:24	87
3:8	86n15
3:19	104n44

2 Peter

2:17	90n23

1 John

1:5	84n12, 90n23
2:8	84n12
2:11	84n12
3:12	25n67
4:1	5n10

Jude

Jude 11	25n67
Jude 13	90n23

Revelation

2:10	104n44
2:20	100n36
14:1	25n67
15:1-8	25n67
16:10	90n23
17:4	174
20	97
21-22	135
21:3-4	135n15
21:24	135n15
22:2	135n15

1 Clem

5:6	97n14

Subject Index

Abraham, 25n67, 36, 141, 142, 152–58 *passim*
absolutism, religious, 187
accountability. *See* responsibility
Acts and Epistles, 179–80
Adam, 146, 152, 156
    second, 155. *See also* Christ
advocacy, 72. *See also* readings
Afghanistan, 188, 192
al Hitar, Hamoud, 197n44
al Khatib, Omar, 206–07
al Qaeda, 185, 197n44, 199
al-Zarqawi, 189–90
America, 194–95. *See also* United States
amnesty, in Bible, 105n48
Anabaptists, 53, 59, 60;
    Mennonite tradition, 159, 210
analogy, 24–27, 30, 34, 151, 157, 193n37
Anselm, Saint, 163, 164, 169
anthropology, moral, 52
Artaxerxes, 99n24
atonement. *See* theories of atonement
authorities, 83, 173, 175
authority, 53, 58, 167;
    biblical, xxi, xxii, 6–9 *passim*, 18, 21, 23, 39–40, 52–56, 58;
    moral, 14–15, 30–31, 33, 36

badges, ethnic, 154
ban. *See* herem
baptism, 107, 155, 174, 175
Barabbas, 83, 205

Barth, Karl, 71
Bartlett, Bruce, 185n5
belief, and public theology, 63
bias, anti-theological, 20, 46, 49, 145
Bible, 24n65, 36, 45, 144. *See also* Scripture
bin Laden, Osama, 185
Blair, Tony, 194n35
Brandl, Colonel Gareth, 200
Brighton bomber, 203–5
brutality, God embroiled in, 140
Bush, George W., 185, 192–94 *passim*

Cain, 146, 181
Calvin, John, 59
Calvinism, 54, 165
Canaan, 139
Canaanites, 142, 147,
canon, 11, 15, 25, 32, 35n101, 53–55; Hebrew, 140. *See also* story, canonical
capital punishment, 19, 95, 115, 165
care, 106–8, 110, 111
casuistry, 17–21; criticism of, 19–21
character, 30, 37, 43; formation, 5, 27–29, 52
Chechnya, 200
Christ. *See also* Jesus; Jesus Christ
    abandonment, 86
    absolute lordship, 65
    all summed up in, 76
    and alien values, 34
    and Christian practice, 58
    and new creation, 68

SUBJECT INDEX

Christ (*continued*)
  anonymous presence of, 107
  biblical witness to, 7, 55
  challenge of, 165
  climax of story, 152
  crucifixion of proclaimed, 180
  death and resurrection, 155, 162
  death of, 183
  ethical paradigm, 59
  fulfilment of hope, 157
  God made known in, 134
  God revealed in, 150
  God's self-disclosure, 7
  in biblical narrative, 73
  in creeds, 169
  law, goal of, 155
  life, death, resurrection, 150, 152
  lord, lordship, 55n31, 65, 105, 129, 135
  love of, 18, 28, 29, 59, 60
  made a sinner, 87
  means discipleship, 60
  needed to make sense of Bible, 46n10
  new creation, 156
  nonviolent, 166–69
  reconciling the world, 180
  removed veil of ignorance, 152
  reveals God fully, 150
  risen, 122, 150, 158
  sinless, 85, 183
  sinner, 87, 183
  ultimate meaning in, 122
  victim, 87, 149
Christendom, 33, 70, 160, 168–69
christocentrism, ethical, 30n82, 59
Christology, 60, 167, 168, 169
Christus Victor, 162, 168. *See also* narrative Christus Victor
Christian ethics, 2–6, 18, 29, 62, 72–74, 160. *See also* ethics; morality
church, 40, 74, 75, 76, 119, 160, 215;
  and Scripture, 40–44;
  and victims, 112
cistern, 98, 103
civilizations, clash of, 197n45, 202
claims, metaphysical, 122–23

commitments, costly, 127
communities, 202, 215;
  of faith, 112, 113, 213;
  religious, 111, 197
community, 36, 43, 47n12, 111, 112–14, 119, 201
  and Spirit, 4–5, 60
  formation, 30–36,
  prisoners' need of, 109
  specialist, 9, 30, 45, 66, 125
compromise, and violence, 147, 187, 200n54
conference, restorative justice, 123–24, 125, 126, 199–200, 204, 207
consensus and pluralism, 77
convictions, Christian, religious, xviii, xix, 65, 70, 119
court system, 124, 125
covenant, 102n37
creation, 122, 135–37
credibility, Christian, 66–70
crime, xvii, 80–81, 91–92, 94, 102;
  against humanity, 139
crisis, regarding Bible,
  of acquaintance, 41–44;
  of authority, 52–55;
  of confidence, 44–52;
  of interpretation, 56–61
criticism, biblical, 47;
  historical, 11, 47;
  ideological, 49. *See also* readings
critique, Christian,
  of law, 152;
  of prisons, 107–08;
  social, 36
cross, 121–22, 134, 163, 171–72
crusade, 192–94
currency, common, 71–72

Da Vinci Code, 44, 54
darkness, 84, 89, 90, 134. *See also* evil
data, in ethics, 4
death, 103, 172–74, 181
deserts, just, 123, 213
determination of position, 68
devil. *See* Satan

dialogue, xv, 199, 200, 202
dilemma, 9, 28
    hermeneutical, 12, 48, 129, 130, 151
dimensions of public voice, 77–78
disadvantaged, the, 101
discernment, 6n14, 11, 22, 28, 29, 71, 77
    communal, 30, 31, 33, 60
discipleship, 31, 59, 60, 61, 68, 75, 159
discourse, distinctive, 74–76
ditheism, 129
diversity, 66
    in biblical morality, 10, 18
    in biblical story, 11–12, 136
Dutch Reformed Church, 35

earth, 146–47
ecclesiology, 168
Eden, 49
Egypt, Israel in, 100
Elijah, 82, 90, 145
elite, scholarly, 44
Emmaus road, 56, 177
empowerment, 125, 201
encounters, face-to-face, 206, 207, 208
engagement, victims with offenders, 116
Enlightenment, the, 44, 69
Enuma Elish, 135
Ephraim, 141
epistemology, postmodern, 60
ethics, 2–6, 62, 63n3, 68, 74n30, 167
    and Christian story, 73
    social, 72
Eve. *See* Adam
evil, 63, 84–88, 89–92 *passim*, 123, 135, 171, 172–73, 182;
    power of, 121–22, 134, 161, 169–70
exegesis. *See* hermeneutics
experience, 3, 6, 53n26, 85n13, 86–87, 105, 198, 205
    and authority, 53n26
    and narrative, 32
    eschatological, 78

human, 71, 74, 80, 86, 145, 148, 159, 181
    moral, 21
    of God, 150, 158
    of imprisonment, 97, 100
    of Jesus, 84, 176, 182
    of victims, 112–13, 116, 124, 125
    of violence, 149
    religious, 144, 188
exposition, xii, 56, 210, 213

faith, xix, 8, 15, 34, 53, 89–90, 107, 154, 201, 202
    absolute, 185n5
    and criticism, 47n12
    and lament, 89
    and public theology, 70, 72
    and terrorism, 187, 188
    and victimization, 112, 165
    Christian, 49n16, 62, 68, 72, 74, 121, 134
    community of, 30, 33, 54, 74, 113, 137
    and Bible [text], 36, 45
    in reason, 47
    language of, 70, 72, 75, 76, 77, 78
    of George Bush, 185n5, 193n34
    rule of, 46n10,
faithfulness, 52, 156, 180
Fallujah, 200
fear, 34, 89, 124, 181, 186, 194
    culture of, 94
    in scholarship, 21
    of crime, 93
feudalism, 164
Fitzgerald, Dr. Garret, 200n54
focus, in public theology, 67
formation, moral, 35, 52
framework, 7, 20, 21, 23, 72, 152
    conceptual, 149, 195
frameworks, 67
freedom, 81, 105–6, 134, 155, 183
fundamentalism, 51

genocide, 19, 139, 147
gentiles, 153–54, 156
Gethsemane, 82, 173, 176, 177

Ginzburg, Yitzak, 199
God, 54–55, 65, 121, 147, 156, 158n82
  absence of, 90
  active in Jesus's death, 180, 181
  as perpetrator, 138, 139
  as violent, 137–41, 148, 149, 167
  authority of, 54
  avenger, 140
  casts off righteous violence, 149
  character of, 73
  compromises with violence, 149
  concern for justice, 110
  disarmed, 145
  distance of, 84–88 *passim*
  freedom-loving, 99
  identity of, 129, 146, 149
  initiative in Jesus's death, 179–81
  knowledge of, 47n12
  nonviolent, 134n12, 135–36
  presence of in Jesus's death, 90–91
  reflected in restorative justice, 122
  reign of, 170, 171–71, 174
  revealed in Jesus's death, 134
  revelation of, 67n14, 107, 121, 132–34
  self-disclosure, 144, 149n64
  sets prisoners free, 104
  silence of, 90
  transcendent immanence, 148
  Trinity, 167
  will and purpose of, 174
gods of near east, 141
Good Samaritan, 111
gospel, truth of, 73
  gospels, 2n3, 55, 59, 67, 83
grace, 28, 51, 53, 122, 135, 154–55
  common, 76
guilt, 81, 113, 116, 163, 200, 203

habits, 70, 210
harm, xiii, xv, 87, 88, 117, 124–25, 200, 211
hatred, 88, 103, 170, 202–3
healing, xv, 88, 116, 118, 112, 123, 212

Jesus brings, 90, 105, 170, 172, 215
herem, 139, 140
hermeneutics, 9–13, 31, 49, 51, 53, 57. *See also* interpretation
Herod, 143, 173, 175
history, 22, 23, 25, 47–48, 129, 131, 178, 208
  and atonement theory, 162, 164, 165, 167
  biblical, 143, 150
  God in, 3, 8, 25, 43, 61, 130–32 *passim*, 152, 171
  of church, 15
  of ethics, 30
  of prisons, 95–97
  salvation, 2, 157
Holy Spirit, 4–5, 46, 67. *See also* Spirit
holy war, 135, 130, 188–89, 190, 192, 194. *See also* terrorism, religious; violence, redemptive
honor, God's, 162, 163n12, 166, 167
hope, 126, 157
humanity, 4n6, 68, 72, 99, 155, 202, 212
  and offending, 81
  and God, 8, 92, 134, 149, 162
  and Jesus with, 86, 87, 88
  and sin, 181, 182, 183
  new, 157, 183

icon of God, 132
identity, 43, 47n13, 73, 74–75, 76, 78
  changed by violence, 149
ideals, xviii, 17–20, 37, 211
idolatry, 69n19, 139, 142, 155
image, 23, 52, 79, 99, 136, 169
images, 37
  biblical, 22–23, 37
  idolatrous, 47n12
  of violent God, 137, 139, 144, 150
imperative, categorical, 71
imperatives, 15, 23, 35. *See also* moralism
imprisonment, 94–96

and power of death, 103
as oppression, 99–103
cause of suffering, 98–99
in Bible, 97–105 *passim*
injustice,
   and satisfaction atonement, 165, 167
   in Bible, 101, 111
   Jesus's confrontation with, 176
   prisons an apparatus of, 103
   victims of, 86, 88
intelligibility of positions, 70
interpretation, 10–13, 38, 45, 48, 56, 59–61, 74, 105n48
   allegorizing, 143
   biblical, 49n16, 137, 143, 152, 209
   in community, 27, 31–32
   postmodern, 47, 47n12, 50, 51
   theological, 47n12, 160, 162
   see also hermeneutics
IRA, 200n54
Iraq, 196n41
Ireland, 94, 201. *See also* IRA
Irenaeus, 46n10
Israel, 99–100, 104, 129, 138–39, 142, 153–54

jailer, Philippian, 107
Jemaah Islamiyah, 185
Jeremiah, 98, 151
Jericho, 142, 143
Jerusalem, 81, 175, 177;
   new, 135
Jesus,
   and interpretive procedure, 56
   and lament, 81–86, 89, 90, 92
   and meaning of Scripture, 56, 59
   and neighbor-love, 110–11
   and power of evil, 88, 168, 171, 173–74
   and powers, 84, 105, 170, 172, 173, 179, 182
   and sin, 86, 90, 91, 182, 183
   and violence, 167, 182. *See also* Jesus, nonviolence
   baptism of, 174, 175
   creator, 120–21, 133

   criminalization of, 83, 86
   death and resurrection, 135, 155, 165, 176, 178, 212
   death of, 87, 90–91, 162, 165, 166, 171–72, 174–81
   dereliction of, 82, 83
   embodiment of God, 121, 133–34, 210
   estrangement, 86, 89, 90
   ethic, 19n53, 133
   face of God, 55, 121, 134
   Gethsemane prayer, 176
   hard sayings, 18, 68
   hour, 174, 178
   in biblical drama, 59
   innocence of, 83, 86
   key to reality, 121, 135
   lays down life, 178–79
   life and teaching, 68, 167, 169, 170
   life, death, and resurrection, xxi, 7, 121, 124, 150, 152
   nonviolence of, 133, 134n12, 159–61
   nonviolent icon, 132
   passion of, 84
   proclamation of release to captives, 105
   restores world, 121
   resurrection, 170
   reveals God's love, 135
   separated from God, 85
   Servant, 173, 174
   solidarity with humanity, 87
   stories of, 32
   story of, 61, 135, 136
   truth, 51,
   use of parables, 58
Jesus Christ,
   enacted restorative justice, 214
   explodes sin's deception, 157
   goal of Scripture interpretation, 59
   God made known in, 120
   governs ethical judgments, 2
   hermeneutical lens, 57, 152
   ultimate meaning in, 135
Jesus Seminar, 54

John's Gospel, 178
Jubilee, 105n48
jihad, 193
Judaism, 17, 129n3, 152, 154. *See also* law
Judas, 173
judgment [God's], 90, 106, 111, 130, 161
justice, 3, 92, 101, 129, 141, 156
   and advocacy readings, 48, 49
   and Christian community, 38
   and church, 36–37, 41
   biblical, xvi, 24n65, 99, 108, 142
   criminal, 101, 114–16
   system, xv, xvii, 84, 102, 114
   God's, 69n19, 130, 131, 134, 161–66 *passim*, 212
   relational, xviii
   social, 36, 101
   violent, 161
   youth, 117
justification, 13, 115, 154, 165, 187
   by faith, 59, 154
just peacemaking, 196n42
just war, 68, 195n39, 196n42

Kant, 71
King, Martin Luther, 41–42
kingdom, God's 168
Korahites, 139
Koran, 197n44

Lamech, 147
lament, xii, 113
language, 6, 43, 50, 137–38, 144, 185, 188, 210
law, 16, 69, 102–3, 212, 213
   and order, 115, 164, 188
   criminal, 83, 96, 102
   letter of the, 15, 28
   natural, 4, 71, 77
   of nature, 123
   Old Testament, 18, 58, 99–100, 110,138
   Paul's treatment of, 151–58, 180
   rule of. *See* rule of law
Lazarus, 81
learning, Christian, 64

legalism, 16, 19
legislation, 115, 117
Lewis, Bernard, 197n45
liberalism, 47
life, 61, 64
   Christ-like, 61
   spheres of, 64
lifestyle, Christian, 63n3
literalism, 18
Lord Jesus Christ, 129. *See also* Jesus; Christ
Lord's Prayer, 176
love, 18, 19, 24n65, 91, 122, 123, 161, 210
   command, 37
   Christ-like, 18
   God's, 28, 61, 73, 121, 134, 162, 178, 180
   and public concern, 76
   human family resisting, 87
   Jesus alienated from, 85
   of enemy, 133, 155, 171
   of God, 47n12, 155
   of neighbor, 2n3, 65, 68, 110–11, 155
   supererogatory, 63n3
Luther, Martin, 45, 59

Magee, Patrick, 203–5
Māori, 101
Marcion, 129
McKinley, Michael, 184
meaning, in Scripture, 48–49, 50–51, 56, 58–59
mercy, 211, 212
   God's 28, 106, 141, 156, 158, 163
method,
   ethical, 13–14, 16–20, 27, 35, 37, 38
   interpretive, 32, 36, 45, 46, 56, 160
Middle Ages, 45n9
Midianites, 139
militarism, spirituality of, 193n33
mission, 119, 170, 171, 174, 176, 185
modesty, 67, 201
monotheism, incoherent, 132
moralism, biblical, 15–17

morality, 14, 62n1–n2
Moses, 56, 57, 58
murder rate, 93n1
myth of redemptive violence, 130

narrative, 16, 58, 69n19, 122, 132, 145
   biblical, 73, 138, 140, 144, 146, 170
   dominant genre, 16, 58
   of crucifixion, 84, 90
   of gospels, 174n55, 178
   queries about, 35–36
   that explains God's violence, 137–38. *See also* story
narrative Christus Victor, 166, 170–72
needs of victims, 123–26
neighbor, 110n3, 111
neutrality, fallacy of, 46–47
new creation, 58, 68, 156
New Perspective, 151–52
New Testament, 59, 67
New Zealand, 69n19, 76, 93, 94, 102, 115, 214–15
   and restorative justice, x, 117, 120
   victims' movement, 115
Noah, 147
nonviolence, 35, 63, 130, 131, 132, 159
   Jesus Christ's, xxi, 133, 134n12, 160, 166
norm, 18–21 *passim*, 33, 35, 68, 168
Northern Ireland, 201–2

obligation, 2, 62, 63n3, 92
   of God, 141, 165
offender and victim, experience, 89, 116
offenders, 81, 91, 92, 102, 115, 204, 205
offending, 81, 116
Old Testament, 59, 67n14, 147–48
Operation Shock and Awe, 186
order, moral, 120, 123
Origen, 143

Pacific Islanders, 101
pacifism, 130, 131, 132
pain, 88, 89, 99, 108, 113, 123
   victims' 88, 92, 182, 191, 203–5, 116–17
Pakistan, 188
parables, 58, 111, 213
paradigm, 16, 23, 158, 194, 196, 211
   biblical, 24, 26, 30n81
   restorative, 118, 212
paradox, 174
Parole Act, 115
participation, 62n1, 73, 89, 183, 188, 213
   Christian, 66, 129, 164
Passion Narrative, 86, 176
Paul, 56, 97, 107, 120, 121, 151–58, 163, 178
   and Silas, 105
   New Perspective on, 151–52
pay-back instinct, 181–82
peace, 121, 135–36, 159
peacemaking, just, 196–97
penal substitution, 163–65
Penitentiaries, 96
Pentecost sermon, 179
people, holiness of, 207
Perle, Richard, 193n32
perpetrators, 87, 88, 131, 189–91, 195, 198, 200–02, 204–05
   and victims, 91, 116, 121. *See also* offenders
Peter, 88, 97, 177, 179
Philippi, 105
philosophy, moral, 3
Pilate, Pontius, 83, 173, 176, 179
Pisidian Antioch, 179
pluralism, 11–12, 12, 14, 37, 48, 70
   and consensus, 77
police, 84, 196–96
policy, 65, 68–69, 73, 76, 94, 100, 212
   foreign, 186, 196
populism, penal, 212
powers, 168, 170, 171, 173, 174, 179, 189

SUBJECT INDEX

practices, 32, 60, 74, 154
    restorative, xv–xvi, 118–19, 122, 204, 213, 213, 215
praxis, 33, 74, 75, 77
prevention, of religious terrorism, 196–97
principle, of creation, 122, 135
principles, 17, 19–21, 53, 72–73, 78, 196n42, 204
Prison Fellowship, 105
prisons, 89, 126, 195, 197n44
problems, 9–12, 113–14
process, of restorative justice, 118
propaganda, 190–91
protest, of lament, 89–90, 91
psalms, 81, 82, 85, 92, 140
punishment, 95, 96, 99–100

Quakers, 96
questions,
    about violence, 161, 186
    formative, 33–36, 141
    methodological, 27
    of victims, 112, 117, 123–24

Rahab, 143
readings, 10, 12, 48–50, 53, 152
reality,
    created, 121, 135
    ultimate, 126, 160
reasoning, 22–27, 142, 195
reception of public theology, 69
reconciliation, 155, 191, 201
redemption, 89, 149, 151, 181
reformers, 53, 59
reign, God's 38, 167–68, 169, 170–71, 176
relationships, 123
    and crime, 91–92, 123
    interpersonal, xvi
    offenders and victims, 116–17, 121
religion, 65n12, 69–70, 144, 185–87, 193n33, 194, 197
responsibility, 111, 132, 147, 150, 174
    communal, 30, 99, 101–2, 202

of offenders, 88, 124, 125, 200, 205
restitution, 99, 125
restoration, 88–89, 92, 117, 123, 125, 199
resurrection, 168, 170, 172, 180
retribution, 92, 108, 130, 142–43, 148, 199
revelation, 2–4, 23n62, 25, 71–72, 75–76, 149, 156
    divine, 22, 144–45, 149n64, 150n67
    in Jesus Christ, 45, 160, 173n47
    of God, 67n14, 107, 121, 134, 149, 150
revenge, 148, 170, 182, 199, 206–7
righteousness, 2, 151, 152, 154, 156, 163, 212
rights, xviii, 68, 69, 115
    and imago Dei, 72
    human, 68n16, 71, 197
rule of faith, 46n10
rule of law, 83, 115, 197
rules, 15–16, 17, 18, 20, 21, 37

safety, of victims in conference, 124
salvation, 58, 105n48, 151, 162, 164–65, 167, 170–72, 182
Satan, 169, 173, 174, 193n29, 200
    and Christus Victor, 162, 168
scandal, 158
scholars, 14, 26, 28, 45–46, 48, 144, 163
    Islamic, 197n44
scholarship, 21, 32, 57n33, 60, 64, 160
    critical, 46, 51, 54
    Pauline, 151–52
scripture, 8, 30, 39–44 *passim*, 53, 56, 61, 67, 158. *See also* Bible; Narrative
    academic study of, 46–47
    fulfilled by Jesus, 177–79
    God's violence in, 137–41
secularism, 65, 72, 74
Sensible Sentencing Trust, 115
Sentencing Act, 115
sermon, 38, 39, 42, 43, 179

settlement, Constantinian, 169, 168
shalom, xvi, xvii, 212
shame, 81, 125, 211, 213
Shanab, Abu, 199
Shirlow, Peter, 201
sin, 87, 91, 146, 134–35, 150, 155, 180
  absorbed by Jesus, 182
  and God, 131, 150, 157
  and Hosea, 141
  and law, 153–57 passim
  and non-human creation, 147
  manifested by violence, 159
situation, 4, 25–27, 30, 32, 35, 37, 165, 190–91
  God enters, 90
  offender and victim, 116
  restorative justice, 116, 122
slavery 19, 49n16, 100, 164
solidarity, 32, 86–88, 211
Sodom, 141, 147
Son of Man, 175, 178
sources, of public theology, 66–67
speech, 55, 124
Spirit, 39, 50, 60, 155, 157. *See also* Holy Spirit
state, 36, 37, 67, 69n12, 115, 193n33
  and offenders, 114–15
  and prisons, 108
  and violence, 63n3, 160
  as victim, 114
stigma, 108
stories. *See* narrative; story
story, xix, 120–21, 136–37, 148–49, 152,
  biblical, 7, 73, 137, 145, 149, 211–13
  canonical, 136, 156, 157. *See also* narrative
strategies, 70, 71–74, 141–46
submission, 165, 167, 180
suffering, 86, 87, 89, 91, 98–99, 112, 123
  and atonement, 164, 165
  and terrorists, 192, 205
  of Jesus, 174–75, 176, 181
symbolism of terrorist acts, 189

text,
  biblical, 15, 42, 43, 45–49, 50–51, 57, 143–44
theodicy, 132
theology, xvi, xvii, xx, 4, 45n9
  atonement, 162–70 passim
Torah. *See* law, Old Testament
theories of atonement, 162–69, 171, 180. *See also* narrative Christus Victor
tradition, 3, 71, 53n26, 75–76, 136n19
traditions, xix, 42–43, 65n12
transformation 28, 29, 33, 34, 52, 56
  of offenders, 92, 115, 207
  structural, 24, 208
truth, 51, 52, 60, 71, 74, 77, 124
  biblical, 51–52, 58, 60
truth claims, 120–23, 132, 134–35
truth-telling, 124–25
Tuffnell, Jo, 203–04
typologies, for ethics, 14
typology, 25n67, 37

United States, 94, 96, 115, 188, 194n36, 196

values, 21, 23, 34, 49, 58, 61, 205
  Christian, xvi, 2, 4n6, 65, 68, 72–73
  of church, xviii, 119
  restorative, 118–20, 126–27, 198–99, 204
Vautier, Dr. Clyde, 39
veil, 56–57, 91, 121, 134, 150, 152
vengeance, 124, 131, 146, 150, 199
  and Jesus, 88, 145
victimization, 81, 112, 113, 115–17, 123–25, 165, 202
  of Jesus, 88, 182
Victim-Offender-Reconciliation-Project, 212
Victim Support, 114
Victims' Rights Act, 115
victims, 80–81, 135, 141, 182, 198, 200
  and Jesus, 91, 134, 170
  and lament, 86, 88, 89

victims (*continued*)
    and perpetrators, 201–2
    satisfaction atonement, 165, 167
    and offenders, 87, 88, 92, 205, 211
    of imprisonment, 100n30
    of injustice, 101
    of redemptive violence, 143
    of religious violence, 204
    support needs of, 113–14
    symbols of confrontation, 189
vindication, 124, 153, 154, 176, 190
violence, 63n3, 88, 91, 92, 93, 103–4
virtues, 4, 28, 29, 32, 62n1, 126, 201
vision, 8, 14, 38, 72, 73, 78, 167, 190
    moral, 29, 31
voice, 41, 63, 70, 71, 144, 208
    Christian public, 69n18, 77
    God's, 40, 55

war, xii, 169, 191–92, 194–95. *See also* holy war, just war
    between good and evil, 187, 189
    Christian participation in, 129, 130
    in Bible, 137–40, 147
weapons, 138, 184, 187, 196n41

Weaver, Denny, critique of, 171–72
welfare and public theology, 63
Wesley, John, 164
wisdom, 5, 16, 34, 41, 43, 57, 77
Women's Refuge, 114
world, 26, 29–34 *passim*, 43, 46, 58, 59, 123
    and God, 52, 74n30, 76, 112, 131, 136, 137, 178, 180
    and humans, 132, 152
    biblical, 11, 25, 30, 142
    restored by Jesus, 121, 134, 158
    sinful, 142n38, 165, 178
World Trade Center, 194
World War II, 196
worldview, 43
worship, 61, 81, 92, 113, 159

Yahweh, 138, 140–41, 142, 147, 148, 174
Yemen, 197n44
Yoder, John Howard, 33

zeal, 151n71, 192
Zedekiah, King, 95n5
Zehr, 210–11, 212

Author Index

Achcar, Gilbert, 193n29, 196n41
Adler, Warren, 60n43
Alibhai-Brown, Yasmin, 200n53
Allison, Dale C., Jr., 16n42, 129n3, 145n48
Anderson, Paul N., 128, 144n43
Armstrong, Karen, 128n2
Augsburger, Myron S., 59n39
Aulén, Gustaf, 162n10
Austin, Greg,, 185n5

Bainton, Roland H., 188n11
Barclay, Oliver, 20n57
Baxter, Christina A., 163n17
Bellinger, William H., Jr., 177n72
Belousek, Darrin W. S., xxn10
Berger, Peter L., 185n2
Birch, Bruce C., 2n1, 13n34, 15, 29n77, 31n83–n84, 32, 36n103, 37n104, 73n27
Bloesch, Donald G., 17n47
Blumenfeld, Laura, 199n50, 206–7
Boersma, Hans, 75n32, 142n38
Boston, Jonathan, 21n58
Boulton, David, 185n2
Bowen, Helen, 118n13, 198n47
Boyack, Jim, 118n13, 198n47
Braithwaite, John, 80n1, 118n12, 126n25
Brandon, James, 197n44
Brenneman, Laura, xii
Brinsmead, R. D., 163n17
Broughton, Geoff, xxn10
Brown, Raymond, 85n13, 86n17
Burke, Jason, 189, 190

Cahill, Lisa Sowle, 4n7, 9n24, 28n72, 30n81, 31n86, 34n96, 35n100, 52n25
Cavanaugh, William T., 69n21
Cayley, David, 108, 109n55, 212n4
Charry, Ellen T., 45n9, 64n6
Chase, Kenneth R., 130n5
Childress, James F., 13n36, 17n47, 21, 38n107
Childs, Brevard S., 59
Church Council on Justice and Corrections, 120n15,
Cloke, Ken, 193n31
Collins, John J., 139n28, 139n30, 143n42, 144, 150n67
Consedine, J., 120n15
Cook, David, 7
Cosden, Darrell, 62n2
Culbertson, R. G., 104n41
Cuzzo, Maria S. W., 195n38

Davies, W. D., 5, 16n42, 37n106
Davis, Ellen F., 136n19, 150n68
Deckert, Marion G., 63n3
De Vries, Simon J., 137n20
Donaldson, Terence L., 151n71
Donfried, Karl P., 48n14
Douma, Jochem, 2n2
Duff, Nancy J., 34n98, 163n16
Dunn, J. D. G., 11n29

Eakin, Hugh, 188n13
Ellens, J. Harold, 132
Etzioni, Amitai, 197n45

AUTHOR INDEX

Fairchild, Mark R., 151n71
Farmer, William R., 177n72
Fiddes, Paul S., 90n22, 163n15, 163n17
Finger, Thomas N., 162n10
Fisk, Robert, 200n55
Flett, John, 64n7, 73n29
Flood, Derek, xxn10
Forrester, Duncan B., 63, 67, 70n22, 73n26, 95n3, 123n19, 126n24
Foucault, Michel, 96
Fowl, Stephen E., 9n25, 11n29, 12n32, 13, 25n66, 28, 32n88, 34, 50
Fuller, Daniel P., 19n51
Fuller, Reginald H., 37n105
Furnish, Victor P., 7n17, 8n21, 16n42, 16n44

Gascoigne, Robert, 77-78
Geering, Lloyd, 197n46
Goldhammer, John D., 185n5
Goldingay, John, 16n43
Gorringe, Timothy J., 163n17, 165, 169n37
Griffith, Lee, 95, 99n25, 103, 105n48, 107, 186n6, 187n7, 188n15, 194, 196n41
Gunton, Colin, 50n18
Gustafson, James M., 5, 8, 9n23, 13n34, 14n39, 17n45, 24n64, 26n71

Hari, Johann, 193n32
Harvey, A. E., 10n27, 19n53
Harvey, Nicholas, 62n2
Hauerwas, Stanley, 6n15, 9n25, 31n84, 33n91, 35n101
Haughey, John C., 134n14
Hays, Richard B., 12, 30n82, 33, 38n107, 43, 53n26, 57, 59n36
Henley, John A., 34n98
Hicks, David, 62n1
Hirsch, Michael, 197n45, 202n57
Holder, Rodney, 71n23

Holloway, Jeph, 72n24-n25, 73n28, 74n30
Hopkins, Julie M., 164
Horsely, Richard A., 26n69-n71
Hoyle, Carolyn, xvii, xviii
Hudson, Barbara A., 102

Jansen, John Frederick, 176n71
Jenson, Robert W., 39n2, 42, 46n10
Jewett, Robert, 151n71, 192n27, 193n30, 194n35
Johnson, Abigail, 42n4
Jones, L. Gregory, 41, 42n3-n4, 50, 59n36; see also Fowl, S.
Juergensmeyer, Mark, 185n3, 187n8, 189n21, 190, 197n46, 200n52

Kaye, Bruce, 20n57
Kerber, Guillermo, 205n63
Kille, D. A., 128n2
Kilner, John F., 5n12
Klein, Joe, 193n34
Knapp, G. L., 97n9
Koontz, Ted, 75n31, 78n34
Kreider, Alan, ix, 69n20, 168n33

Lampman, Lisa B., 81n2, 112n6
Lederach, John P., 192n26, 196n40
Lindars, Barnabas, 6n14
Lindbeck, George, 8, 11n30, 12n31
Lischer, Richard, 33n91
Long, E. LeR., Jr., 5n13, 14n38, 194, 194n35
Longenecker, Richard N., 17n45, 17n47, 19n51

Mabee, Charles, 128n2
Malina, Bruce J., 51n22
Marcus, Joel, 85n13
Marrow, Stanley B., 173n47
Marshall, Christopher D., xviin4, xixn9, 9n24, 32n89, 33n92, 67n15, 68n16-n17, 72n25, 92n25, 95n2, 100n29, 105n49, 109n55, 110n1, 111n5, 118n13, 123n20, 134n14, 159n1, 161n7,

162n8, 180n89, 193n29,
198n47, 205n63, 209, 213n6,
214n7–n9, 215
Marshall, I. Howard, 7, 7n17–n18,
10n26, 18
Martinkus, John., 205
Masters, Catherine, 185n1
Mathieson, Don, 17n47, 20n56
Mauser, Ulrich, 134n13
McCold, P., 122n18
McCurdy, Diana, 200n54
McDonald, Patricia M., 136n16,
137–39, 147
McEntire, Mark, 138n25, 140,
140n35, 141n37, 142,
149n62
McGrath, Alister E., 2n2, 29n76, 44,
45n7, 47n13, 55n31
McKanan, Dan, 130n5
McKim, Donald K., 39n1, 54n27
McKittrick, David, 203n60
McTernan, Oliver, 187n10, 192n26,
200n52, 201n56, 202n57
Meeks, W., 30n80, 31, 35n101,
60n41
Mika, Harry, 126n26
Miles, Jack, 138n22
Miles, Margaret R., 3n5
Moltmann, Jürgen, 60, 64
Moltmann-Wendel, Elisabeth,
163n16
Morris, Leon, 163n13
Mott, Stephen C., 17n46
Myers, Ched, xxn10

Nath, Pamela S., 208n70
Nelson-Pallmeyer, Jack, 134n12,
140n31, 144, 145, 150n67
New, David S., 197n43
Newbigin, Lesslie, 65, 73n26
Niditch, Susan, 139, 140n34
Noakes-Duncan, Thomas, xxn10,
215n10

Oldfield, Duane, 193n34
Ollenburger, Ben C., x, 31n87,
55n30
Olson, Mark, 97, 104

Olson, Dennis T., 49n17

Packer, J. I., 10n26, 163n13
Padgett, Alan G., 52n24
Patrick, M. W., 110n2
Patte, Daniel, 51, 163n16
Peachey, Dean E., 213n5
Perkins, Pheme, 24n65
Pinnock, Clark H., 122n17, 160
Placher, William C., 149n64

Ramm, Bernard, 17n47
Ramsey, Michael, 55n31
Rasmussen, Larry L., 2n1, 13n34,
15, 29n77, 31n83–n84, 32,
36n103, 37n104
Rawnsley, Andrew, 194n35
Redekop, Vernon, 204
Ricoeur, Paul, 2n3
Rodd, C. S., 9n24

Schantz, Brad, xii
Schlabach, Gerald, 195n39
Schluter, Michael, 20n55, 20n57
Schrey, H., xviiin7
Schüssler Fiorenza, Elisabeth, 24
Schüssler Fiorenza, Francis, 11n30,
30n81
Schwager, Raymund, 133, 134n12,
138, 147, 148n57, 148n60,
150n66
Scroggs, Robin, 7n16, 11n29, 13n35,
25, 26n68, 28n74
Selengut, Charles, 188n11, 188n16,
190n23, 197n46, 199n51,
202n58
Shupack, Martin, 65n11
Sleeper, C. F., 13n34
Smail, Tom, 163, 163n17
Smiles, Vincent M., 151n71
Snyder, T. Richard, 96n7, 102n37,
108n54
Spohn, William C., 13n36, 21n59–
n60, 22, 23n61–n62, 29n78
Stacey, David, 59n38
Stackhouse, Max L., 63n5, 65n12
Stassen, Glen H., 194n36, 196n42
Steinmann, Rebecca, 205n63

Stern, Jessica, 187, 188, 188n12, 188n14, 189, 195n37, 199n48–n49, 203n59
Strang, Heather, 115n9, 118n12, 124n21, 126n25
Suskind, Ron, 185n5, 192n28, 193n34,
Swartley, Willard M., xii, xvin2, 7n17, 10n28, 57n34, 59n39

Talbot, T., 163n17
Tate, W. Randolph, 51n21
Thompson, James W., 29n79
Tiessen, Terrance, 19n52
Trulear, H. D., 113n8

Utley, Jon Basil, 192n25

Vanhoozer, Kevin J., 46, 47n11–n12, 48
Verhey, Allen, 5n13
Volf, Miroslav, 130n5, 161

Wachtel, T., 122n18
Wansink, C. S., 99n22–n23
Ward, Kevin, 185n2

Weaver, J. Denny, xi, 129, 162, 163n12, 163n16, 164n20, 166–172, 174, 174n52
Welch, D., 93n1
Westerholm, Stephen, 29n75
Wilder, Amos N., 34n98
Wilson, Richard A., 205n63
Wink, Walter, 130, 134n12, 135, 136n16, 149n63, 192n27, 193n33
Wolterstorff, Nicholas, 46n10, 55, 64
Woolford, Andrew, xvn1
Wright, C. J. H., 20n57
Wright, N. T., 6n15, 45n8, 54, 57n33, 58n35, 61, 133n11

Yoder, Perry, xi
Yoder, John Howard, 6n14, 20n54, 23n63, 30, 31n83, 33, 34n95, 36n102, 37n104, 131

Zehr, Howard, x, xvi, xvii–xviii, xixn8, xx, 112, 113n7, 118, 125, 210-13, 215
Zifcak, Spencer, 205n63
Zimbelman, Joel, 33n94

www.ingramcontent.com/pod-product-compliance
Lightning Source LLC
Chambersburg PA
CBHW030822230426
43667CB00008B/1332